THE BFRB RECOVERY WORKBOOK

of related interest

The Ultimate Anxiety Toolkit
25 Tools to Worry Less, Relax More, and Boost Your Self-Esteem
Risa Williams
Illustrated by Jennifer Whitney and Amanda Way
ISBN 978 1 78775 770 7
eISBN 978 1 78775 771 4

The Ultimate Time Management Toolkit
25 Productivity Tools for Adults with ADHD and Chronically Busy People
Risa Williams, LMFT
Illustrated by Jennifer Whitney
ISBN 978 1 83997 178 5
eISBN 978 1 83997 179 2

ADHD an A–Z
Figuring it Out Step by Step
Leanne Maskell
Foreword by Ellie Middleton
ISBN 978 1 83997 385 7
eISBN 978 1 83997 386 4

The A–Z Guide to Exposure
Creative ERP Activities for 75 Childhood Fears
Dawn Huebner, PhD and Erin Neely, PsyD
ISBN 978 1 83997 322 2
eISBN 978 1 83997 323 9

The BFRB RECOVERY WORKBOOK

Effective Recovery from Hair Pulling, Skin Picking, Nail Biting, and Other Body-Focused Repetitive Behaviors

Marla W. Deibler, PsyD, ABPP
and **Renae M. Reinardy, PsyD**

Jessica Kingsley Publishers
London and Philadelphia

First published in Great Britain in 2024 by Jessica Kingsley Publishers
An imprint of John Murray Press

1

"My Matrix" exercise reproduced from Polk and Schoendorff 2014 with kind permission from New Harbringer Productions.
"Choice Point" exercise adapted from The Weight Escape: How to Stops Dieting and Start Living by Joseph Ciarrochi, Ann Bailey, and Russ Harris. Copyright © 2014 by Ann Bailey, Joseph Ciarrochi, and Russ Harris. Reprinted by arrangement with The Permissions Company, LLC on behalf of Shambhala Publications, Inc., Boulder, Colorado, shambhala.com.
Image on page 89 © Tyler Eichorst printed with permission from HabitAware Inc.
Image on page 187 and compass, hiking, and map icon source: Shutterstock.
Graph on page 196 and table on page 198 are reproduced from Linehan 2014 with kind permission from Guildford Publications, Inc.
Every effort has been made to trace copyright holders and to obtain their permission for the use of copyright material. The author and the publisher apologize for any omissions and would be grateful if notified of any acknowledgements that should be incorporated in future reprints or editions of this book.

A CIP catalogue record for this title is available from the British Library and the Library of Congress

ISBN 978 1 83997 655 1
eISBN 978 1 83997 656 8

Printed and bound in the United States by Integrated Books International

Jessica Kingsley Publishers' policy is to use papers that are natural, renewable and recyclable products and made from wood grown in sustainable forests. The logging and manufacturing processes are expected to conform to the environmental regulations of the country of origin.

Jessica Kingsley Publishers
Carmelite House
50 Victoria Embankment
London EC4Y 0DZ

www.jkp.com

John Murray Press
Part of Hodder & Stoughton Ltd
An Hachette Company

Contents

STEP IV: LIVE YOUR BEST LIFE

Acknowledgements

It is with much gratitude that we acknowledge our families, friends, and colleagues who gave us the space and support we needed to pour our clinical experience, research knowledge, and integrative psychotherapy training into this workbook. This was a labor of love in service to the body-focused repetitive behavior (BFRB) community, including those who wish to live life unfettered by their BFRB, those who wish to support a loved one with a BFRB, and professionals who wish to more effectively treat these conditions.

Some of our most touching, inspiring, and formative career experiences occurred during conferences and retreats held by the Trichotillomania Learning Center (TLC), under the loving care of Christina Pearson. Without Christina, we would likely still be decades behind in learning how to support those experiencing BFRBs. To her, we are all indebted.

Our early career development in treating BFRBs and related disorders was influenced by our talented colleagues at the Behavior Therapy Center of Greater Washington, led by Dr. Charles Mansueto. Their knowledge, humor, and compassion, in addition to the clients who shared their experiences with us along the way, led to our easy decisions to specialize in treating these conditions for the decades to come.

We are thankful to have had many opportunities to present professional workshops and provide clinical training and consultation to further increase awareness of BFRBs and improve treatment outcomes through the support of organizations, including the TLC Foundation for Body-Focused Repetitive Behaviors, the International OCD Foundation, the Anxiety & Depression Association of America, and the Association for Contextual Behavioral Science. These experiences have allowed us to not only share our knowledge but continue to grow personally and professionally.

Finally, thank you to Jane Evans for reaching out in search of this book which we had not yet fully realized we would write, and, by extension, to the entire team at Jessica Kingsley Publishers for all of their hard work to bring this to fruition.

While there is more work to do, it has been amazing to witness the developments in better understanding and supporting this community as evidenced by the growing list of healthcare providers and organizations which strive to serve those impacted by these conditions. May these efforts continue until no one with a BFRB feels alone or goes without support.

Introduction

WHAT IS RECOVERY?

So, you want to work on recovery from your body-focused repetitive behavior (BFRB)? Chances are, this is not the first time you've thought about wanting to change your BFRB. And it's probably not the first time you've taken action to do something with the intention of changing your BFRB. You're likely wondering what this book contains that will help you to achieve this—something different from what you've tried previously. In this book, you'll have the opportunity to explore many different strategies, some of which you have tried before and some of which you have not. You'll be examining your BFRB in a new way, shifting perspectives on how you relate to your inner experiences and choosing interventions specific to your own BFRB pattern. So, throughout your journey here, stay curious and be gentle with yourself.

Before we get started, let's talk about the word "recovery." "Recovery" is defined as: the process of becoming well again; the process of improving or becoming stronger again; the action or process of getting something back that has been lost or stolen (Oxford University Press n.d.). This word can often be found in reference to physical injury/illness or to addiction. It is, however, a word that carries a heavy load. One that implies that something has been missing or lost, not whole, wrong, in a state of suffering, or in another undesirable state. It's a word that implies efforts toward regaining a previous self. We'll use this word—as it is familiar and widely used—but we'd like to encourage you to consider a different definition of "recovery," one that you, alone, can define for yourself.

In the spirit of this BFRB work together, we will be approaching the word "recovery" in a future-oriented manner—toward a future self—a self who embodies all of the personal characteristics and values you hold dear. One who does not look back but looks forward. One who is able to live a meaningful, fulfilling life, unfettered by your BFRB.

Life with a BFRB is a journey, and each person's experience is unique. What lies ahead in this book will guide you in the navigation of the variety of terrains you will encounter on your own path. We hope that you will come to appreciate your travels, both the smooth, well-traveled routes as well as the rocky roads less traveled, with your BFRB in tow.

Chapter 1 provides an overview of BFRBs (the science-y stuff). Each chapter thereafter is divided into three core content areas:

- **Explore**: Explore sections will provide you with information to better understand concepts and recognize the ways in which these concepts directly relate to your own lived BFRB experience.
- **Practice**: Practice sections will actively engage you in skills-building exercises and provide new learning experiences to expand your BFRB toolbox and enrich your sense of well-being.
- **Action Plan**: Action Plan sections will highlight your commitment to investing in yourself and the life you envision on your BFRB journey.

Welcome. We're glad you're here.

All pages marked with ✶ can be downloaded from www.jkp.com/catalogue/book/9781839976551.

STEP I

GET TO KNOW YOURSELF

CHAPTER 1

All About Body-Focused Repetitive Behaviors

What Are Body-Focused Repetitive Behaviors?

Before our work begins, let's review what is currently known about these behaviors. All animals groom, both human and non-human. Grooming behaviors serve important functions, including hygiene, stress reduction, and aspects of socialization with others. So, what makes these behaviors "disordered"?

Body-Focused Repetitive Behaviors (BFRBs) are any repetitive self-grooming behaviors that involve biting, chewing, pulling, picking, or scraping one's own hair, skin, or nails that result in damage to the body and have been met with multiple attempts to stop or decrease the behavior. BFRBs that meet the diagnostic criteria set out in the *Diagnostic and Statistical Manual of Mental Disorders, Fifth Edition (DSM-5)* cause notable distress or impairment in daily functioning and are not better accounted for by another medical or psychiatric condition. These behaviors are diverse in nature in that they are complex and experienced differently from person to person. BFRBs may include the following behaviors, among others:

- trichotillomania: hair pulling
- excoriation disorder: skin picking
- onychophagia: nail biting
- onychotillomania: nail picking/chronic manicuring
- trichophagia: eating of hair
- dermatophagia: eating of skin
- morsicatio buccarum: cheek biting
- morsicatio labiorum: lip biting
- morsicatio linguarum: tongue biting
- trichotemnomania: cutting of one's hair
- rhinotillexomania: nose picking.

BFRBs throughout History

While BFRBs have only been diagnosed as "disorders" in recent decades, the acknowledgement of these behaviors extends much further into our history. The first written mention of these behaviors was by Aristotle in 340 BCE (Aristotle, Ross, and Brown 2009) when in his work *The Nicomachean Ethics* he referenced the habit of plucking out hair and gnawing nails. The first documentation of behaviors in the medical literature was made by Hippocrates (460–377 BC), who referenced the effects of stress on the skin and described cases of hair pulling behavior caused by stress (Franca *et al.* 2013). Erasmus Wilson (1875) coined the term "neurotic excoriation" to describe difficult to control skin-picking behavior. And, in 1889, French dermatologist François Henri Hallopeau first used the term "trichotillomania" to describe hair-pulling behavior. This behavior was also described in literary works, including the Old Testament of the Bible and by Shakespeare in *Romeo and Juliet*.

Trichotillomania first appeared in the *Diagnostic and Statistical Manual of Mental Disorders, Third Edition, Revised (DSM-III-R)* in 1987 (American Psychiatric Association 1987). And, in the *Diagnostic and Statistical Manual of Mental Disorders, Fifth Edition (DSM-5)*, excoriation (skin picking) disorder first appeared as its own diagnostic category, and the diagnostic criteria for trichotillomania were modified (American Psychiatric Association 2013).

The Nature of BFRBs

BFRBs are among the most misunderstood and under-addressed psychiatric diagnoses, and yet these behavioral struggles are commonly reported "habit behaviors" that individuals seek to change. Research indicates that trichotillomania occurs in approximately 1 in 50 people. A meta-analysis (a statistical analysis that combines and examines the data of multiple studies that have sought to answer the same scientific question) demonstrated a prevalence of 1.14 percent across 30 studies and 38,526 individuals (Thomson *et al.* 2022). A survey of 10,169 community adults indicated that 1.7 percent report current trichotillomania (Grant, Dougherty, and Chamberlain 2020). This data is consistent with a cross-cultural prevalence rate (how common or uncommon a condition is across differing cultures or geographical regions) of 1.4 percent, demonstrated in 7,639 individuals in Brazil (Bezerra *et al.* 2021).

Excoriation (skin picking) disorder is also common. A study of 10,169 US community adults indicated that 2.1 percent have experienced excoriation disorder within their lifetime (Grant and Chamberlain 2020). This occurrence rate is consistent with cross-cultural data indicating a prevalence rate of 3.03 percent in a study of 2,176 individuals in Israel (Leibovici *et al.* 2014).

Although there have been fewer investigations of other BFRBs, those that have been published suggest that they, too, are common, with 20–30 percent of the population engaging in nail biting (Halteh, Scher, and Lipner 2017) and 3.05–5.7 percent of US adults reporting mouth, lip, or cheek biting (Shulman, Beach, and Rivera-Hidalgo 2004; Teng *et al.* 2002). Studies of other BFRBs across cultures also suggest high rates of prevalence. In a study of 3,475 individuals in Turkey, 17.6 percent of university students and 29.2 percent of high school students reported nail-biting behavior (Erdogan *et al.* 2021), and in a study of 2,636 children aged 4–15 in India, 8.8 percent reported nail biting and 2.01 percent reported lip biting (Hegde and Xavier 2009).

Only recently have there been insights into the manifestation of BFRBs across gender and ethnic groups within the US population and beyond. Early studies examining gender differences in trichotillomania suggested that the disorder was more common in females (Christenson, MacKenzie, and Mitchell 1994). More recent data indicates that trichotillomania, and more broadly other BFRBs, are likely to have a more equal gender distribution (Grant and Chamberlain 2020; Grant *et al.* 2020; Leibovici *et al.* 2014; Thomson *et al.* 2022). In regards to ethnicity, a study of 539 adults with trichotillomania and excoriation disorder indicated that 14.1 percent of participants self-identified as Black, Asian, or Minority Ethnic, while 85.9 percent identified as white Caucasian; furthermore, individuals identifying as Black, Asian, or Minority Ethnic reported greater frequency of symptoms and were less likely to have received treatment, highlighting the need for further study and increased access to clinical resources and care (Grant *et al.* 2021a).

Although inclusion diagnostic criteria have been debated in studies, some degree of BFRB or what may be considered to be subclinical symptoms of a BFRB (i.e., symptoms that do not meet full criteria for diagnosis) are very frequently acknowledged. For example, in a study of 4,335 US college students, 59.55 percent reported subclinical BFRBs (Houghton *et al.* 2018). In a meta-analysis of 30 studies, including 38,526 individuals, 8.84 percent of participants reported subclinical hair pulling (Thomson *et al.* 2022). And in an online study of 1,378 individuals, 23 percent reported a "probable" BFRB (6% nail biting, 14% lip/cheek biting, 2% hair pulling) (Solley and Turner 2018). Taken together, research suggests that you are not alone in your experience of living with a BFRB; millions of others across the world share this experience.

Onset and Course of Symptoms

BFRBs can begin at any point in an individual's life. Historically, studies have estimated that BFRBs typically start between 11 and 15 years of age, with trichotillomania beginning at 11–12 years of age and skin picking beginning at 14–15 years of age (Christenson and Mackenzie 1994). More recent data suggests that the average age of onset of trichotillomania may be somewhat later (17.7 years of age), with females experiencing onset (14.8 years of age) prior to males (19.0 years of age) (Grant *et al.* 2020), ages that are somewhat higher than those seen in clinical practice. Very young children (ages 0–6 years) may experience hair pulling as well, often referred to as "baby trich," which tends to manifest as self-soothing behavior and is thought to be different from trichotillomania in older children and adults in that it may be transient in some cases, rather than more enduring/chronic (Flessner *et al.* 2010). Generally, BFRBs are considered to be chronic, and their course tends to wax and wane in intensity over time. This course is dependent upon many individualized factors.

Chronic nail conditions, including nail biting and picking, are under-recognized complex disorders that cause damage to the periungual skin (i.e., the skin surrounding the nail) and nail. Like other BFRBs, these conditions can also cause significant psychological, social, and physical consequences with failed attempts to control the behavior. Furthermore, people rarely seek out treatment to decrease these behaviors (Lee and Lipner 2022). Onychophagia or compulsive nail biting is thought to decrease with age, affecting 45 percent of children through early adolescence (Gupta and Gupta 2019) and 20–30 percent of the general population (Halteh, Scher, and Lipner 2017; Pacan *et al.* 2014).

The BFRB Experience

Those who pull hair may pull from the full range of areas on which hair grows, including but not limited to scalp hair, eyelashes, eyebrows, pubic area, arms, underarms, legs, beard, and mustache, with the most frequent pulling areas being the scalp, eyebrows, eyelashes, and pubic hair (Woods *et al.* 2006). Skin-picking sites also span across the body and may include upper extremities, trunk, lower extremities, face, and scalp (Kwon *et al.* 2020). Individuals often pick and/or pull from more than one area of the body. Beyond pulling or picking on one's own body, it is not uncommon for individuals to pull or pick from objects not on their own body. These sites may include wigs, dolls, blankets, a throw-pillow fringe, and pets (fur and whiskers), as well as other people (spouses, younger siblings, children).

The cause(s) of BFRBs are not well understood. It is widely believed that BFRBs are a neurobiological set of behaviors and share both biological and environmental underpinnings; in other words, BFRBs are a set of behaviors relating to the nervous system that likely involve a combination of many factors, including one's biological makeup and one's environment. Studies have suggested that genetic susceptibility is likely a factor contributing to the manifestation of symptoms (Johnson and El-Alfy 2016). Other factors that have been preliminarily looked at include neuroanatomical differences, neurochemistry, immune dysregulation, and emotion dysregulation, as well as learning and models of behavioral reinforcement (several of these concepts will be discussed in further detail later in this book).

Several efforts have been made over the past two decades to try to delineate categorical differences within the umbrella of BFRBs (Christenson and Mackenzie 1994; Flessner *et al.* 2008; Grant *et al.* 2021b; Pozza, Giaquinta, and Dèttore 2016). Often referred to as subtyping, these studies have sought to examine the heterogeneous nature of these disorders in order to better inform treatment. For more than a decade, mental health research (National Institute of Mental Health Research Domain Criteria framework; NIMH RDoC) and diagnostic psychiatry (DSM) have prioritized a move toward a more dimensional perspective of psychiatry (i.e., descriptive characteristics or symptoms on a continuum) and away from a categorical approach. Furthermore, other studies have attempted to identify unique personality traits specific to those with BFRBs, identifying potential targets such as perfectionism/trait incompleteness (i.e., a sense of "not just right"), sensory over-responsivity to external stimuli, alexithymia (emotional processing deficits), and neuroticism (anxiety, anger, hostility, depression, self-consciousness, impulsiveness, and vulnerability to stress) (Aydin *et al.* 2022; Falkenstein *et al.* 2018; Keuthen *et al.* 2016; Ricketts *et al.* 2021). Attention to a thorough analysis of the ways in which each individual's BFRB manifests, rather than attempting to place individual experiences into categories, may be more useful and informative for an individualized case conceptualization and treatment plan. The characteristics commonly associated with the ways in which individuals engage in their BFRB and the qualities of hair, skin, or nails that are targeted will be discussed in detail as you are led to explore these aspects of your own BFRB in Chapter 3.

BFRBs can have significant physical effects on the body. Trichotillomania and excoriation disorder can lead to pruritus (itching), infection, repetitive motion injuries, tissue damage, scabbing, open wounds, skin discoloration, scarring, and disfigurement. If hair is ingested, there is a risk of gastrointestinal distress, trichobezoar (i.e., build-up of hair in the digestive tract), and in extreme cases, gastrointestinal blockage. Approximately 30 percent of those who pull hair engage in trichophagia (i.e., eating of the hair) and 1 percent of those individuals progress to develop a trichobezoar that requires surgical extraction (Frey *et al.* 2005).

Tongue chewing may result in soreness, keratinization and hyperkeratosis (i.e., skin cell changes often resulting in patches of thickened skin), and changes in pigmentation (Delong and Bukhart 2013). Nail biting may result in damage to the cuticles and nails, bacterial and viral infection, cellulitis, abscess, injury to the soft tissue lining the mouth, dental problems, temporomandibular dysfunction (i.e., disorders of the jaw), and osteomyelitis (i.e., bone infection) (Pacan *et al.* 2009). Cheek biting can result in lesions and ulcers in the oral mucosa (Ngoc *et al.* 2019).

BFRBs also have an emotional impact on those who experience them. Hair-pulling behavior is associated with increased feelings of pleasure, relief, and decreased boredom across the pulling cycle, trending toward unwanted emotions such as anger and anxiety as time passes (Bottesi *et al.* 2016). The long-term impact of the behavior over time can lead to shame, sadness, frustration, and decreased levels of calmness (Bottesi *et al.* 2016), low self-esteem, feelings of unattractiveness, strained relationships, depressed affect, and secrecy (Stemberger *et al.* 2000). Emotional reactivity and emotion dysregulation have been associated with skin picking (Snorrason, Smári, and Ólafsson 2010, 2011).

Because mild nail biting is so common, the behavior is likely under-reported and the impact can be underestimated. With severe cases of nail biting and picking, people report a diminished quality of life, increased distress, and significant nail damage to the fingers or toes. In some cases, this form of BFRB can result in infections, dental complications, plate abnormalities, ridging, cuticle damage, permanent shortening of the nail plate, or partial or complete loss of the nail (Lee and Lipner 2022).

Due to the embarrassment and shame associated with the physical consequences of BFRBs, individuals who engage in these behaviors may go to great lengths to camouflage or cover up the affected areas. Some of these efforts may include wearing wigs, hats, scarves, headbands, hairbands, various hair products and hair styles, makeup, Band-Aids, false eyelashes, acrylic nails, clothing that conceals, and shaving. Avoidance behaviors are also quite common in the effort to keep the behaviors private. These behaviors may include avoidance of bright light, wind, water (e.g., beach, swimming pools, rain), medical care, and hair salons. In a survey of 1,697 individuals with trichotillomania, common avoidances included vacations, job duties, school attendance, school responsibilities, studying, social events, and group activities (Woods *et al.* 2006).

Co-Occurring Disorders

It is common for individuals with BFRBs to have a diagnosis of one or more additional psychiatric disorders. Research suggests that 55–79 percent of adults with trichotillomania have one or more co-occurring disorders, with common comorbidities including anxiety, depression, obsessive compulsive disorder (OCD), attention deficit hyperactivity disorder (ADHD), posttraumatic stress disorder, panic disorder, excoriation disorder, bipolar disorder, substance use disorder, eating disorder, and tic disorder (Chesivoir *et al.* 2022; Grant *et al.* 2020; Woods *et al.* 2006). Co-occurring disorders are also present in the majority of individuals with a diagnosis of excoriation disorder and commonly include depression, anxiety, substance use disorder, bipolar disorder, ADHD, OCD, and posttraumatic stress disorder (Kwon *et al.* 2020) in addition to generalized anxiety disorder, panic disorder, eating disorder, trichotillomania, and tic disorder (Grant and Chamberlain 2020). While there is limited information on other BFRBs and co-occurring disorders, a study of 450 children found that nearly 75 percent of children who engaged in nail biting also experienced ADHD, with other significant comorbidities including oppositional defiant disorder, separation anxiety disorder, enuresis (urinary incontinence or involuntary urination), tic disorder, and OCD (Ghanizadeh 2008).

Pharmacological Treatment

Presently, there is no Food and Drug Administration (FDA)-approved medication for the treatment of BFRBs, and there is insufficient evidence to implicate the involvement of a specific agent or class of medication. The most commonly prescribed psychotropic medications for BFRBs are serotonin reuptake inhibitors (SRIs, SSRIs), as there is robust evidence for their use in the treatment of OCD. This being said, research suggests that these medications do not effectively treat BFRB symptoms. Small randomized controlled trials (RCTs) of SRIs have shown modest BFRB results (Farhat *et al.* 2020; McGuire *et al.* 2014). A meta-analysis of 13 small studies, including 298 adults and 43 youth, also concluded modest results (Hoffman *et al.* 2021).

A small trial of clomipramine vs. desipramine brings into question the possible efficacy of tricyclic antidepressants with predominant serotonin reuptake inhibition in adults (Swedo *et al.* 1989). Neuroleptic (antipsychotic) medications may be beneficial in reducing trichotillomania symptoms, although there has only been one small RCT evaluating its efficacy (olanzapine) (Van Ameringen *et al.* 2010). Glutamate modulators (N-acetylcysteine; NAC) have also come to light as a possible agent of utility in adults with BFRBs (Grant, Odlaug, and Kim 2009; Grant *et al.* 2016) but have not evidenced benefit in youth (Bloch *et al.* 2013). It also bears mentioning that a small RCT evidenced no benefit for the use of cannabinoids (dronabinol) (Grant *et al.* 2022).

Overall, although there have been no medications to date that have demonstrated clear efficacy for the treatment of BFRBs, medications can be helpful for some in their function as emotion modulators or as treatment of other co-occurring symptoms that impact or otherwise maintain BFRB symptoms and may help to maximize the efficacy of BFRB-targeted behavioral therapy in such cases.

Psychological Treatment

Behavioral therapies are among the most evidence-based treatments in the field of behavioral health, and they are based on a strong foundation of theoretical concepts. A 2020 meta-analysis (Farhat *et al.* 2020) of 24 treatment trials indicated that behavior therapy has the strongest evidence to date across multiple RCTs for reducing trichotillomania symptoms. Psychological interventions that have demonstrated promise for the effective treatment of BFRBs include: Habit Reversal Training (HRT), Comprehensive Behavioral Treatment (ComB), Acceptance and Commitment Therapy (ACT), Dialectical Behavioral Therapy (DBT), and technology-assisted treatments.

HRT is a simple behavioral intervention that aims to change the pattern of behavior through new behavioral practices. Although HRT may include differing components of treatment, core elements include:

- psychoeducation and functional analysis
- awareness training
- competing response training
- stimulus control.[1]

1 These core elements will be discussed in further detail later in this book.

Core component HRT studies and others that have included additional elements (e.g., relaxation training, social support, cognitive restructuring) have demonstrated reduced BFRBs (hair pulling, nail biting) following treatment and after a period of time following treatment cessation (Azrin, Nunn, and Frantz 1980a, 1980b; Lerner *et al.* 1998; Rahman *et al.* 2017; Teng, Woods, and Twohig 2006; Twohig *et al.* 2003). However, a meta-analysis of RCTs concluded insufficient support for HRT due to limited study and methodological weaknesses (Lee, Mpavaenda, and Fineberg 2019). While HRT may be a useful, simple behavioral procedure, it fails to directly address unhelpful thinking, emotional suffering, unwanted sensations, the impact of experiencing a BFRB on one's relationships, or avoidance behaviors enacted as a result of experiencing a BFRB.

ComB treatment for BFRBs is a broader, individualized, flexible cognitive-behavioral approach based on factors that cue and maintain BFRBs. Treatment components include:

- assessment and functional analysis (sensory, cognitive, affective, motor/awareness, place/environment)
- identification and selection of target domains
- implementation of specific Cognitive Behavioral Therapy (CBT) interventions
- evaluation, termination, and relapse prevention.[2]

ComB is arguably the most widely used treatment for BFRBs and has been the dominant model of clinical training. There have been two investigations of ComB. An uncontrolled study, which resulted in reduced trichotillomania symptom severity (62% no longer met diagnostic criteria post-treatment) and improved quality of life, although neither experiential avoidance (attempts to control or avoid unpleasant, unwanted internal experiences) nor depression improved (Falkenstein *et al.* 2016). The only RCT to date (a comparison of ComB treatment vs. minimal attention (placebo treatment)) resulted in subject-reported improvements in symptom severity, with maintenance at three- and six-month follow-up; however, no significant changes in symptom severity or alopecia were rated by the interviewer (Carlson *et al.* 2021). ComB is a well-organized, highly individualized treatment approach that may include a variety of traditional cognitive and behavioral therapy interventions. Empirical support for this treatment is limited as there have been few studies conducted to date and there is limited interpretation of existing data. While ComB includes a wide range of traditional CBT techniques, it includes a traditional cognitive-therapy-based view of cognition focusing on cognitive restructuring and does not make use of the "third wave's" evolution of CBT, which focuses on mindful awareness and the relationship one has with one's inner experiences.

ACT is a process-oriented behavioral therapy, steeped in metaphor, that operates on the premise that psychological suffering is the result of experiential avoidance of one's own unwanted cognitions, emotions, and bodily sensations. ACT aims to help individuals become fully engaged in the present moment and move toward what matters

---

2 These core elements will be discussed in further detail later in this book.

most to them in the service of living a rich, meaningful life, even in the presence of uncomfortable private experiences. ACT's six core processes include:

- present moment
- acceptance
- cognitive defusion
- self-as-context
- values
- committed action.

ACT for BFRBs has been studied as an adjunct to behavioral therapy procedures as well as a standalone treatment, in both individual and group treatment formats, with adults and with adolescents, demonstrating improvements at treatment cessation as well as at follow-up (Asplund *et al.* 2021; Crosby *et al.* 2012; Haaland *et al.* 2017; Lee *et al.* 2018; Lee *et al.* 2019; Woods, Wetterneck, and Flessner 2006; Woods *et al.* 2022). With the recent adoption of ACT across the field of mental healthcare, BFRB research has seen significant growth in this area in recent years, although the robust demonstration of its efficacy is still in progress and the mechanism for therapeutic change remains unclear. Unlike HRT and ComB, ACT directly addresses the experiential avoidance associated with BFRBs and seeks to improve psychological flexibility.

DBT is a skills-based psychotherapy that is intended to help individuals manage intense emotions, unwanted behaviors, and interpersonal difficulties through the processes of acceptance and change. This is an integrative psychotherapy model that adapts Zen practices, behavioralism, social behavioralism, and practices of CBT, to include problem-solving strategies, life-skills training, exposure, and contingency management (Heard and Linehan 2019). There are four core modules in DBT which include:

- mindfulness training
- distress tolerance
- emotion regulation
- interpersonal effectiveness.

There have been three investigations of DBT skills training as an adjunct to HRT. A small pilot study of DBT (mindfulness, distress tolerance, and emotion regulation skills training)-enhanced HRT demonstrated improvements in trichotillomania symptoms, mood severity, and emotion regulation after 11 sessions and at three-month follow-up (Keuthen *et al.* 2010). At six-month follow-up, some maintained their improvements, while others demonstrated some loss of gains (Keuthen *et al.* 2011). An RCT of DBT (mindfulness, distress tolerance, and emotion regulation skills training)-enhanced HRT resulted in improvements of trichotillomania severity, functional impairment (impairment in daily functioning), and experiential avoidance at treatment completion; however, emotion regulation capacity change (significant change in the ability to regulate one's emotions) was unclear and some subjects reported loss of treatment gains at three- and six-month follow-up (Keuthen *et al.* 2012). Unlike other BFRB treatment protocols, DBT focuses on skills training to improve emotional regulation, distress tolerance, and impulsivity. It is also a highly structured model that is easily implemented. While DBT shows promise in treating BFRBs, its efficacy remains unclear, as there have been so few investigations evaluating this treatment model, all four modules of DBT have not been applied in the treatment of BFRBs, it has not been evaluated as a standalone treatment for BFRBs, and there have been no comparisons with other active treatment conditions.

Technology-assisted treatments provide accessible internet, application-based, or device-delivered interventions to improve access and treatment outcomes for those experiencing BFRBs. Internet-delivered interventions have shown promise in an online ACT-enhanced behavior therapy for adolescents and are an area of growth in the expansion of access to evidence-based care (Petersen *et al.* 2022; Twohig *et al.* 2021). A study of an awareness training device, HabitAware, has garnered interest in the use of such devices to assist in treatment (Stiede *et al.* 2022). The use of technology holds the potential for utility in the treatment of BFRBs, as their use may decrease barriers to treatment (e.g., cost, accessibility) and may guide the practice of skills in the individual's natural environment, among others. Although this is an area of interest and growth, research to date has shown only modest outcomes with early website-based CBT programs and high disengagement with self-guided programs. A survey of treatment preferences for BFRBs also indicated a preference for face-to-face interactions and concerns about confidentiality and security (Arabatzoudis, Rehm and Nedeljkovic 2021).

Why An Integrative Behavioral Treatment Model?

Although there has been useful foundational research in the treatment of BFRBs and the current behavioral therapy standard of care is helpful for some, robust long-term outcomes remain inadequate for a significant number of those living with a BFRB. The following remain unaddressed or under-addressed:

- chronic nature of the disorders
- readiness for treatment and setting realistic treatment expectations
- maintaining motivation to consistently utilize strategies
- awareness and automaticity
- addressing vulnerabilities and comorbidities
- impact on self-worth and self-efficacy
- interpersonal impact of the disorders
- experiential avoidance and psychological inflexibility
- skills deficits: adaptive responses to unwanted internal discomforts
- oversimplification of case conceptualization and treatment plan
- lack of dissemination and standard of care and access to care.

The goal of Integrative Behavioral Therapy (IBT) is to improve quality of life by changing one's relationship to BFRB experiences and broaden tools to more effectively manage them. Based upon the shared underlying behavioral principles of all of the aforementioned evidence-based treatments to date in addition to applicable integrative treatment models which emphasize the importance of motivation and stages of change, IBT provides a unified treatment protocol, utilizing the full range of scientifically supported psychological interventions to maximize and maintain treatment success. Beginning with a thorough functional analysis to conceptualize the function(s) of an individual's BFRB and the way(s) in which it is maintained, IBT integrates the essential theoretical and treatment elements of HRT, ComB, ACT, DBT skills, and the Transtheoretical Model (Prochaska and DiClemente 2005) into an individualized treatment plan. This program was initially developed as a 14-week group, in which participants are introduced to the full range of behavioral skills and encouraged to find what works for them, based on their functional analysis and hands-on experience practicing the skills. However, the program can be modified for individual therapy or be used in a self-guided manner, as we will do in this workbook. Please note that self-guided work is not intended to be a substitute for mental health treatment with a licensed professional.

Common Questions and Answers

Q: Are BFRBs a form of OCD?

A: No. Although BFRBs are commonly misdiagnosed as OCD, they are different conditions. BFRBs may resemble OCD in that there may be a sense that one is driven to repetitively engage in the behavior, but the two disorders have different symptoms and require different treatments. The two disorders are, however, likely related to one another in terms of genetics.

Q: Are BFRBs caused by childhood trauma, maltreatment, or abuse?

A: Not necessarily. Although research has attempted to demonstrate an association between BFRBs and trauma, there is little evidence to suggest that BFRBs are an indication of deeper issues or unresolved trauma. It is, however, not unusual for those who struggle with BFRBs to experience anxiety or depression as the result of a trauma history, which contributes to their difficulties in managing the behavior (Houghton *et al.* 2016).

Q: Are BFRBs considered to be a form of self-mutilation or non-suicidal self-injury?

A: No. Self-harm, also referred to as non-suicidal self-injury (or NSSI), include behaviors that cause intentional harm to the body, such as cutting or burning. The function of self-harm is not intended to result in suicide, but rather is a goal-directed, intentional means of coping with intense emotional pain or suffering. Self-harm behavior is often reported to lead to feelings that override the emotional numbing of overwhelm associated with distress intolerance. BFRBs, by contrast, may occur in a goal-directed, intentional manner or they may occur outside of one's awareness of the behavior. One of the main differences between self-harm and BFRBs is that self-harm behaviors are intentionally carried out to cause pain (and relief), while BFRBs are unwanted behaviors that individuals struggle to stop. The function of BFRBs is not to cause harm to oneself and is not intended to produce pain. Although the specific function(s) can vary from person to person, overall it is an unwanted means by which individuals self-regulate or self-soothe when uncomfortable internal states arise (thoughts, feelings, emotions, bodily sensations). Although the long-term effects of these behaviors are unwanted (e.g., hair loss, embarrassment), the immediate consequences perpetuate the behavior pattern (e.g., feels satisfying, serves as a distraction).

Q: Are BFRBs just "bad habits" that can be stopped with enough willpower or with punishment?

A: No. BFRBs are complex disorders that often require skilled interventions. No amount of willpower, alone, is likely to be sufficient to effectively cease the behavior. Punishment does not help to decrease the behavior and has the potential to intensify the shame and guilt individuals living with BFRBs often experience. Compassion, understanding, and psychological interventions are often necessary to learn to live life fully with a BFRB.

Q: Are people always aware of their BFRB?

A: No, not always. BFRBs can occur with little or no awareness. Many individuals experience both focused and unfocused BFRBs. These unfocused behaviors typically occur when people are engaged in another activity, such as reading, doing work at home, or watching television.

Q: Do BFRBs respond well to anti-anxiety or antidepressant medications?

A: There is currently no FDA-approved medication for the treatment of BFRBs. Medications may be helpful in treating co-occurring conditions, which in turn may help to reduce BFRB symptoms.

Q: How are trichotillomania and other BFRBs diagnosed?

A: BFRBs are diagnosed by clinical interview with an informed healthcare professional, who may also administer questionnaires to further assess BFRB symptoms. Although in the case of trichotillomania tests such as a scalp biopsy may be used to rule out alopecia when hair-pulling behavior is denied or is occurring outside of an individual's awareness, there are presently no medical "tests" to diagnose BFRBs, such as blood tests or imaging studies.

Q: Is there a cure for BFRBs?

A: There is presently no known cure, but many do experience recovery and live full, happy, meaningful lives. We aim to help you do just that.

Getting Started

As you embark on the road to recovery, we invite you to approach your BFRB with curiosity on the path we'll travel together. Let's begin by noticing where your journey began and where you are right now in this moment.

When did your BFRB begin and how did you understand it at the time?

....

....

How does your BFRB impact your life?

....

....

What do you find has helped, and what hasn't helped?

....

....

How has your BFRB impacted your self-view, daily life, and relationship with others?

....

....

Why do you want to change this behavior?

....

....

What is your goal in using this workbook?

....

....

CHAPTER 2

Building Motivation and Resilience

It is important to bring motivation and resilience with you on your life's journey. The fact that you are here demonstrates that you already possess some of these qualities. You've likely had experiences with your BFRB that have left you feeling frustrated, disappointed, overwhelmed, knocked down, or defeated. But here you are! You're getting back up! With these ups and downs, your BFRB has likely waxed and waned. Perhaps you're wondering what's going to be different this time. What magic does this workbook hold that will banish your BFRB forever? Right now, let's look at where you want to go in life.

EXPLORE

What Matters Most

Oftentimes in psychological treatment, the client's goal in therapy is to decrease or get rid of the problem that has brought the individual into treatment. Typically, the client has struggled with the problem and has come to a mental healthcare provider to join forces with them in this difficult battle. Let's consider a different path, and, instead of focusing on ridding yourself of what your mind and body does, let's begin by focusing on what really matters most to you in your life. After all, you are much more than your BFRB.

The goal of this exercise is to help you to identify your values. That is, what matters most to you. This is highly personal—what matters most to you may be different from what matters most to another person. There are no right or wrong answers. Let's explore this. Consider the following questions:

Who is important to you in your life?

....

....

What is important to you?

What excites or inspires you?

What kind of person do you want to be? What qualities do you want to bring to what you do?

In moments when you are doing something you enjoy, what is it about those moments that feels good?

In moments when you feel good and relaxed and comfortable with just being you, what is it that you are thinking, feeling, and/or doing?

How does reflecting on these questions right now make you feel? Do you notice any thoughts showing up, or emotions, bodily sensations, or urges?

What Matters Most—Values Identification

Let's take a closer look at what matters most to you in the spaces and places you spend time. Here is a word bank—a list of descriptive words. Read each word and notice what words stand out to you—words that feel like they capture something that is important to you. Circle those words.

Acceptance
Achievement
Adaptability
Adventure
Aesthetics
Affection
Ambition
Assertiveness
Attentiveness
Balance
Belonging
Bravery
Calm
Camaraderie
Candor
Capability
Caring
Charity
Cleanliness
Collaboration
Comfort
Commitment
Communication
Community
Compassion
Competence
Confidence
Connection
Consistency
Contribution
Control
Cooperation
Country
Courtesy
Creativity
Curiosity
Decisiveness
Dedication
Democracy
Dependability
Determination
Dignity

Diligence
Discipline
Discretion
Diversity
Duty
Eagerness
Education
Effectiveness
Efficiency
Elegance
Empathy
Empowering
Energetic
Engagement
Entertainment
Enthusiasm
Environment
Equality
Ethics
Excellence
Excitement
Expertise
Fairness
Faith
Fame
Family
Fearlessness
Fitness
Flexibility
Focus
Freedom
Friendship
Generosity
Genuineness
Goodwill
Grace
Gratitude
Growth
Happiness
Hard work
Harmony
Health

Helpfulness
Heroism
Honesty
Hope
Hospitality
Humility
Humor
Imagination
Improvement
Independence
Individuality
Innovation
Insightfulness
Integrity
Intellect
Intimacy
Justice
Knowledge
Leadership
Learning
Liberty
Logic
Love
Loyalty
Mastery
Mindfulness
Modesty
Morality
Motivation
Nature
Openness
Optimism
Order
Organization
Partnership
Passion
Patience
Peace
Perfection
Perseverance
Playfulness
Pleasure

Positivity
Power
Pragmatism
Preparedness
Pride
Privacy
Productivity
Professionalism
Purpose
Relationships
Reliability
Religion
Resilience
Respect
Responsibility
Restraint
Safety
Security
Self-care
Simplicity
Sincerity
Spirituality
Stability
Strength
Success
Support
Thoughtfulness
Tolerance
Trust
Truth
Understanding
Uniqueness
Unity
Warmth
Wealth
Willingness
Wisdom
Wonder
Zeal

Value Sorting—Spaces and Places

Next, in the values categories below, write the words from the word bank that most fit those categories for you. Of course, this is not an exhaustive list. If you come up with additional words that are not listed in the bank, feel free to add them to the list. Words may be listed in more than one category, if that is what is meaningful to you.

Relationships	Work/ Education	Leisure/Play	Physical Health	Emotional Health
1.	1.	1.	1.	1.
2.	2.	2.	2.	2.
3.	3.	3.	3.	3.
4.	4.	4.	4.	4.
5.	5.	5.	5.	5.
6.	6.	6.	6.	6.
7.	7.	7.	7.	7.
8.	8.	8.	8.	8.
9.	9.	9.	9.	9.
10.	10.	10.	10.	10.

On a scale of 0–10, with 0 being "not at all" and 10 being "completely consistent," how closely do you think you are living in a manner that is consistent with these values within these different areas of your life.

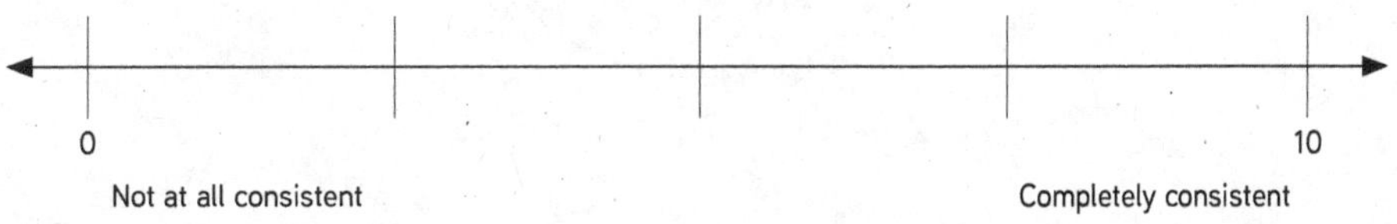

Relationships	Work/ Education	Leisure/Play	Physical Health	Emotional Health
Rating =	Rating =	Rating =	Rating =	Rating =

Finding a Balance: The Busy Lives We Lead

Do you ever feel like you don't have the time to do all of the things you'd like to do (or feel the need to do)? That's most of us. People live such busy lives. And, when life slows down a bit, many of us have the tendency to actively find things to keep us busier than we care to be. It can be a difficult balance. Think about how you typically spend your time. What percentage of your time do you presently devote to the important areas of your life: Relationships, Work/Education, Leisure/Play, Physical Health, and Emotional Health? There are no correct or incorrect answers, and you don't have to be happy with the way in which you manage your time. This is just a reflection of your current life as you live it.

Divide up that time accordingly on the pie chart below:

It might look something like this:

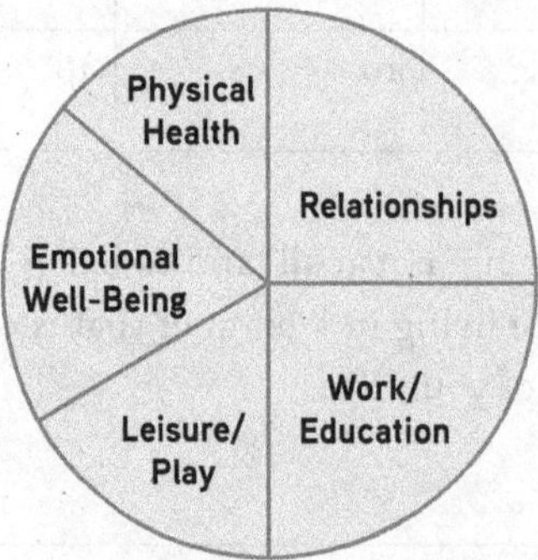

In an ideal world, how do you imagine you would like to spend your time and energy? Even if your mind is telling you that your ideal balance is not possible, what would that pie chart look like?

How does your actual pie chart compare to your ideal pie chart? No judgments here, although you may find that critical voice in your mind scrutinizing any differences you see. The goal here is to help you to gain a better understanding of your daily life and what it would look like if you could achieve a more satisfying balance.

....

....

....

....

....

....

PRACTICE

Getting a Bird's-Eye View of What Makes You Tick

Great! You have an idea of what's important to you—the inside stuff: that which is in your heart and mind, that which no one would know unless they asked. Now, let's get a bird's-eye view, "the big picture," of those important things, those values, by plotting them on a matrix (Polk and Schoendorff 2014), an exercise from Acceptance and Commitment Therapy (ACT). Have no fear—there are no complex mathematical computations coming. This just gives you a place to step back and take a look at what makes you tick—what motivates you and what may hold you back from living the life you want.

Based on what you explored above, record the values you identified and sorted in the values sorting exercise in the bottom-right quadrant of your matrix:

My Matrix

★

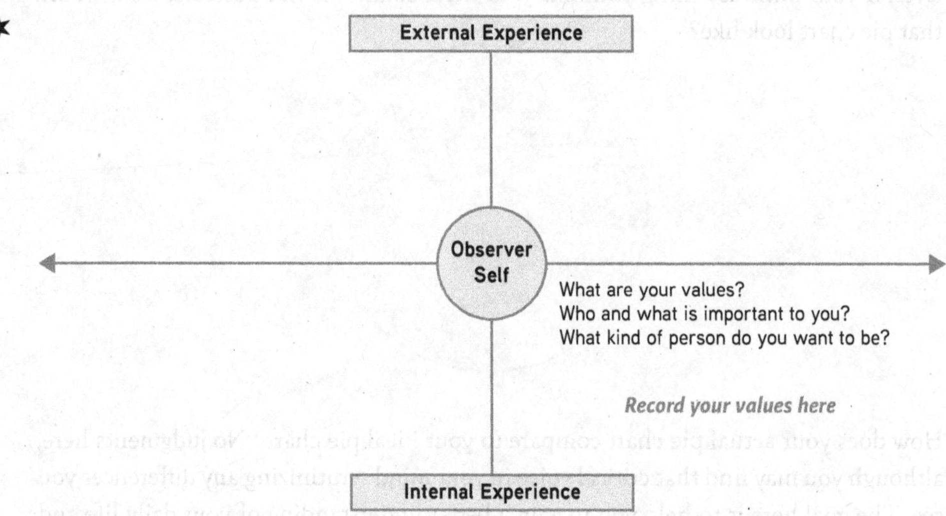

Your matrix might look something like this:

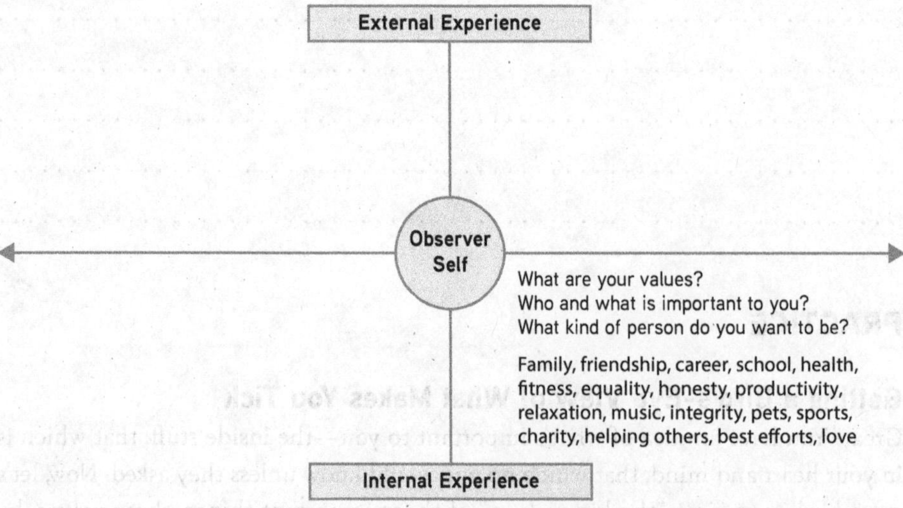

Now that we know what matters most to you—who, what, and the qualities you ideally want to bring to what you do in your life—let's take a look at the ways in which you live those ideals. Keep in mind that no one lives out their values 100 percent at every moment of every day, no one. Let's take a look at what it looks like when you do.

If you were being filmed as you went about your everyday life, what would the camera capture? What would we see you doing that moves you towards your values? We'll call these towards moves. For example, if family is important to you, maybe you would be seen playing with your children or talking with your parents. If kindness is valued, perhaps you'd be seen gathering donations for a charity or smiling at a stranger on the street. What do you do in the service of your values? Record some of the behaviors that are consistent with what matters to you below:

Value	Towards Move
Example: Self-care	*Example: Taking a yoga class*
Example: Environmental preservation	*Example: Recycling*

Now, let's add these towards moves to the upper-right quadrant of your matrix:

My Matrix

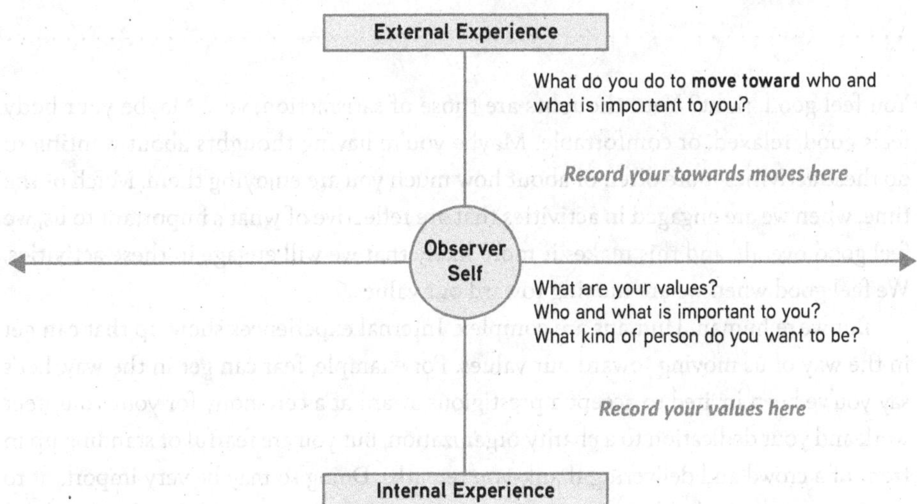

Your towards moves might look something like this:

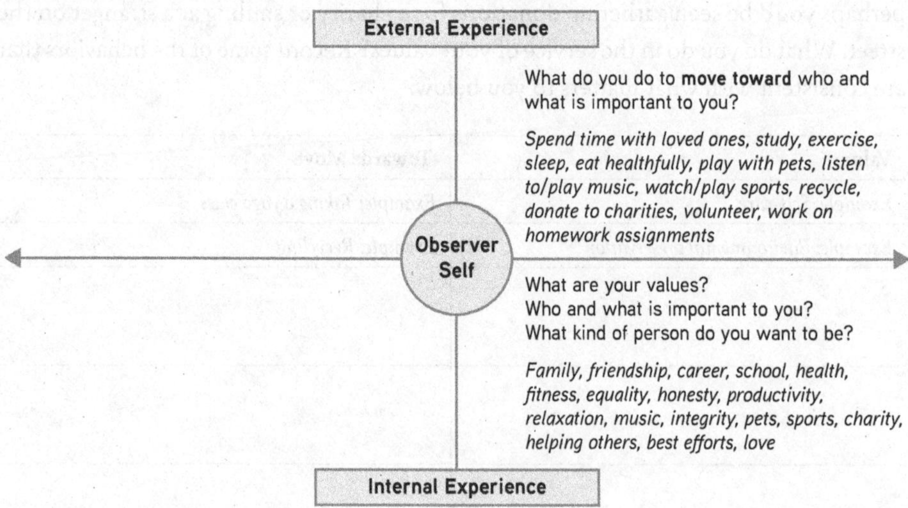

Think about the experience of carrying out these towards moves. Notice the emotions you experience when you are doing things that are consistent with what's important to you. Notice the thoughts that show up in your mind. Notice your bodily sensations. What shows up when you are doing these things?

....

....

....

....

You feel good, right? Your thoughts are those of satisfaction, yes? Maybe your body feels good, relaxed, or comfortable. Maybe you're having thoughts about wanting to do these activities more often or about how much you are enjoying them. Much of the time, when we are engaged in activities that are reflective of what's important to us, we feel good overall, and this makes it more likely that we will engage in these activities. We feel good when we are moving toward our values.

But we're human. Humans are complex. Internal experiences show up that can get in the way of us moving toward our values. For example, fear can get in the way. Let's say you've been invited to accept a prestigious award at a ceremony for your volunteer work and your dedication to a charity organization, but you are fearful of standing up in front of a crowd and delivering thank-you remarks. Doing so may be very important to you because charity holds great meaning to you, as does this organization, but fears and intense worries arise about what might go wrong. You may feel physical symptoms of anxiety, such as a racing heartbeat, stomach discomfort, and shortness of breath. And, as a result, you don't want to go because you don't want to feel this way and you don't want the worries about what could possibly go awry to actually happen, no matter how unlikely.

Internal experiences, such as fear, can take us away from what matters most to us. Let's take a look at your internal experiences and how they may take you off course.

How about those TIMES?

Our minds are like machines, constantly receiving, analyzing, and processing information from our senses. These processes are internal, private experiences that only the individual has the ability to observe and acknowledge. We are all experiencers experiencing experience. Let's think about these private experiences; think about your thinking. Sometimes, these experiences are helpful to us, alerting us to something important upon which we must act. Other times, these experiences are unpleasant, unwanted, and unhelpful, interfering with what is important to us. We sometimes get stuck struggling with these experiences in our minds, ruminating, trying to avoid them, push them away, or make them stop. Let's focus on that. We'll use a mnemonic to help identify these pesky experiences. Identify your T-I-M-E-S (adapted from Harris 2008).

What shows up inside your mind and body that gets in the way of what matters most to you?

Thoughts (e.g., self-criticism, giving permission to engage in my BFRB)

....

....

Images (e.g., imagining someone noticing and questioning my hair loss, picturing an area of skin damage in my mind)

....

....

Memories (e.g., recalling experiences of embarrassment, remembering a time of being ridiculed)

....

....

Emotions (e.g., anxiety, shame, sadness, frustration, fatigue)

....

....

Sensations and urges (e.g., itchy head, burning eyelids, rising sense of tension/urge)

....

....

Now, let's add these TIMES to the bottom-left quadrant of your matrix:

My Matrix

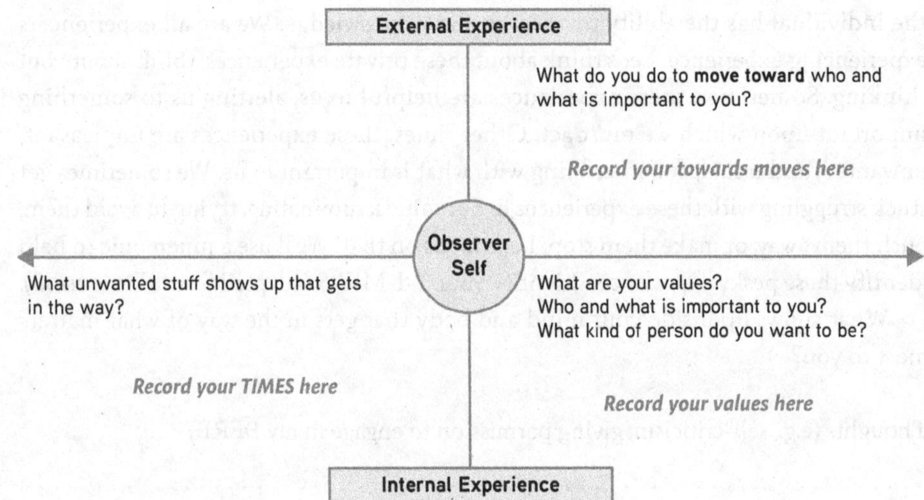

Your TIMES might look something like this:

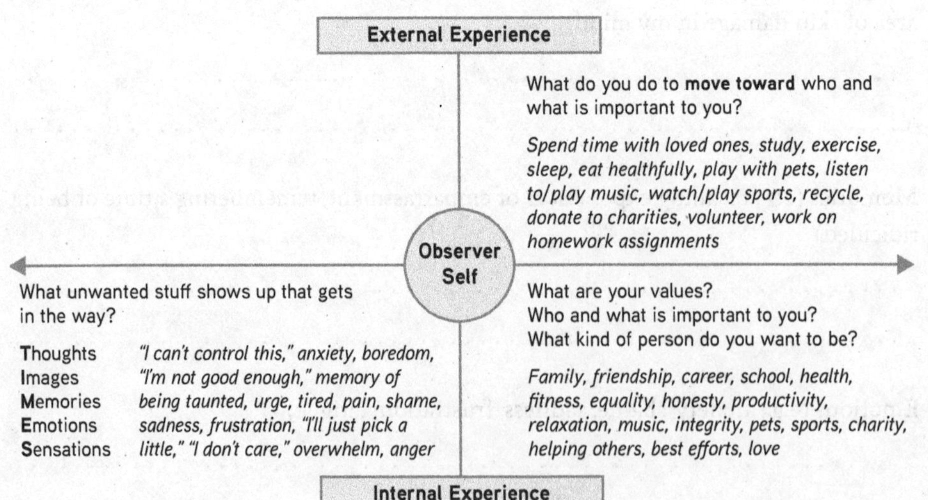

Connect the DOTS

When these unwanted TIMES show up, we sometimes choose to act in ways that attempt to avoid them, push them away, or get rid of them. Of course we do! It's natural to want to avoid unpleasant experiences. Sometimes, we work really hard to try to do this. These efforts are effective to varying degrees, often resulting in relief from the TIMES; however, this relief is temporary. The TIMES are persistent and they re-emerge after a period of time.

Let's examine the actions you carry out to try to rid yourself of your TIMES. These are your "away moves"—in your efforts to get rid of your TIMES, they take you away from what is important to you. We'll use another mnemonic, D-O-T-S (Harris 2008), to help identify how you attempt to manage these unpleasant private experiences.

Distracting yourself: Are there things that you do to try to distract yourself from the TIMES, such as engaging in specific activities or avoiding people, places, or spaces that trigger the TIMES?

....

....

Opting out: In what ways do you decline or avoid opportunities that may trigger your TIMES? Think about the "no thank yous" and the "not nows" in your life.

....

....

(Over)**T**hinking: How do you talk to yourself when the TIMES show up? Do you reason, worry, blame yourself or others, think things through, or use other thinking strategies to deal with the TIMES?

....

....

Substances and other strategies: Do you ever turn to alcohol or drugs? Caffeine or nicotine? Food? Or do you do other things to try to manage or dampen the TIMES?

....

....

These are your DOTS. Now, let's add these DOTS to the top-left quadrant of your matrix:

My Matrix

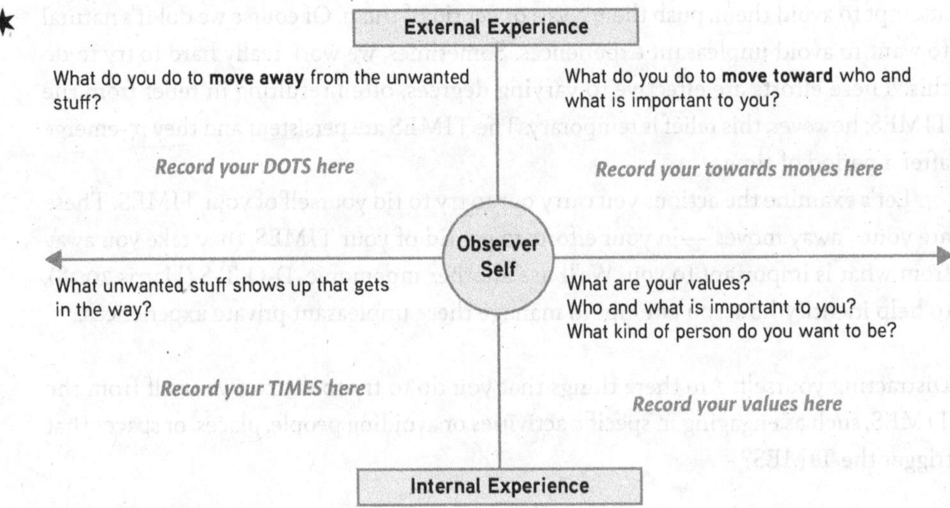

Your DOTS might look something like this:

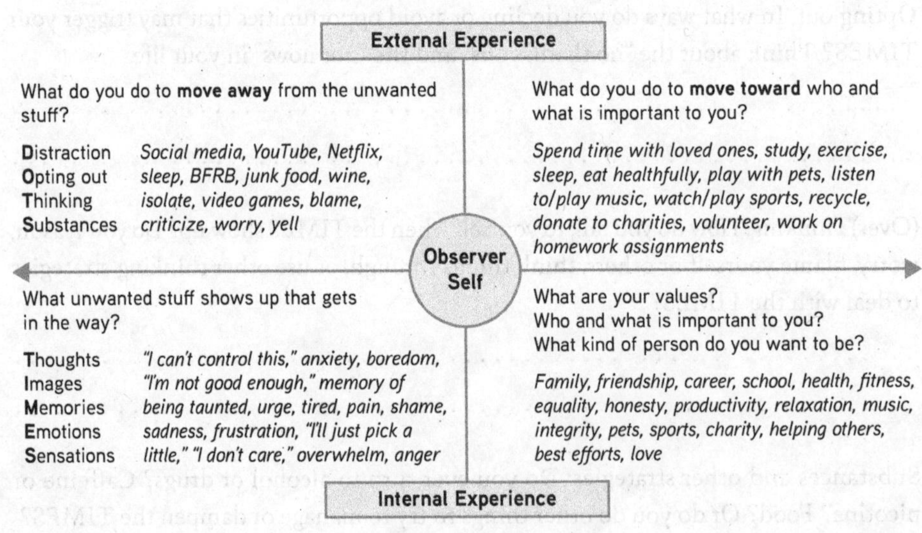

EXPLORE

The Secret about BFRBs

Here's the thing about BFRBs—these behaviors are intended to make you feel better, but ultimately, they make you feel worse and trap you in the cycle of the behavior.

We all want to feel good about ourselves and our choices. When we are hanging out on the right side of this matrix, doing the things that move us toward what matters most to us, the reward centers of our brains light up with satisfaction. We're aligned with our values. But, inevitably, our internal world distracts us with experiences that are unwanted. Maybe we have uncomfortable thoughts about how we look or we question whether the people around us like us or approve of something we said or did. Maybe we imagine the possibility of making a mistake that leads to catastrophic consequences for us or for others. Maybe our minds bring up memories of shameful experiences or of feeling regretful for not having made a choice we had wanted to make but didn't. Maybe we're distracted by unwanted feelings, like fear, anger, or other intense emotions. Or maybe we notice an uncomfortable bodily sensation, like pain, tingling, or the felt urge to engage in a BFRB.

Of course, we don't want this discomfort. Not only does it feel bad, but it distracts us from what's important to us and from feeling good. So, naturally, we try to get rid of it, to push it away. Those are the DOTS. We try to distract ourselves from our discomfort. We opt out of things to try to avoid bringing on those TIMES. We try to reason with it to try to force it away or otherwise try to think ourselves out of having this internal discomfort. And we may try to use substances of all sorts to try to push away our discomfort and try to make ourselves feel better. We're stuck on the left side of this matrix. Moreover, while we are going to great lengths to get rid of these internal discomforts, we are also moving away from what's important to us; we have lost sight of what matters to us and/or are not doing the things that matter to us because we are focused on our own distress. These are detours from our destinations.

It makes sense that we intrinsically try to make ourselves feel better in any way we can. Does it work? Yes, it does, sometimes. And research teaches us that intermittent reinforcement (reward that occurs inconsistently) is the greatest way to ensure a pattern will continue; thus, we keep doing what we've been doing. Unfortunately, these discomforts typically return. Think about the TIMES that bother you most. Have you ever banished one from your mind forever? We'd venture to guess that's a no. It's a futile effort. They come back. There's the rub.

Your BFRB Monster

Picture this: your BFRB is a scary monster. Imagine what it looks like—its color, texture, size, shape, and facial expression. Imagine what it sounds like. Does it sneer? Does it growl? Does it speak? Now imagine that you are engaged in a tug of war with this monster. You are standing on the edge of a steep cliff. The monster is also standing on the edge of a cliff, but this cliff is across from you. And, between you and the monster is a vast darkness down below. You feel terrified of falling into the abyss. So you pull the rope with all your might and the monster pulls in return. You pull and it pulls, and you pull and it pulls. Sometimes, you pull the monster closer to the edge of its cliff, but just as you do, it tugs back and pulls you closer to the edge of yours. You're exhausted, yet you continue to struggle with all your might. Just then, you realize that this is an unwinnable struggle. You won't be able to pull the monster into the chasm. And you are terrified of it pulling you in and falling to your end. What can you do?

You can drop the rope.

Yes, it's true that this will not make the monster go away. It will still be there on the other side, scary as ever. But if you drop the rope, it doesn't have the same power over you. It can't pull you in and you are free to move about, turn your attention to other things, and rest those aching muscles.

Here's the thing—when most people struggle, they are convinced that they are not succeeding because they aren't trying hard enough. If you're reading this book, you've struggled with your BFRB and have worked so hard to control it, yet it continues to return, doesn't it? How many times have you thought that if you could just stay more motivated or have more "willpower," you could stop your BFRB for good? You just need to try harder, right?

What if that isn't it at all? What if the struggle itself is the problem and not the BFRB?

Are You on the Struggle Bus?

Imagine this: you're a bus driver, driving your bus on the journey of life. You've got your navigation set to specific destinations, destinations that you really want to reach. Unfortunately, you have a rowdy group of passengers who make a lot of noise and, at times, cause trouble on your bus. They yell at you. They tell you that you're a terrible driver. They tell you that you can't be trusted to take them anywhere. Some passengers demand that you turn off course, in other directions that would take you away from your destinations. Others insist that you stop the bus and let someone else drive. They tell you that you can't be trusted to make the right turns or keep them safe and happy on the journey. You find yourself increasingly irritated, and you want them to stop. What do you do? Do you do what they say, turning left instead of right, heading to another destination rather than where you want to go? Do you yell at them and insist that they cut it out? Do you pull over and tell them to get off the bus? What if they refuse and just become louder and more bothersome? What if this just intensifies the conflict?

What happens if you choose to respond in this way—paying more and more attention to them, trying harder and harder to make them stop? You're not focused on driving the bus. You may not even be driving the bus to your destination anymore because you are caught up in trying to control the situation. Ironically, you are actually in less control, totally off course from your journey.

What if you were to let them be there, without responding to them? What if you were to just focus on driving the bus, even if that is sometimes difficult? You may not like their behavior and you may not want them there, but if you don't give them attention by responding to them, arguing with them, or struggling with them, they would likely seem much less problematic. Maybe they would even quiet down because you aren't fueling their antics, or maybe if you pivoted your attention to your drive, you'd perceive the situation as tolerable and you'd get to experience the satisfaction of getting to where you're going. That's perseverance, resilience, satisfaction—and maybe even pride. Sometimes, stopping the struggle itself makes all the difference.

So what does that mean for our work here together? We invite you to approach this journey differently than you may have intended and maybe differently than you have in the past. Rather than setting the expectation that this book will enable you to stop your BFRB, we invite you to:

- set an intention to use this book as a guide—to allow yourself the space to reflect on a wide range of experiences, both internal and external, without judgment
- set an intention to become an observer of your BFRB rather than a critic
- set an intention to approach your BFRB with curiosity for observing it in order to learn more about the experience rather than trying to struggle with it to make it stop
- set an intention to adopt a stance of willingness to experience everything there is to experience, even the tough stuff, rather than a resistant or willful stance
- set an intention to change your relationship with your BFRB and the private experiences that drive and maintain it.

Willfulness vs. Willingness

As you've seen in your matrix, we can get so caught up in struggling with unwanted private experiences—those unpleasant thoughts, images in our minds, memories, emotions, and sensations—that we have a natural tendency to want to get rid of them, push them away, avoid them, and do anything we can to make them stop. In doing so, we become willful... toward ourselves. We shut down, we opt out, we give up, we refuse to try, and we disengage from the world and from that which is most meaningful to us in our lives.

Have you ever found yourself so frustrated that you tell yourself you don't care anymore and give yourself permission to engage in your BFRB? Or have you found yourself feeling so ashamed of your hair loss or skin/nail damage that you decide to decline a social invitation and stay home? Do you turn to your BFRB or other DOTS when those TIMES show up in your mind? This is willfulness. Consider some moments in which you became willful.

What was the willful behavior and what TIMES were you trying to push away?

....

....

Willfulness, in this regard, is the refusal to be open to your own experience. It's *you* rejecting *you*. You can learn to be more accepting of yourself and of all of the busywork of your mind and body, even that which is unwanted, by practicing willingness.

Willingness is the act of being fully open to one's own experience. It's the act of being accepting of whatever shows up, even if you don't like or want it. It's the act of allowing it to be there, to let it come and go freely, refraining from the struggle to push it away. By practicing willingness, you will be more available to flexibly consider your experiences, have greater freedom to consider possibilities, and learn to better sit with your mind and body's constant stream of stuff. And everyone's got a constant stream of stuff. It's how we work!

The concept of willingness is included in the radical acceptance often referred to in Dialectical Behavioral Therapy (DBT). In a nutshell, it is being able to accept that we all experience some sort of pain in our human experience. How we deal with that pain has an impact on our well-being. Ongoing distress occurs when we deal with our pain in shortsighted or unhealthy ways, which leads to suffering. Willingness, however, is finding understanding and acceptance, even when things are not going the way we want. The cycle of suffering is broken by embracing these experiences, even though we may not approve of them. The process of willingness to accept reality is what opens us up to new experiences and allows us to let go of shame, guilt, anger, and other distressing emotions. This is not an easy process since we are often conditioned to stay stuck in our suffering. We will continue to build on this skill throughout the workbook.

Be on the lookout for your mind's signals that it is becoming willful. What are some willfulness signals you might observe? Might you think, "I can't...," or "I won't...," for example? What do you notice?

....

....

PRACTICE

TOOLS FOR THE TERRAIN

- Half-Smile and Willing Hands
- A Letter to Your BFRB
- Setting Intentions with Others

Half-Smile and Willing Hands

When you notice these signals, acknowledge them: "There's willfulness." Just label it. And practice having an openness stance. You might tell yourself, "It's okay to feel frustrated. I can keep trying, even though I feel this way." Or you might say to yourself, "Shame doesn't feel good, but I can still go to the party and also enjoy seeing my friends, even if this feeling is there."

Practicing physical signals of willingness can also be helpful. Unfold your arms, relax your facial muscles, drop your shoulders, hold your head up, make eye contact with others, and adopt a half-smile—just turn up the corners of your mouth. Position your arms in an open, welcoming stance; we call this "willing hands." This, too, can go a long way toward willingness and well-being. Research actually shows that the simple act of smiling can improve one's experience and overall mood.

How can you practice willingness?

....

....

A Letter to Your BFRB

Living with a BFRB is hard. It can affect so many areas of your life. Consider the ways in which your BFRB has impacted you. As you embark on this journey to change your relationship with your BFRB and diminish the impact it has on your life, take a moment to write a letter to your BFRB. What have you lost or missed out on? How has it made you feel? How has it held you back? And what might life look like without this struggle? Allow these thoughts and feelings, though they may be difficult, to be here, acknowledged on this page.

....

....

....

....

....

....

....

....

....

....

....

....

....

Setting Intentions with Others

Oftentimes, BFRBs impact relationships. They can impact close relationships if they are kept "secret." They can also impact relationships with those who know about your BFRB in the way these individuals interact with you around the topic of your BFRB. (We will be addressing improving the relationships in your life in Chapter 14.) For now, consider how you might prefer to interact with others as you embark on your work with this book.

Consider whether others in your life, who are "in the know," are helpful or unhelpful in how they interact with you regarding your BFRB. What do they say or do?

....

....

How does this influence your thoughts/beliefs about yourself, your BFRB, and your relationship with them?

....

....

How do you respond to them (in action)?

....

....

How would you like to interact with them? For example, you may choose to ask others to give you nonverbal cues to help with bringing the BFRB into your awareness or by offering you a tool when they notice your behavior? Or you may want others to give you the space you need to work on this yourself. However you would prefer to engage with others regarding your BFRB is okay. You may even change your preferences around this as time passes. That's okay, too!

....

....

ACTION PLAN

Building Motivation and Resilience

What key points in this chapter really spoke to you? What are the highlights *you* most want to keep in mind that are important for you and your BFRB?

....

....

What did you learn about yourself as you **explored**?

....

....

What **practices** will you commit to working on this week to move you toward your destination?

....

....

What is your **action plan**? What steps will you take to put these practices in place?

....

....

When and how often will you engage in these practices?

....

....

CHAPTER 3

Understanding Your BFRB and Your TIMES MAP

EXPLORE

Mindfulness

Understanding your BFRB starts with a curiosity for wanting to understand it and increasing awareness of the behavior and its patterns. As BFRBs sometimes occur outside of conscious awareness, practicing the skill of noticing your BFRB pattern, what is sometimes called awareness training or attentional training, is vital to setting the stage for behavior change. This action of noticing may begin with developing a mindfulness practice.

Mindfulness is a concept that is often misunderstood. It is not simply meditation, nor is it a practice of relaxation, but it *can be* meditative and it *may feel* relaxing. Mindfulness is a state of awareness. It is a process by which you are present in the moment, fully aware of both internal and external experiences. It is a process by which you pay attention to all of your senses and become an observer of your experience, moment by moment. Mindfulness is a practice. It is a skill to be cultivated, so don't be surprised if you find it to be a bit of a challenge at first. Think of your mind as a puppy that needs training. In order to get your mind to sit, it requires patience, kindness, and practice.

As busy as we can sometimes be in our daily lives, our minds have developed an amazing ability to be on "autopilot." That is, we are able to carry out a well-rehearsed task while our minds are caught up in something completely different. For example, have you ever been driving down a highway to discover that you have missed your exit because you were tangled up in thoughts about something else entirely? Perhaps you were thinking about something that happened earlier in the day or you were planning what you needed to do later in the day. Yes, the mind is an amazing thing; it has the ability to be in one place externally and in another place internally.

Yet, when we allow ourselves to be on "autopilot" in this way, we are less aware of our environment and of ourselves. And we tend to experience higher levels of stress and lower levels of daily satisfaction. Learning to be mindful—to slow down and attend to the present moment—creates the opportunity for greater awareness and greater joy.

Research demonstrates that developing a mindfulness practice leads to improvements in attention and concentration, positive affect, and emotional well-being, as well as reductions in levels of anxiety, depression, worry, rumination, and emotional reactivity. When we are able to slow down, we learn how to mindfully respond rather than react impulsively to our internal or external environment.

Mindfulness is a useful tool for learning to become more aware of and engaged in the present moment—to become an observer of your own experience without getting caught up in, analyzing, or judging those observations. By becoming more aware of the present moment, we learn to have greater awareness of those "autopilot" behaviors, including BFRBs and other habitual, overlearned actions. With awareness comes opportunity for change.

TOP TIP

Develop a regular mindfulness practice.

PRACTICE

TOOLS FOR THE TERRAIN

- Five-Minute Mindfulness
- Observing and Recording Your BFRB Experience
- Understanding Your BFRB Cycle
- Your BFRB Cycle

Five-Minute Mindfulness

Take 5–15 minutes out of each day to practice mindfulness. Consider scheduling the practice into your daily activities. There are many places you can find great mindfulness exercises—on YouTube, via a Google search, and in smartphone apps such as Headspace, Calm, and Ten Percent Happier. Here's an introductory exercise to get you started. You can record and listen to this or invite someone to practice it with you.

Let's take a few minutes to settle into the moment. Get comfortable in your seat. Feel your feet on the floor, uncross your legs, and gently close your eyes. You can rest your hands on your lap or by your sides. If closing your eyes doesn't feel right for you, you can look down past your nose with a soft gaze at a fixed spot so that your visuals don't distract you for the next few minutes. We're going to work on cultivating peacefulness, being fully present in the moment, and setting our intention to be in the here and now.

The inability to be in the moment occurs when we resist being in the present, allowing our minds to rush forward to something in the future—like something we are looking forward to or not looking forward to, or being pulled into the past by something that's worrying us. Take a few minutes to be here in the present, instead of in the past or future with the stressors in your life, to focus on being open to introspection.

Take a few deep breaths and just notice what's going on in your body. Notice your feet on the floor. Notice your body touching the chair. Notice your breath. Can you loosen and let go of any tension or tightness you notice in your body that is the physical manifestation of the stress you carry around? Imagine that this tension just melts away into your seat. Imagine creating a little bit of ease and a little bit of space.

Let your eyelids be heavy and your brows soften. Let the muscles of your face relax and your jaw loosen. Relax your throat. Drop your shoulders and allow your arms and hands to feel heavy and warm, resting down below. Notice your breath as you breathe comfortably and easefully, breathing down into your belly. Let your exhalation be long and slow. Just let yourself be here in the present moment. If you notice your thoughts wandering, that's okay, just bring them back to noticing your breath and any sensations in your body.

Ask yourself, with every exhale, if you could let yourself let go just a little more. And, when you notice something that shows up on the inside, just acknowledge it. If you notice anxiety or worry, for example, just say to yourself, "There's anxiety," or, "There's worry." You can let it be there, creating space for it instead of reacting to it. Don't push it away. Allow it to be there. Just acknowledge it and turn your attention to letting go of any bodily tension with every exhale. Just be here in the moment. Take a few minutes to sit in this silence.

Then, when you're ready, take a few deeper breaths and allow yourself to bring your awareness back into the room. Take a few moments to notice how you feel. Notice that there's a little more space and a little more openness and presence. Acknowledge your efforts and gently return your attention to your surroundings.

Observing and Recording Your BFRB Experience

Every person is unique, with a particular set of BFRB triggers, behavioral functions, and reinforcing factors. In order to successfully target these behaviors, we must first examine these behavior patterns. Keeping a record or behavior log of your observations—like a scientist—will help you to begin to examine the patterns of your BFRB. You'll then use that as a component to inform your roadmap to effectively choose the most appropriate strategies specific to your needs. Think of this as improving your aim in a game of darts. You're much more likely to hit the bullseye if your eyes are open and you are focused on the target than if you threw the dart in the direction of the bullseye with your eyes closed. Monitoring on a regular basis can also be a way of tracking your progress over time and increasing your awareness of the behavior and its patterns.

In monitoring your BFRB, the goal is to gather specific data that will be helpful to you in planning your individualized intervention strategies. Record the day and time of day you notice engaging in the behavior, the duration of the BFRB episode, the area of the body targeted, where you were and what you were doing, any thoughts, images, memories, emotions, or bodily sensations noticed, when you noticed the behavior, and why you stopped engaging in the behavior. Your log may look something like the following example:

Date	Time of Day	Duration	Body Area	People, Places, and Spaces	Thoughts, Images, Memories, Emotions, Sensations	When Did You Notice?	Why Did You Stop?
4/1	*7am*	*15 mins*	*Face*	*Bathroom sink, washing face, brushing teeth, mirror*	*"I want these blemishes gone." Imagining a blotchy face getting negative attention from others, remembering a time when someone asked about my face, embarrassment, tired, "I can pick these to help them heal"*	*Noticed the urge to pick when looking at my skin*	*Stopped after picking off scabs*
4/2	*10am*	*40 mins*	*Eyebrows*	*Sitting at desk at work, alone, computer*	*"This work project is overwhelming." "Why is my internet so slow today?" Frustrated, fidgety, anxious*	*Noticed after several hairs were pulled*	*Stopped when I had to start typing*
4/2	*6pm*	*25 mins*	*Upper arms*	*Reading a book, sitting in an armchair with a nearby reading lamp, alone in the room*	*"My skin should be smooth." Image of unblemished, smooth skin, focused on reading, leaning on the arm of the chair, feeling small bumps*	*Noticed when I saw blood on my fingertips*	*Stopped when I saw blood*
4/2	*11pm*	*20 mins*	*Scalp*	*Alone, in my bed*	*"I'm going to be tired tomorrow." Unable to fall asleep, restless, tired, frustrated*	*I found hair on my pillow when I woke up*	*I was not able to stop as I was unaware of my pulling at the time*

Use the BFRB Information-Gathering Log to record your observations over the course of several days to one week.

BFRB Information-Gathering Log

Date	Time of Day	Duration	Body Area	People, Places, and Spaces	Thoughts, Images, Memories, Emotions, Sensations	When Did You Notice?	Why Did You Stop?

Understanding Your BFRB Cycle

Now that you are exercising curiosity and recording your observations, let's take a closer look at the factors involved in your BFRB pattern so that you may better understand what maintains it. We'll begin by examining the "antecedents" to your BFRB. Identifying your antecedents is fundamental to creating an effective roadmap for your personalized intervention strategies. Antecedents are the factors that "set the stage" or make it more likely that you will engage in your BFRB. They are the cues or triggers. Understanding antecedents, behaviors, and consequences are core elements in Habit Reversal Training (HRT), Comprehensive Behavioral Treatment (ComB), ACT, and DBT, which have all been well-respected treatment approaches for BFRBs. This workbook has adapted what we have learned from these and other BFRB treatments to help you build a personalized and integrative treatment for your BFRB.

1. Behavior Antecedents
Antecedents serve as cues or triggers for the behavior.

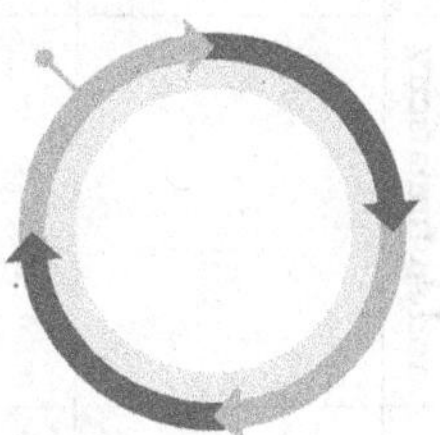

Antecedents can be both internally derived, from within your body and mind, or derived from your external experiences in the environment. They can be both underlying factors and immediate factors that impact the behavior. Determine your TIMES MAP to guide you on the path to successful strategies. Your TIMES MAP includes the antecedents that you notice prior to engaging in your BFRB.

Thoughts—Thoughts that show up in your mind **I**mages—Images that come to mind in your mind's eye **M**emories—Narratives from past experiences **E**motions—Emotions that you notice yourself experiencing **S**ensations and Urges—Bodily sensations or urges	Internal Experiences
Movement and Automaticity—Movements, body postures, and activities **A**wareness of Vulnerabilities—Biological influences such as genetics, co-occurring medical conditions, sleep, nutrition, exercise **P**eople, Places, and Spaces—Where you are, who and what is around you	External/Contextual Experiences

External/contextual experiences (the MAP) provide a path to uncomfortable internal experiences. Internal experiences that are uncomfortable are responded to by performing the BFRB in an effort to gain comfort/relief from discomfort.

Use the TIMES MAP Self-Assessment Summary to summarize what you notice as you proceed through the exploration that follows.

TIMES MAP: Self-Assessment Summary

Thoughts	Images	Memories	Emotions	Sensations and Urges	Movement and Automaticity	Awareness of Vulnerabilities	People, Places, and Spaces

Your Antecedents—TIMES MAP

1. Antecedents

Antecedents serve as cues or triggers for the behavior.

Antecedents may include:
Thoughts
Images
Memories
Emotions
Sensations and Urges

Movement and Automaticity
Awareness of Vulnerabilities
People, Places, and Spaces

(ANTECEDENT) THOUGHTS

Thoughts are conscious cognitive processes. They include those that show up in our minds—we call these "automatic thoughts." They also include beliefs and collections of cognitions about something in particular (e.g., concepts about ourselves, others, our ability to take effective actions)—we call these "schemas." Consider what you are thinking just before your BFRB occurs.

- What thoughts do you notice before engaging in your BFRB?
- Do you sometimes give yourself permission to engage in your BFRB at a given moment?
- Do you have particular thoughts or beliefs about your BFRB, about its consequences, or about hair, skin, or nails?
- What thoughts or beliefs do you have about your ability to control your BFRB?
- What thoughts or beliefs do you have about experiencing a relapse of your BFRB after a period of being able to resist engaging in the behavior?

....

....

(ANTECEDENT) IMAGES

Images include the pictures that appear in your mind's eye. Note that some individuals have the ability to vividly imagine images and/or moving images in their minds while others cannot, and others experience an ability to imagine somewhere in between the two ends of the imagination continuum. If you are someone who experiences mental images, consider any images that come to mind before engaging in your BFRB.

- What images do you notice before your BFRB?
- What imagined scenes, "clips," or "movies" do you notice before your BFRB?
- Are thoughts or emotions coming up in response to these images?

- If so, what is showing up?

....

....

(ANTECEDENT) MEMORIES

Memories include the mental experiences that show up in your mind from the past. These may show up as stories you tell yourself from past experiences or as narratives that you recall from the past. As with other mental experiences, these do not necessarily involve your BFRB but they may. Explore the memories you have in mind just prior to carrying out your BFRB.

- Do you notice any memories coming to mind before your BFRB?
- What are those memories?
- How do those memories show up for you? Do they involve thoughts, images, emotions, sensations/urges, or any of your five senses in your mind's eye?

....

....

(ANTECEDENT) EMOTIONS

Emotions are a complex set of reactions, which are often simply referred to as feelings. BFRBs may be carried out in response to a wide range of emotional antecedents. Consider the range of emotion(s) you experience immediately preceding your BFRB.

- What emotion(s) do you notice before your BFRB?
- Do you notice any emotion(s) in particular that precede your BFRB, such as anxiety, boredom, indecisiveness, tension, fatigue, sadness, shame, guilt, anger, excitement, frustration, and/or any other emotion?

....

....

(ANTECEDENT) SENSATIONS AND URGES

Sensations and urges involve any experiences pertaining to the five senses, as well as the rising sense of tension—urge—that many individuals experience prior to carrying out a BFRB. Examine the possible antecedent sensations and urges by considering these experiences before your BFRB occurs.

- Do you notice any sensations before your BFRB occurs or when searching for the target area from which you are going to pull/pick/bite/etc.?
- Do you notice any sounds?
- Do you notice any smells?

- Do you notice any tastes?
- Do you notice any tactile sensations (i.e., sensations on your fingers or other areas of the body)?

....

....

Explore any felt sense of an urge—a rising sense of tension prior to engaging in your BFRB. Urges are complex. They can involve a range of internal experiences.

- Do you experience an urge?
- How often would you estimate you are aware of experiencing an urge?
- How would you describe that urge experience? What does it feel like?

....

....

(ANTECEDENT) MOVEMENT AND AUTOMATICITY

MAP areas provide contexts in which TIMES are prompted—they are situational and increase the likelihood of antecedent TIMES. Movements include the body postures that precede your BFRB and the ways in which your body is moving that contribute to the facilitation of the behavior (i.e., that make it easier to carry out your BFRB). This also includes your level of awareness of the behavior. Research indicates that some individuals experience a sense of urgency to which they respond by engaging in the BFRB in order to relieve that sensation—we call this "focused or goal-directed behavior." Others do not notice this sensation and carry out the BFRB with little to no awareness of an urge or of any other antecedents prior to beginning the behavior—we call this "automatic or unfocused" behavior; some people refer to this as a trance-like state. Many individuals experience both focused and automatic behavior at different times and to varying degrees.

Explore your movements, including how your body is positioned or moving just prior to your BFRB.

- What activities are you doing just prior to your BFRB?
- In what ways does your body more easily facilitate your BFRB?
- Do you notice postures, or hand, arm, or other body movements or positions that make your BFRB target area(s) more accessible or that otherwise more easily lead to your BFRB?
- Are you touching or physically searching for a target?
- Do you use your hands or fingers to feel, stroke, or select a target hair, skin, or nail?

....

....

Explore your experience of automaticity vs. mindful awareness.

- What is your level of awareness of your pre-BFRB state?
- Do you sometimes begin to engage in your BFRB without awareness, as if you were on "autopilot"?
- How often would you estimate that this automaticity occurs?

....

....

(ANTECEDENT) AWARENESS OF VULNERABILITIES

Underlying vulnerabilities often pave the way to BFRBs. Explore the underlying factors that may leave you more susceptible to your BFRB.

- Do you have an underlying genetic predisposition of which you are aware (e.g., a relative who pulls, picks, bites, etc.)?
- Do you have an underlying medical condition (e.g., dry scalp, eczema, or other condition of the hair, skin, or nails) that influences your urge to engage in the BFRB?
- Do you have attention deficit hyperactivity disorder (ADHD) and/or would you describe yourself as a particularly fidgety individual or in need of movement much of the time?
- Do you have a co-occurring mental health condition (e.g., anxiety disorder, depression, etc.) or are you someone who is particularly emotionally sensitive or responds intensely to triggering situations?
- Do you notice any changes in your BFRB in relation to sleep, such as an increase when sleep is not restorative?
- Do you notice any changes in your BFRB in relation to your nutrition?
- Do you notice any changes in your BFRB in relation to substance use (e.g., alcohol, drugs, prescription medications, caffeine, other substances)?
- Do you notice any changes in your BFRB frequency or intensity with fluctuations of hormones (e.g., stages of the menstrual cycle, pregnancy, menopause, birth control pills, hormone replacement therapy, testosterone supplementation)?
- Do you notice any changes in your BFRB in relation to engagement or non-engagement in exercise?

....

....

(ANTECEDENT) PEOPLE, PLACES, AND SPACES

People, places, and spaces include all of the people, places, and spaces in your surroundings that precede the behavior—namely where you are and who and what is around you. Explore your people, places, and spaces before the behavior occurs.

- Is there a particular time of day that your BFRB is more likely to take place?
- Where are you just prior to your BFRB?
- Are you alone, with others, or in either setting?
- Are there specific people around you?
- Are you engaged in a particular activity or activities?
- Are there tweezers, needles, pins, razors, or other implements near you that you might use to facilitate your BFRB?
- Is there a mirror or other reflective surface of which you may make use to visually examine a target area?

....

....

Fill in the TIMES MAP Self-Assessment Summary with the information you've gathered from exploring your BFRB antecedents.

Your Behavior

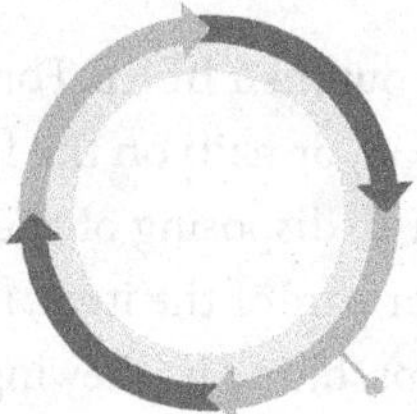

2. Behavior
The behavior is carried out in a specific sequence of events in an attempt to avoid the experience of discomfort and to self-regulate.

The second stage of the BFRB cycle is the behavior itself. The behavior is carried out in a multi-step chain of events. By increasing your awareness of each link in the behavior chain, you will increase your ability to recognize each link in the chain and create an opportunity to intervene and break that link. Let's explore the behavior chain:

1. THE SEARCH

Searching for your target hair, skin, or nail typically involves a habitual process, such as visual examination or touching the target area to feel for a particular characteristic (e.g., rough skin, wiry hair, gray hair, jagged nail, rippled cheek tissue). Consider the factors involved in your search.

- What are the target areas?

- Do the target areas have specific characteristics?

 ....

 ....

2. THE ACTION

Carrying out your BFRB (e.g., picking, biting, pulling, etc.) is completed in a specific manner. Explore the way in which you engage in the action of carrying out your BFRB.

- Are there multiple steps to carrying out your BFRB (e.g., twirling long hair, feeling the texture of the ends of the hairs, looking at the ends of the hairs, identifying hairs with dry/split ends, pulling those hairs out, etc.)?
- If so, what are those steps?
- Is your BFRB carried out slowly or quickly?
- If hair, is it pulled in individual hairs or in multiples?
- What is the frequency of your BFRB?
- How long are the episodes of pulling, picking, biting, etc.?
- What is the intensity?

 ....

 ....

3. THE DISPOSITION

Individuals engage in a wide range of behaviors after carrying out their BFRB. For some, a simple disposition, such as dropping the item (i.e., hair, skin, or nail) on the floor is done, while, for others, there are additional behaviors prior to disposing of the item. Those behaviors may include visually examining the item or part of the item, feeling it with the fingers or playing with it, running it across the lips, biting it, chewing it, or swallowing it. Consider what you do with the item once it is removed.

- Once the target is removed from the body, what do you do with that hair, piece of skin, or nail?

 ....

 ....

Your Behavior—TIMES MAP

Exploring your BFRB behavior in the same way you examined the BFRB antecedents will give you additional details for your TIMES MAP and will help you to further understand your BFRB cycle. Let's look at these experiences during the behavior sequence itself—the search, the action, and the disposition. Notice what is happening internally and externally as your BFRB is being carried out. And notice if there are any changes over the duration of the BFRB episode.

(BEHAVIOR) THOUGHTS

Explore the thoughts you have while you are engaged in your BFRB, both when the behavior has just begun and after a period of time.

- What thoughts do you notice?
- Do you notice further permission to engage in your BFRB?
- Do you notice self-criticism or other commentary about your BFRB, your appearance, what others may think of you, or your ability to control the behavior?
- Have your thoughts changed in any way since starting to engage in your BFRB? How?

....

....

(BEHAVIOR) IMAGES

Explore the images or moving images that come to mind while you are engaged in your BFRB, both when the behavior has just begun and after a period of time.

- What images do you notice during your BFRB?
- What imagined scenes, "clips," or "movies" do you notice during your BFRB?
- Are thoughts or emotions coming up in response to these images?
- If so, what is showing up?
- Do these experiences change over the duration of your BFRB episode? How?

....

....

(BEHAVIOR) MEMORIES

Explore the memories you have in mind as you are carrying out your BFRB.

- Do you notice any memories coming to mind during your BFRB?
- What are those memories?
- How do those memories show up?
- Do they involve thoughts, images, emotions, or any of your five senses in the mind's eye?
- Do these experiences change over the duration of your BFRB episode? How?

....

....

(BEHAVIOR) EMOTIONS

Explore the emotions you experience while you are engaged in your BFRB.

- What emotions do you notice?
- Do you notice any emotion(s) in particular at the outset of your BFRB?
- Do you notice any changes in emotion(s) experienced over the duration of your BFRB episode? What are those changes?

....

....

(BEHAVIOR) SENSATIONS AND URGES

Explore your sensory experiences while you are engaged in your BFRB, both when the behavior has just begun and after a period of time.

- Do you notice any sounds?
- Do you notice any smells?
- Do you notice any tastes?
- Do you notice any tactile sensations?
- Do you notice what you see?
- Do you notice any bodily sensations?
- Do you notice any changes in an urge sensation?
- Do any of these sensations or urges change over the duration of your BFRB episode? How?

....

....

(BEHAVIOR) MOVEMENT AND AUTOMATICITY

Explore your movements, including how your body is positioned or moving over the course of carrying out your BFRB.

- Is your body positioned in such a way that it makes it easier for you to engage in the behavior?
- Do body movements facilitate searching for a target? How?
- How do you move your body as you carry out the behavior?
- Do body movements facilitate disposition?
- Are there any other body movements that you notice over the course of your BFRB episode?

....

....

Explore your experience of automaticity vs. mindful awareness while you are engaged in your BFRB.

- How aware are you of your BFRB as you are carrying out the behavior?
- Are you aware of the behavior at the outset or do you become aware once you are already engaged in your BFRB?
- Are you on "autopilot" some of the time?
- When does that level of awareness change?

....

....

(BEHAVIOR) AWARENESS OF VULNERABILITIES

The underlying vulnerabilities you identified as antecedents may continue to drive the behavior once it has begun. Explore the ways in which these vulnerabilities influence your experience of the BFRB as it is being carried out (e.g., genetic predisposition, underlying medical condition, ADHD or fidgetiness, co-occurring mental health condition or emotional responsiveness, sleep, nutrition, substance use, fluctuations of hormones, exercise).

....

....

(BEHAVIOR) PEOPLE, PLACES, AND SPACES

Explore the people, places, and spaces in your surroundings while you are engaged in your BFRB.

- Where are you when you are carrying out your BFRB?
- Have you moved to another location specifically to carry out your BFRB?
- Are you alone or with others?
- Are there specific people around you?
- Are you engaged in an activity? What?
- What's happening around you?
- Are you using implements, such as tweezers, needles, pins, razors, or other items to carry out your behavior?
- Is there a mirror or other reflective surface that you are using as you engage in your BFRB?
- Is there a preferred hand or finger(s) used to carry out your BFRB?

....

....

Your Consequences—TIMES MAP

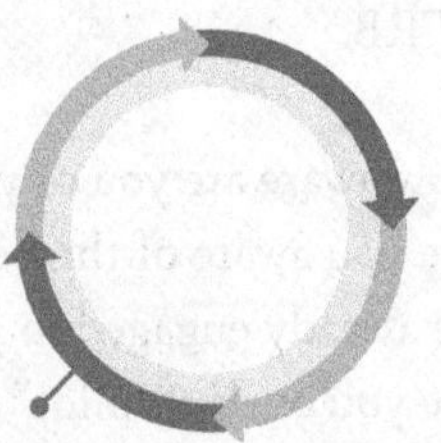

3. Consequences
Both positive and negative consequences occur, which serve to reinforce the stimulus-response pattern.

The consequences of your BFRB can be complex and self-reinforcing as they change over time. Exploring your BFRB consequences in the same way you examined your BFRB antecedents and behavior will give you additional details for your TIMES MAP and will help you to further understand your BFRB cycle.

Let's look at the consequences of your BFRB. Notice how you experience the consequences both internally and externally. Notice the consequences of your BFRB, both short-term and long-term. As you explore the Consequences TIMES MAP, consider, "What happens immediately following the behavior and does this change as time passes?"

(CONSEQUENCES) THOUGHTS

Explore your cognitive experiences immediately after picking, pulling, biting, etc. and after a period of time.

- What thoughts do you notice?
- Do your thoughts change in any way over time?
- Do you notice thoughts of satisfaction or gratification?
- Do you notice self-criticism or other commentary about the behavior, your appearance, the damage, what others may think of you, or your ability to control your BFRB?

....

....

(CONSEQUENCES) IMAGES

Explore the images or moving images that come to mind after you've ceased the behavior, both immediately following your BFRB and after a period of time.

- What images do you notice?
- What imagined scenes, "clips," or "movies" do you notice?
- Are thoughts or emotions coming up in response to these images?
- If so, what is showing up?

- Do these experiences change as time passes?

....

....

(CONSEQUENCES) MEMORIES

Explore the memories that come to mind after you have completed your BFRB, both immediately and after a period of time.

- Do you notice any memories coming to mind after your BFRB?
- What are those memories?
- How do those memories show up?
- Do they involve thoughts, images, emotions, or any of your five senses in your mind's eye?
- Do these experiences change as time passes?

....

....

(CONSEQUENCES) EMOTIONS

Explore the emotions you experience immediately following your BFRB and after a period of time has passed. It is not uncommon for more immediate emotions to involve positive experiences, such as pleasure, satisfaction, or relief of tension. As time passes, you may notice unwanted emotions, such as guilt, shame, anger, and frustration.

- What emotions do you notice immediately following your BFRB?
- What emotions do you notice as time passes?

....

....

(CONSEQUENCES) SENSATIONS AND URGES

Explore your sensations and urges immediately following your BFRB and after a period of time.

- Do you notice sounds, sights, smells, tastes, tactile sensations, or bodily sensations after your BFRB has ceased?
- Do any of these sensations change following your BFRB episode? How?
- Do you notice any changes in an urge?
- Does your sense of tension diminish over time or change in any other way?

....

....

(CONSEQUENCES) MOVEMENT AND AUTOMATICITY

Explore your movements, including how your body is positioned or moving after you've carried out your BFRB, both immediately and after a period of time.

- How do you position or move your body once you've completed your BFRB?
- How do you position or move your body as a result of your BFRB?
- Do you attempt to use your body to cover up damage that may have resulted from your BFRB?

....

....

Explore the automaticity vs. mindful awareness of your BFRB once it has ceased.

- Are you fully aware of the BFRB that has occurred once it has ceased?
- Are you sometimes unaware that you have engaged in your BFRB (e.g., noticing evidence of your BFRB after sleeping or after a trance-like state)?

....

....

(CONSEQUENCES) AWARENESS OF VULNERABILITIES

Underlying vulnerabilities may influence your BFRB, and, in turn, your BFRB may impact your existing underlying vulnerabilities. As a result of your BFRB, your underlying vulnerabilities can be exacerbated or otherwise impacted. Explore the ways in which your vulnerabilities are affected by the consequences of carrying out the BFRB (e.g., genetic predisposition, underlying medical condition, ADHD or fidgetiness, co-occurring mental health condition or emotional responsiveness, sleep, nutrition, substance use, fluctuations of hormones, exercise).

What are the ways in which your underlying vulnerabilities have been impacted? Have there been any positive impacts as a result of your BFRB? What are the negative impacts to your vulnerabilities as a result of your BFRB and have these effects changed over time (e.g., intensifying your anxiety or depression, maintaining the skin irritation caused by psoriasis, etc.)?

....

....

(CONSEQUENCES) PEOPLE, PLACES, AND SPACES

Explore the people, places, and spaces in your surroundings immediately following your BFRB and after a period of time has passed.

- Do your surroundings change in any way (place, people, implements)?
- Are your relationships impacted?
- Is your home, school, or work impacted?
- Are your leisure activities impacted?
- Are your finances impacted?
- Is your healthcare impacted?

. . . .

. . . .

Your BFRB Cycle

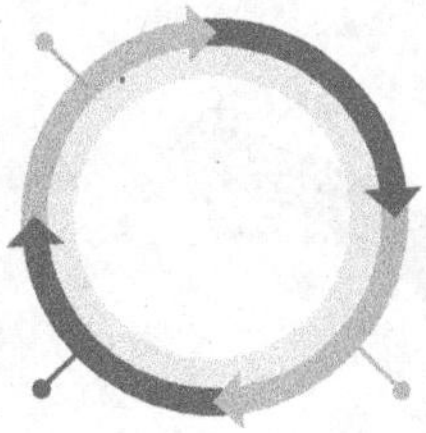

1. Antecedents
Antecedents serve as cues or triggers for the behavior.

Antecedents may include:
Thoughts
Images
Memories
Emotions
Sensations and Urges

Vulnerabilities may include:
Movement and Automaticity
Awareness of Vulnerabilities
People, Places, and Spaces

2. Behavior
The behavior is carried out in a specific sequence of events in an attempt to avoid the experience of discomfort and to self-regulate.

3. Consequences
Both positive and negative consequences occur, which serve to reinforce the stimulus-response pattern.

Let's back up and take a look at the "big picture." What makes you vulnerable to your BFRB? What are the antecedents? How do you carry out the behavior? What are the short- and long-term consequences? What functions might your BFRB be serving? What needs might it be meeting? How does this perpetuate the cycle?

. . . .

. . . .

Use the following chart to construct your BFRB cycle.

★ My BFRB Cycle

1. Antecedents

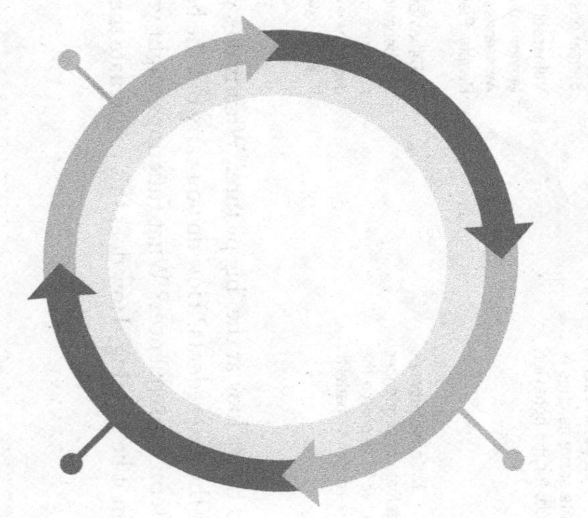

Antecedents may include:
Thoughts
Images
Memories
Emotions
Sensations and Urges

Movement and Automaticity
Awareness of Vulnerabilities
People, Places, and Spaces

2. Behavior

3. Consequences

EXPLORE

Processes That Maintain BFRBs

Patterns of responding to antecedents in certain ways continue to occur because those responses are reinforced over time. Sensitization (a heightened awareness of a trigger) can occur when, through repeated exposure to a trigger, the response becomes progressively amplified. In other words, specific triggers can elicit more intense responses (BFRBs) over time. This occurs with the processes of over-attending, over-valuing, and over-responding.

THREE PROCESSES THAT CAN KEEP YOU STUCK IN YOUR BFRB CYCLE

- Over-attending to BFRB antecedents leads to their amplification.
- Over-valuing antecedents gives them more power over you and your BFRB.
- Over-responding to your antecedents by engaging in your BFRB in an effort to try to control or get rid of your urges and discomforts perpetuates the response.

Over-attending occurs when you pay a lot of attention to a particular antecedent—more than is due. It's a natural response to give unpleasant BFRB cues and other unpleasant stimuli attention. We do this as we innately seek comfort in mind and body. By bringing discomforts to your attention, you can choose to act in such a way that is protective, ridding yourself of discomfort. However, sensitization happens when we become hypervigilant or over-attentive to these triggers when we notice them. We begin to notice them more easily. As a result, we learn to notice them more often and with greater sensitivity in an attempt to protect ourselves from discomfort.

When we become more attuned to the presence of these unwanted triggers, we can assign them more meaning and importance than is warranted. For example, if you tend to pick at your face in the bathroom mirror when washing your face, you may come to think, "I can't be around mirrors," and believe that mirrors are items that will never be able to be seen without picking. Over-valued ideation is the term that we use to describe strongly held thoughts or beliefs that we have difficulty challenging or that we struggle to see from another perspective, despite evidence to the contrary. And this can impede progress. For example, although seeing your reflection in a mirror may be evocative and may be a significant cue for your BFRB, there have likely been times when you have seen your reflection and were able to refrain from picking behavior. Be mindful of giving a thought or a past experience more meaning or power than it deserves. Don't believe everything you think.

Over-responding is a natural inclination. Our natural response to discomfort is to try to avoid or push away that which makes us uncomfortable. And we will do that over and over again. This pattern of responding to a trigger is reinforced by reducing our discomfort (at least in the short term), which strengthens that stimulus → response pattern (in other words, we will do it more because we got something out of it). But, in the case of your BFRB pattern, it's not working for you. That's why you're here—to learn new, healthy responses.

ACTION PLAN

Understanding your TIMES MAP

Assessment is a continual process. As you continue to progress through this workbook, continue to practice curiosity—use your BFRB Information-Gathering Log to record your observations. Add to your TIMES MAP as you notice, more and more, the nuances that are unique to you and your BFRB. *This* is the MAP that will guide you in your journey.

What key points in this chapter really spoke to you? What are the highlights *you* most want to keep in mind that are important for you and your BFRB?

....

....

What did you learn about yourself as you **explored**?

....

....

What **practices** will you commit to working on this week to move you toward your destination?

....

....

What is your **action plan**? What steps will you take to put these practices in place?

....

....

When and how often will you engage in these practices?

....

....

★ BFRB Information-Gathering Log

Date	Time of Day	Duration	Body Area	People, Places, and Spaces	Thoughts, Images, Memories, Emotions, Sensations	When Did You Notice?	Why Did You Stop?

TIMES MAP: Self-Assessment Summary

★

Thoughts	Images	Memories	Emotions	Sensations and Urges	Movement and Automaticity	Awareness of Vulnerabilities	People, Places, and Spaces

CHAPTER 4

Setting Yourself Up for Success

EXPLORE

Change Is a Process

There is a science behind behavioral change. It is important to think about change as a process rather than a final outcome. A well-known integrative psychotherapy model that looks at how people change is called the Transtheoretical Model created by James Prochaska and Carlo DiClemente in the late 1970s (Prochaska and DiClemente 2005). This model has studied change across a wide range of physical- and mental-health-related behaviors, such as smoking, anxiety, eating disorders, alcohol and substance abuse, and preventative medicine. Through multiple studies, the transtheoretical model outlines four core constructs including the stages of change, self-efficacy, decisional balance, and the processes of change.

The stages of change emphasize the concept that behavioral change occurs over time. It is recommended you build upon and practice different types of skills at different stages to modify behavior more effectively. This journey of change is typically summarized through a series of five stages.

Stages of Change

Precontemplation	People in this stage are not intending to take action to change their behavior anytime soon. This lack of intention may be due to a sense of feeling demoralized from previous attempts to change or not understanding the consequences of the behavior. *"What's the point, I will never be able to control my skin picking."*
Contemplation	In this stage, people typically intend to change their behavior in the coming months. They are beginning to identify the pros and cons but have some ambivalence. *"I really want my cuticles and nails to heal, but I am just too busy with other things right now and can't focus on this."*
Preparation	This is the stage in which people start to get very serious about taking the next steps and are likely to take action in the next few days/weeks. There may be plans to return to some action step they tried recently, reach out to a provider, or read a self-help book. *"Okay, let me see what I can learn and apply from this new workbook."*

cont.

Action	People in this stage are making active changes in their day-to-day lives to modify a behavior. This is the stage in which people work toward an acceptable level of health to reduce the consequences of a condition or behavior. *"I am learning more about my emotions and I am coping in new ways! My hair pulling has reduced and I am working on spending time with people I enjoy instead of staying home and looking for imperfect hairs in the mirror."*
Mainte-nance	New patterns of behavior are sustained and have become part of a lifestyle. There is less temptation to engage in the behavior and there is improved confidence in oneself to continue on this journey. *"Wow, I have learned and practiced how to better care for myself and live a life consistent with my values. Nothing is ever perfect, but I believe I can keep going, continue to learn, and use skills when urges arise to further reduce my BFRB."*

These are all important stages in your quest to change behavior. It is also important to remember that relapse or other forms of regression rarely mean that you would go all the way back to the beginning. Change does not always occur in a linear fashion, so try to remind yourself that it is okay if you notice a nonlinear path as you observe your own patterns. This is usually the case when changing any behavior, not just BFRBs. Many individuals and programs have limited success because they do not look at change as it occurs in stages and identify what skills might be a good fit at that particular time.

Can you recognize in which stage you currently find yourself?

....

....

How long have you been in this stage? Do you recall being in any of the other stages?

....

....

In which direction do you think you are currently going?

....

....

Can you recognize any patterns in your stage/readiness to change?

....

....

The great news is that there are skills you can practice to move you from one stage to the next! Research has found that these tend to fall into ten processes of change that are stage-matched to reduce resistance, build upon progress, and decrease the frequency of unhelpful behaviors. When you work through the cognitive, affective, and evaluative strategies early on, it increases the likelihood of success in trying to use behavioral processes like stimulus control. This could explain why you have gotten stuck in trying to change your behavior in the past.

Fewer than 20 percent of people trying to change a behavior are in "action mode" and thus action-oriented therapies may not be successful in helping those in an earlier stage. It is common for people to try to jump ahead before they have a good foundation to build upon. This is why many struggle to make or sustain the desired change. Throughout the workbook, we will help you learn many integrative psychotherapy tools to work through these different processes. This chart will help you consider which type of skills to focus on depending on where you are in your stage of change.

Processes of Change

Process	When to Use It	Examples of How to Practice
Consciousness raising	Precontemplation, contemplation	Build awareness. Learn more about your BFRB. Monitoring when and how your picking, pulling, or biting occurs and the consequences of the behavior. You may even talk to others about their observations.
Emotional arousal/ dramatic relief	Precontemplation, contemplation	Identify, experience, and express feelings and emotions. Attend to difficult emotions and feel inspired that relief is possible after appropriate action is taken.
Environmental reevaluation	Precontemplation, contemplation	Notice the impact on relationships and the social environment. Observe how BFRBs negatively affect relationships and how working toward change will have a positive effect on your interpersonal and social functioning.
Self-reevaluation	Precontemplation, contemplation	Build a positive self-image. Examine your values and how building healthy behaviors is a part of who you are and how/why you aspire to grow.
Social liberation	Contemplation, preparation	Find behavioral change environments. Increase your social opportunities and seek out support groups or social media pages that encourage and reinforce healthy behaviors and lifestyle.
Self-liberation	Preparation, action, maintenance	Discover purpose, decision-making, and commitment. Believing, committing, and recommitting to actions to improve self-care, replace BFRBs, and live with purpose and meaning.
Countercon-ditioning	Preparation, action, maintenance	Substitute unwanted BFRB behaviors. Learn healthier alternative behaviors, such as distress-tolerance skills, sensory substitutes, exercise, assertiveness training, mindfulness, and increasing pleasurable activities.

cont.

Process	When to Use It	Examples of How to Practice
Stimulus control	Preparation, action, maintenance	Manage environmental cues. Observe your environment and identify cues that trigger unwanted BFRBs and emotions. Reduce, replace, or reconstruct triggering environments, cues, or situations.
Helping relationships	Preparation, action, maintenance	Accept and seek support. Build social connection through caring, trusting relationships that support healthy change. Accept help from a broad range of social networks including friends, family, support groups and a variety of professionals.
Contingency management	Action, maintenance	Reward yourself. Rewards work better than punishments in increasing the likelihood that skills will be repeated. Celebrate the process and your progress toward healthy life changes.

In addition to the stages and processes of change, it is helpful to evaluate the pros and cons of changing your behavior (decisional balance), examine your beliefs about your ability to do so (self-efficacy), and consider how you plan to handle temptation to engage in your BFRB during your triggering situations. Let's take a few minutes to explore those questions.

What are the pros of changing your BFRB?

....

....

What are the cons of changing your BFRB?

....

....

How much confidence do you have in your ability to develop a new relationship with your BFRB? How can you maintain your gains in triggering situations?

....

....

If you have felt frustrated in your journey with your BFRB, you may have taken too simplistic of an approach toward changing this behavior. An integrative perspective will help you to understand that change is a complex process and many people need to apply certain strategies and skills before they will be ready to take on the "action" stage.

BFRBs are common and it is important to remember that they impact people with many different biological, social, and emotional characteristics. That is why you need to develop a program that is specific to your needs at this particular moment in time.

We encourage you to hang in there and match your interventions to your stage of change. We will cover a wide range of skills and strategies in the chapters ahead. What you need along the way will likely change over time, so stay flexible and be kind to yourself.

Resist Punishment

In an effort to modify a behavior, it is easy to take some unhelpful turns. For example, it is not uncommon for individuals to turn toward punishment in an effort to change an unwanted behavior. However, punishing yourself or your loved one for a behavior that is often out of control tends to be ineffective. Taking a harsh or unsympathetic approach has not been shown to be effective in decreasing BFRBs or any unwanted behavior. In fact, it usually just increases suffering. The use of shame, negative comments, or removing pleasurable activities as punishment tends to increase the negative consequences of the behavior and increase emotional stress. This, in turn, may even be a trigger to increase pulling, picking, or biting. As mentioned earlier, rewarding yourself or accepting rewards from others for using skills and strategies is more likely to produce healthy change.

Have you ever punished yourself for your BFRB?

....

....

Has anyone else punished you in some way for your BFRB?

....

....

Do you think you can break out of the pattern of punishment and move in the direction of rewarding yourself/your loved one for making healthy changes? What is your first step?

....

....

PRACTICE

TOOLS FOR THE TERRAIN

- Rewards and Incentives
- Tracking Your Progress

Rewards and Incentives

Rewards are not just for kids. Everyone responds to rewards, whether it be an anticipated reward, such as a paycheck for a job well done, one that is worked toward, such as earning that free cup of coffee after nine qualifying purchases, or the possibility of a reward, such as the idea of winning the lottery. In Cognitive Behavioral Therapy (CBT), behavioral goals are often achieved by using contingency management to reinforce desired behaviors through rewards and incentives. The desired behavior cannot be to just resist engaging in a BFRB but should focus on the use of strategies to improve the health of your mind and body. This takes work (at any age), and efforts should be celebrated! Reward the use of strategies and resist focusing on hair, skin, and nails. That's right—the best way to change a BFRB is to focus on skills, not whether or not you've engaged in the behavior. By monitoring and rewarding the use of skills guided by your stage of change, you may notice you are living a more full, complete, and flexible life. If you have a more sound foundation, it is much easier to experience your BFRB in a new way.

Think about a goal you have worked toward in your life that is *not* BFRB-related.

Can you think of a time in your life when you worked really hard for something important to you?

....

....

What motivated you in that situation?

....

....

How did it turn out? Did you get what you thought you wanted?

....

....

What obstacles came up for you? What got in your way?

....

....

Did you have any unexpected positive experiences as a result?

....

....

How do you feel now reflecting on that experience?

....

....

What are your personal strengths that helped you move toward your goal?

....

....

This demonstrates that you have been able to take action on other goals in your life, even when barriers have arisen. When taking on this new approach in your BFRB journey, there are several things to keep in mind.

Reward Yourself

Set yourself up for success by practicing skills that you believe you will actually use and that fit with what you have learned about the function of your BFRB. Try not to get overwhelmed and know that skills often take practice before you've noticed much benefit or feel like you've mastered them. As you establish your specific goals to monitor and reward yourself, don't forget to give yourself a heavy dose of self-compassion and humor. Keep it simple, both with building your skills and with rewarding yourself. Here is an example of a reward chart. If you are challenging yourself with more difficult skills, you can give yourself bonus points!

★

Skill	Sunday	Monday	Tuesday	Wednesday	Thursday	Friday	Saturday
Practice three-step breathing at bedtime (bonus point)							
Wear a hat while using the computer							
Go for a 20-minute walk							
Use a fiddle toy while watching TV							
Turn off screens 30 minutes before bed							
Do a pleasurable activity							

Create a chart of your own to set yourself up for success:

Rewards Chart

Skill	Sunday	Monday	Tuesday	Wednesday	Thursday	Friday	Saturday

Once you learn what triggers your BFRB (antecedents), you can set specific goals for your situation. You can make a tally mark every time you use those skills. You can earn multiple points on the same skill, on the same day. If you miss a skill that day, or for a few days, ask yourself why that might be, and perhaps you can modify the goal if necessary.

Skill	Sunday	Monday	Tuesday	Wednesday	Thursday	Friday	Saturday
Practice three-step breathing at bedtime (bonus point +1)	✓✓		✓✓	✓✓		✓✓	
Wear a hat while using the computer	✓✓	✓✓	✓✓	✓✓	✓✓	✓✓✓	✓
Go for a 20-minute walk		✓	✓		✓		✓
Use a fiddle toy while watching TV	✓✓	✓✓	✓	✓		✓✓	✓✓
Turn off screens 30 minutes before bed		✓					
Do a pleasurable activity	✓	✓✓	✓	✓	✓	✓	✓

✓ = 45 for the week! Way to go!!

At the end of each week, you can see what skills you are using and what you may need to modify. In this example, there has been much success in several areas. However, you might consider why the sleep-hygiene goal of turning off screens before bed was not frequently met. If you are not able to meet a goal, use troubleshooting. What might be getting in the way of meeting that goal? Do you need to adjust the goal in some way to make it more attainable? Or, do you need to address some barrier to meeting this goal and, if so, what might you do?

....

....

It is important to remain flexible as you assess your goals along the way. If the goal is not being met, consider modifications.

Think about some fun ways to reward your efforts. It may be helpful to come up with small, medium, and large rewards. While building up to large rewards, don't forget about the importance of verbal praise and celebrating what you are learning and practicing every step along the way. Reinforce the small changes and keep a curious mind. New skills can be reinforced through noticing efforts and celebrating positive change.

Reward Ideas

- Recognize and praise the use of skills.
- Relaxing bath.
- Go to a movie.
- Buy a new clothing item.
- Buy a little piece of jewelry.
- Go out to eat.
- Buy yourself flowers.
- Take a weekend trip by yourself or with a friend.
- Go on a special outdoor adventure.
- Get a new book.
- Go to a concert.
- Get a manicure/pedicure.
- Special gathering with a friend.
- Get a massage.
- Delegate chores.
- Special trip to the beach or pool.

What are some fun rewards that you can earn?

....

....

Below is an example of an incentive chart:

Small Rewards May take one day to one week to earn	Medium Rewards May take one to two weeks to earn	Large Rewards May take longer than three weeks to earn
Make special taco dinner *20 points* *Buy flowers* *30 points*	*Go to the movies* *45 points* *Go out to eat* *60 points*	*Get a massage* *120 points* *Weekend trip with friend* *200 points*

Create an incentive plan to reward yourself:

My Rewards

✶

Small Rewards May take one day to one week to earn	Medium Rewards May take one to two weeks to earn	Large Rewards May take longer than three weeks to earn

If you are not keen on keeping a reward chart, know that there are many ways to promote the use of strategies and skills. That is the great thing about this journey, you are allowed to be flexible and creative in order to personalize Integrative Behavioral Therapy to get the greatest benefit to you!

How to Keep Track

- Hand clickers and digital counters can be kept in your pocket to click each time you use a skill.
- Apps, such as Tally Counter or Notes, or a Google Drive spreadsheet, can be used to note each time you use a skill.
- Poker chips are great tools for a point system. Use different colored chips to keep track of points toward a reward.
- Pom-pom jars are colorful visual representations of progress made in using skills to work toward a desired incentive; although, you may find filling up the jar to be a fun motivator on its own!

- Penny transfers are used by transferring a penny from one pocket to another each time you use a strategy. See if you can use up all the pennies in your pocket by using skills throughout the day. To use penny transfers, keep any number of pennies or other small items (let's say ten) in one pocket of your clothing, and each time you use a skill, transfer one penny or item to another pocket. Repeat if needed.

How do you want to keep track of your use of skills?

....

....

....

Example: Pom Pom Jar

Keys to a Successful Reward System

- Keep it simple.
- Reward the use of skills, not the amount of hair, clear skin, or long nails.
- Put time and energy into the system.
- Build it into your routine.
- Be consistent.
- Establish clear goals.
- Set realistic expectations.
- Plan achievable, immediate rewards.
- Choose rewards that will motivate you.
- Follow through.
- Plan ahead.

Tracking Your Progress

It can be helpful to track the changes in your BFRB over time through the use of clinical self-report measures. Some find it motivating to see a pattern of improvement, while others benefit from seeing that there is a waxing and waning pattern but the overall trend is in the direction of symptom reduction. These results can be graphed on a chart each time you complete one of the questionnaires listed below. If this is something that appeals to you, you may want to consider using this type of tracking. A few examples of such measures are listed below.

Trichotillomania Severity and Impairment

The Massachusetts General Hospital Hair Pulling Scale (MGH-HPS; Keuthen *et al.* 1995) is a seven-item self-report measure of trichotillomania symptom severity. Items specifically assess the frequency and intensity of urges, ability to control urges, attempts to resist hair pulling, control over hair pulling, and associated distress.

Skin-Picking Severity and Impairment

The Skin Picking Scale—Revised (SPS-R; Snorrason *et al.* 2021) is an eight-item self-report scale of skin-picking severity. Items assess frequency and severity of urges, time spent engaged in picking, emotional distress, functional impairment, avoidance behaviors, and resulting skin damage.

Quality of Life

The World Health Organization Quality of Life questionnaire (WHOQOL-BREF; The WHOQOL Group 1998) is a self-report questionnaire containing 26 questions rating an individual's perceptions of their own health and well-being. Four content domains include physical health, psychological, social relationships, and environment.

You can use graphing paper or a graph such as the one below to plot your scores over time:

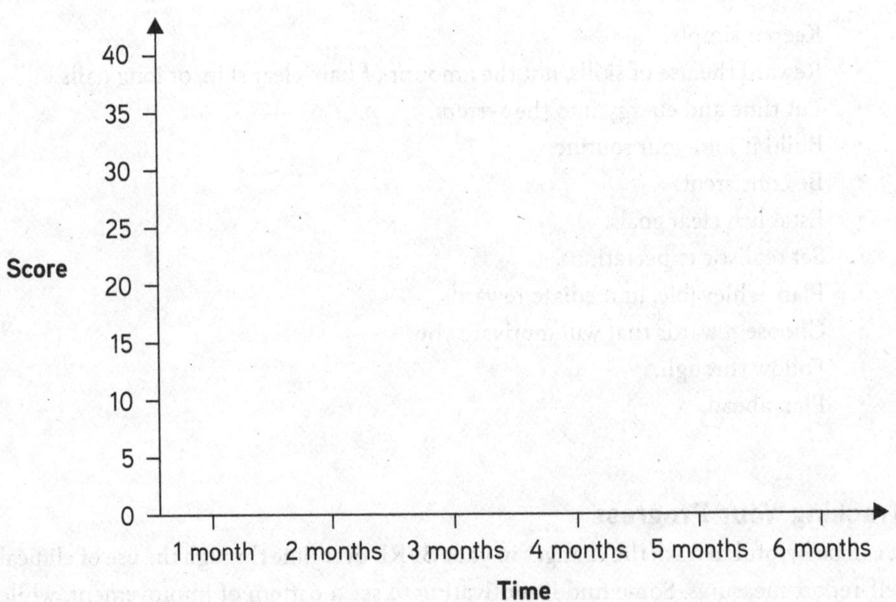

ACTION PLAN

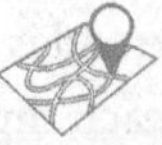

Setting Yourself Up for Success

What key points in this chapter really spoke to you? What are the highlights *you* most want to keep in mind that are important for you and your BFRB?

....

....

What did you learn about yourself as you **explored**?

....

....

What **practices** will you commit to working on this week to move you toward your destination?

....

....

What is your **action plan**? What steps will you take to put these practices in place?

....

....

When and how often will you engage in these practices?

....

....

STEP II

NARROW DOWN THE PATHS ON YOUR MAP

CHAPTER 5

Movement and Automaticity

EXPLORE

The M in **M**AP refers to movement and automaticity. The degree to which you are aware of your body and its movements, including the movements involved in your BFRB, is an important consideration in effectively managing the behavior. Levels of awareness vary from person to person. Many individuals are not always aware of an urge sensation or of how their body is positioned or moves in ways that facilitate their BFRB. Some are acutely aware of their BFRB and carry out the behavior in a goal-directed manner. Others are unaware of the behavior, as if they are on "autopilot," with little to no awareness of the BFRB as it is occurring. Many individuals experience both states of awareness. Thus, it is important to address any automaticity, or lack of awareness, that may be posing a barrier to behavior change.

Movement and automaticity skills aim to increase your bodily awareness and utilize strategies that target body posture and movement. Refer to your Self-Assessment Summary for the antecedents you identified in Chapter 3, and as you review potential strategies you may use, pair your identified antecedent with a strategy to try. You may use this chart to record these pairings:

Antecedent Movement/Automaticity ➔	➔ Movement/Automaticity Strategies
Noticed scalp hair on my lap	*Wear a Keen bracelet, put on a hat*
Resting my head on my hands while at my desk	*Wearing a posture trainer while at my desk*

PRACTICE

TOOLS FOR THE TERRAIN

- Movement and Automaticity Strategies and Skills
- Mindfulness Practices
- Awareness Training Devices
- Awareness-Enhancing Sensory Strategies
- Self-Monitoring
- Self-Check-Ins
- Response Prevention Strategies
- Postural Changes
- Competing Response Training

Movement and Automaticity Strategies and Skills

Training yourself to become more aware of the antecedent urges as well as movements is essential to effective intervention. After all, it's very difficult to stop a behavior if you aren't aware you are engaging in that behavior. And it's often easier to stop a BFRB pattern from progressing before you've begun picking, pulling, biting, etc. Becoming more aware during the antecedent phase of the BFRB cycle provides you with a greater opportunity to intervene. Therefore, learning to become more mindful of the experience is important. There are a number of ways to train yourself to become more aware of the pattern earlier in the BFRB cycle. Consider strategies that can boost your awareness of the behavior sequence prior to behavior initiation.

Mindfulness Practices

Mindfulness practice provides an opportunity to build an awareness of both internal and external experiences at any given moment and to become more present-focused rather than being on "autopilot." Mindfulness exercises can have a broad range of practice focuses, such as noticing your breath, body scanning awareness, or accepting and allowing your internal experiences to come and go without responding, to name a few. There are many great apps, videos, and MP3s available for practicing mindfulness, from instructor-led exercises of varying lengths to apps that provide mindfulness prompts to guide your practice.

Mindful Body Awareness

Body scans are foundational skills of mindfulness training and meditation practices rooted in Buddhist traditions (Anālayo 2020). The purpose of a mindful body awareness exercise, or "body scan," is to help you to become more fully present and focused on the moment, and aware of and comfortable with your bodily sensations, through focused observation. You can record and listen to the following practice or ask someone to read this as you follow along.

> *Let's begin by sitting upright and closing your eyes, if you are comfortable doing so, or casting a soft downward gaze as you take a few slow, cleansing breaths. In and out. Allow your mind to focus on your breath as you inhale deeply and exhale gently, noticing your belly and chest expand and contract as you breathe.*
>
> *Notice the sensations on the top of your head, slowly moving downward. You may imagine a sense of warmth or a soft glow moving downward, slowly covering each part of your body. Just like this, around your forehead and brows, noticing the sensations, eyes, and ears, noticing any movement or sounds, nose, feeling your breath, cheeks, mouth, noticing your tongue, teeth, any tastes or sensations, and around your chin.*
>
> *Continuing to move through your body, notice any sensations down your neck, out to your shoulders, down your arms, and into your hands and fingers. You may notice warmth flowing down into your hands. Notice any discomfort you may feel by just noticing and pausing your awareness on each part of the body.*
>
> *Bring your awareness to the chest and around to the back, wrapping you in comfort as you breathe. Moving across your belly and around your lower back. Notice your posture and any feelings in your abdomen. Across and around your hips, around your pelvis, noticing where your body meets your seat. Down your legs, and into your feet and toes. Covering your entire body. From head to toe, notice your body as you sit in the stillness of the moment. Allow yourself to sit with this experience for a few minutes. When you are ready, notice your awareness returning to the space around you and open your eyes.*

Awareness Training Devices

Awareness training devices, such as HabitAware's Keen, are bracelets with electronic motion sensors trained to detect specific wrist movements and respond via haptic feedback. Worn on the wrist(s), this device can alert you each time you engage in the recorded wrist-based scanning motion. This can be a useful tool for bringing your attention to the initial movements in your BFRB sequence, such as raising your hand to your scalp to search for a target hair or touching your face to feel for bumps. The vibration is a cue to pause and carry out an alternative action.

Awareness-Enhancing Sensory Strategies

Awareness training may also be achieved by bringing attention to automatic behaviors through unexpected sensations. For example, lotions, oils, or perfumes with intense smells worn on the fingers or wrists may help bring attention to hands that are raised to the face. Foul-flavored or foul-smelling nail polish may alert the wearer to fingers at the mouth. Bracelets that jingle or otherwise make noise may bring attention to arms that are raised toward the head or that stray down to pick at the feet.

Self-Monitoring

Keeping a monitoring log of your BFRB as it occurs may not only inform your intervention plans but also improve your behavior awareness and decrease your automaticity. The act of self-monitoring alone can result in a decrease in the BFRB, at least initially, although it's important to note that this alone is not likely to maintain this decrease in your BFRB over time. It's also acknowledged that some individuals find longer-term monitoring to be aversive and neglect the strategy. If you can't bring yourself to use this strategy because it is aversive or it is not practical in the context of your daily activities, there are alternative self-monitoring strategies. Using awareness tools, such as mechanical tally counters or computer/smartphone counting apps, hash marks made with pen and paper, or using penny transfers, can also provide awareness training.

Self-Check-Ins

Schedule "reminders" or "alarms" with your smartphone to check in on your body awareness. Or you may consider apps such as Yapp or Random Reminders that can be used to schedule periodic personalized notifications throughout the day. For example, you may schedule reminders that say, "Where are your hands?" or, "Take a moment to notice your internal and external experience."

Response Prevention Strategies

Response prevention strategies serve to both increase awareness of your BFRB and interfere with the behavior, making it difficult to initiate. Also referred to as "blockers" or "barriers," these include tools such as wigs, hairpieces, hats, headbands, bandanas, scarves, sleep masks, Band-Aids, medical tape, finger cots, gloves, long pants/sleeves, socks, short nails, gel or acrylic manicure, Vaseline, wet hair, lotion, Buff head coverings, hairstyles such as ponytails or braids, rubber thimbles, hoodies, or eyeglasses.

Postural Changes

Changing the way in which your body is postured may eliminate or change the antecedent early in the BFRB sequence and prevent the behavior from occurring. For example, if you tend to pull your hair while driving your car with your window down and your arm/elbow resting on the door, your hair is more accessible than it is if you drive with both of your hands on the steering wheel. Alternatively, you might place the rough part of a Velcro strip on the door to make it an uncomfortable place to rest your arm. Position can also be noteworthy when sitting in an armchair or on the end-piece of a couch. Sitting with your arms on the armrests may bring your hands closer to a BFRB target area; thus, you may choose to sit in an armless chair or on a center-piece of a couch. If you tend to engage in your BFRB in the bathroom sitting on the vanity or leaning in to get a closer look in your mirror, try eliminating facilitating postures by using reminders, such as "no leaning in" sticky notes on the mirror or wearing a posture trainer to prevent leaning. Many people pull pubic hairs or squeeze bumps while sitting on the toilet; try leaning forward so that you cannot see visual triggers or easily explore these areas with your hands. If you engage in your BFRB in bed at night, you might choose to sleep with your hands under your pillow rather than tucked under your head or free to roam about.

Competing Response Training

Competing response training is the process of learning to replace one behavior with another behavior—one that is often physically incompatible (i.e., cannot be performed at the same time). This component of HRT (see Chapter 9) can also be used as a standalone strategy aimed at responding to facilitative movements in order to disrupt the behavior sequence. For example, engaging in behaviors such as fist clenching, differential relaxation, using manipulatives/fidget toys, clasping/folding your hands, or holding an object with both hands can be useful behavioral redirections.

TOP TIP

Manipulatives/fidget toys can be great competing response training tools when conveniently located in "high-risk areas."

ACTION PLAN

Movement and Automaticity

What key points in this chapter really spoke to you? What are the highlights *you* most want to keep in mind that are important for you and your BFRB?

....

....

What did you learn about yourself as you **explored**?

....

....

What **practices** will you commit to working on this week to move you toward your destination?

....

....

What is your **action plan**? What steps will you take to put these practices in place?

....

....

When and how often will you engage in these practices?

....

....

As you experiment with different movement and automaticity techniques, monitor your observations in the Strategies and Skills Observation Log.

Strategies and Skills: Movement/Automaticity Observation Log

★

Date and Time	Antecedent Movement/Automaticity	Strategy/Skill	Observations
June 28, 5:15pm	*Sitting in traffic, looking in visor mirror*	*Dry erase marker note on mirror "Close Me"*	*Closed mirror, returned both hands to steering wheel*

CHAPTER 6

Awareness of Vulnerabilities

EXPLORE

The A in MAP refers to your awareness of BFRB vulnerabilities. Reducing vulnerabilities is all about establishing and maintaining positive self-care and minimizing or eliminating any potential underlying factors that may promote BFRB symptoms. By tending to the overall needs of your mind and body, you will be less likely to experience physiological or psychological discomfort (TIMES) that will be met with unwanted means of trying to regulate these discomforts (your BFRB).

It is important to take care of the mind and the body in order for you to optimally manage the stress you experience in your day-to-day life. Let's look at sleep as an example. When our minds and bodies do not get sufficient sleep, we are at risk for experiencing physical illness such as obesity, heart disease, high blood pressure, diabetes, stroke, physical injury, psychiatric symptoms such as anxiety and depression (Grandner 2019), and exacerbations of other psychiatric symptoms, including trichotillomania and excoriation (skin picking) disorder (Cavic *et al.* 2021). However, unfortunately, when we are faced with increased demands, it is not uncommon to allow self-care to fall by the wayside as we struggle to keep up. For example, have you ever sacrificed much-needed sleep in order to meet a deadline? Or perhaps your diet or exercise habits have taken a hit during periods of strain? If you answered yes, you're not alone.

It is also not uncommon to struggle with some of these foundational habits as the result of physical illness or psychiatric disorders. For example, some physical illnesses such as autoimmune or gastrointestinal disorders can have a direct impact on one's ability to maintain adequate nutrition. Psychiatric disorders, such as anxiety disorders, trauma and stress-related disorders, depressive disorders, and bipolar and related disorders, among others, may compromise the ability to maintain adequate sleep. Unsatisfactory self-care can not only have a direct negative impact on your mind and your body, it can also undermine any efforts you make to engage in self-improvement, such as efforts to reduce BFRB symptoms. This is why it's essential to start with establishing a baseline of healthy habits.

PRACTICE

TOOLS FOR THE TERRAIN

- Sleep
- Nutrition
- Exercise
- Substances and Addictions
- Psychological Factors and Co-Occurring Mental Health Conditions
- Acute and Chronic Stressors and Medical Conditions

Sleep

Sleep is an essential part of our daily lives, helping us to function at our best, both physically and mentally. Adults require approximately seven to eight hours of sleep per night, while school-aged children and adolescents require a minimum of ten hours. Although the function of sleep is not entirely understood, research suggests that sleep plays an important role in growth and development, hormone function, appetite regulation, modulation of immune-system response, muscle and tissue repair, regulation of body temperature and blood pressure, cognition, memory consolidation, learning, decision-making, performance, vigilance, physical health/disease, and psychological state/mood (Grandner 2019; Zielinski, McKenna, and McCarley 2016). Examine your sleep habits:

On average, how many hours of sleep do you get each night?.......................

Do you have a regular sleep schedule? If so, what does that look like?

....

....

Do you have difficulty falling asleep (more than 30 minutes in bed prior to sleep onset)?

....

....

Do you have difficulty maintaining sleep (i.e., awaken throughout the night with difficulty falling back to sleep)?

....

....

Do you regularly awaken earlier than you feel ready to each morning?

....

....

Do you find yourself tired or fatigued during the day?

....

....

Do you regularly take naps?

....

....

Do you experience frequent nightmares or other sleep disturbances that result in awakenings?

....

....

Do you snore/gasp/stop breathing for periods of time during sleep?

....

....

Do you move around a lot during sleep or experience uncomfortable bodily sensations such as numbness or tingling when trying to fall asleep?

....

....

Does too much or too little sleep impact your anxiety, mood, or BFRB symptoms?

....

....

If you are unsure of the relationship between sleep and your psychological health, consider tracking this relationship for a month to examine this association further.

Sleep and Psychological Health Tracker

✶ On a daily basis, record your bedtime, awakening time, total number of hours slept, mood rating (on a scale from 0 = worst mood to 10 = best mood) and BFRB symptoms rating (on a scale from 0 = no symptoms to 10 = severe symptoms). Also record any observations about the night or the preceding day that may have impacted your sleep and psychological health.

	Monday	Tuesday	Wednesday	Thursday	Friday	Saturday	Sunday
Bedtime							
Awakening							
Total Hours							
Mood Rating							
BFRB Rating							
Notes							

Sleep disorders are common. If you notice regular difficulties falling asleep or maintaining sleep or if you experience sleep disturbances such as snoring/gasping/breathing irregularities, excessive bedtime movement, frequent nightmares, or other sleep disturbances, consider consulting with a physician to further evaluate and improve your quality of sleep.

Strategies to Improve Sleep

- Establish a "regular" sleep schedule. Try to get in bed at approximately the same time every night and get out of bed at about the same time each morning—yes, even on the weekends, especially if you have any difficulty with sleep.
- Avoid daytime naps. As tempting as they may be, afternoon or evening naps, especially those that last more than one hour, can make it more difficult to fall asleep at bedtime.

- Avoid caffeine or nicotine, especially in the latter part of the day. Caffeinated beverages, such as coffee, tea, or energy drinks, as well as chocolate, are stimulants and can disrupt sleep.
- Avoid alcohol. Although having an alcoholic beverage in the evening may seem to make you feel sleepy, alcohol disrupts the sleep cycle, resulting in less restorative sleep and middle of the night awakenings.
- Avoid heavy meals just prior to bed. Eating a heavy meal increases the need for digestive activity; however, digestion is naturally slowed during sleep. Thus, eating a large meal prior to going to bed can disturb the process of sleep as well as result in unpleasant digestive symptoms such as gastroesophageal reflux. If you are hungry just prior to bed, a light snack is unlikely to impact your sleep, but you may want to avoid eating a substantial meal several hours before bed.
- Avoid exercise late in the day. Exercise is activating and raises core body temperature. Some individuals find it more difficult to sleep if they have exercised late in the day. If you notice a negative effect of late-in-the-day exercise on sleep, avoid exercising several hours before bed.
- Be mindful of the effects of other substances. Some prescription medications, such as medications for ADHD, steroids, blood pressure medications, and antidepressants, as well as medications that are obtained over the counter, such as cold and allergy medications, can be stimulating or otherwise interfere with sleep or cause daytime sleepiness. Some medications specifically prescribed for sleep, when taken for a prolonged period of time, can result in tolerance (i.e., needing more of the medication to result in the desired effects). The use of illegal drugs may also disrupt sleep. And the existing research examining the effects of cannabis and CBD on sleep demonstrate mixed results (Sleep Foundation 2022).
- Consult with your prescriber or pharmacist if you have any questions about the effects of specific substances you are taking and their potential impact on sleep.
- Keep a devoted sleep space. If possible, only utilize your bed and bedroom for sleep and sex, especially if you experience sleep difficulties. Engaging in other activities, such as reading, watching TV, using your phone, or spending time on your computer, can unintentionally establish an association between your bedroom and activities other than sleep and may make it more difficult to settle down to sleep at the desired time. If you live in a studio apartment or other small living space, this may be unavoidable, but efforts to keep a dedicated sleep space whenever possible may help promote healthy sleep.
- If your sleep is delayed due to the experience of worry or an "active mind," consider taking time in the evening to write a "to-do" list, engage in time-limited problem-solving efforts, plan for those things you need to accomplish the following day, or schedule those tasks for another appropriate time.
- Create a bedtime routine. Quiet time before bed with activities to help you to

"wind down," such as a warm shower, a meditation exercise, gently stretching, or reading a good book can help prepare your mind and body for sleep.

- Maintain a comfortable sleep environment. Creating a dark, quiet space for sleep that is kept at a cool temperature can help with sleep. Be aware that while sound machines or playing music may be useful to drown out other background noises or create a soothing environment for sleep onset, it may also create an unwanted sleep association, rendering it more difficult to sleep without these specific sounds or result in unwanted awakenings when the sounds stop.
- Avoid staring at the clock. If you tend to lie awake at night calculating how long it has been or how little sleep you may get, you may experience frustration and unintentionally undermine your sleep efforts. Consider turning the clock around so that you cannot easily glance at the time. Alternatively, use a clock that must be activated by a motion sensor in order to view the time. Or wear a smartwatch or fitness tracker in "sleep" or "night" mode that you may use as a morning haptic alarm but will not easily distract you with a brightly lit clock at night.
- Avoid lying awake in bed. If you find yourself unable to fall asleep for more than 20 minutes, get up and engage in a quiet or relaxing activity for a brief period, such as walking around your home, gazing out the window, drawing, or getting a drink of water, and then return to your bed. (Take care to avoid screen time or activities involving bright lights, which can be activating and further compromise sleep.)
- If sleep continues to be problematic, consider seeking assistance from a psychologist or therapist who provides evidence-based treatment for sleep—known as Cognitive Behavioral Therapy for Insomnia (CBT-I). These practitioners can support the establishment of good sleep hygiene as well as improve sleep onset and maintenance.

Nutrition

Maintaining adequate nutrition is vital to our overall health and wellness. There is a growing body of research to suggest that there is a complex, bidirectional relationship between nutrition and mental health, with nutrition directly impacting mood and psychological health, as well as mood and psychological wellness impacting individuals' dietary choices (Van der Pols 2018). Furthermore, it is emerging that a Mediterranean-style diet, rich in fruits and vegetables, low in processed foods, and high in healthy fats, is associated with a lower prevalence of psychiatric symptoms (Rucklidge and Kaplan 2016). There is also some data to suggest that although there was no direct relationship to symptom severity or daily dietary patterns, a past-year diet high in fat and sugar was associated with trans-diagnostic impulsivity and compulsivity in individuals with BFRBs (Grant, Valle, and Chamberlain 2021); thus, further examination of the relationship between nutrition and BFRBs is an area of interest. Examine your nutrition:

What does your average daily diet look like? There are many ways to examine this. You might consider total caloric intake, macronutrient ratio of carbohydrates: fats: proteins, or even how your meals visually align with "MyPlate."

....

....

Do you have a regular meal/snack schedule? If so, what does that look like?

....

....

Do you ever struggle with undereating or overeating?

....

....

Do you notice any ways in which your nutrition impacts your anxiety, mood, or BFRB symptoms?

....

....

> If you are markedly underweight, have an intense fear of gaining weight, significantly restrict your food intake, eat large amounts of food in short periods of time, or think your eating habits are out of control, consult with a disordered eating specialist for assistance. For more information, visit the National Alliance for Eating Disorders at http://allianceforeatingdisorders.com.

If you are unsure of any relationship between nutrition and your psychological health, consider tracking this relationship for a month to examine it further. As you do so, notice when and what you eat, amount of time between meals, levels of hunger and satiety, and how you feel overall before and after you eat. Observe any fluctuations in emotional state, physical comfort/discomfort, and your BFRB symptoms throughout the monitoring period. For example, bodily discomfort, such as bloating or feeling very hungry, may be associated with anxiety, distress, or increased BFRB symptoms.

Nutrition and Psychological Health Tracker

✶ On a daily basis, record the food and drink (including alcohol) you consume. Record your mood rating (on a scale from 0 = worst mood to 10 = best mood) and BFRB symptoms rating (on a scale from 0 = no symptoms to 10 = severe symptoms). Also record any additional observations regarding your nutrition, digestion, and psychological health.

	Monday	Tuesday	Wednesday	Thursday	Friday	Saturday	Sunday
Breakfast							
Lunch							
Dinner							
Snacks							
Mood Rating							
BFRB Rating							
Notes							

Strategies to Improve Nutrition

- Establish a "regular" eating schedule, eating meals and snacks at approximately the same time every day.
- Aim to eat a wide variety of foods. Think, "Eat the rainbow."
- Drink plenty of water.
- Make one small dietary change per week and build upon each change, maintaining each as you make additional changes. For example, swap out white bread for wholegrain bread this week. When that becomes a consistent practice, add another small change. Take care not to change too much at once; too many changes at once will be difficult to maintain.
- Be present. The practice of mindful eating can increase satisfaction and limit consumption by improving the recognition of satiety. If you are interested in

developing your mindful eating practice, check out *Mindful Eating on the Go: Practices for Eating with Awareness, Wherever You Are* (2018) by Jan Chozen Bays.

- Tracking your daily food/beverage intake can help to improve nutrition by increasing awareness of dietary patterns as well as providing a sense of accountability for your choices and the impact of them. Try keeping a daily food log.
- Limit unhealthy fats, sugars, and sodium in foods, condiments, and beverages.
- Avoid being overly restrictive. Everything in moderation.
- If the support of a nutrition professional would be useful to you in making changes to your diet, consider consulting with a registered dietitian.

MyPlate is the current set of dietary guidelines for Americans published by the United States Department of Agriculture's (USDA) Center for Nutrition Policy and Promotion. More information on these guidelines can be found at http://myplate.gov.

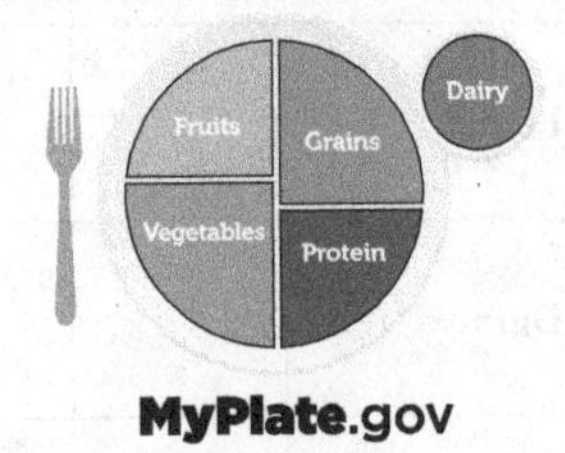

Exercise

Have you ever noticed that you tend to engage in less frequent BFRBs on days you've engaged in vigorous activity? Or have you noticed that when you haven't been particularly active, your BFRB has increased? Is it possible that exercise directly impacts your BFRB?

Exercise is most certainly important to physical health, but did you know that it is also important to psychological health? Exercise can serve many different functions for different people. It can have a positive impact on mood, reduce perceived distress, and improve functioning across a wide range of psychiatric disorders (Budde and Wegner 2018). And anecdotal reports suggest that exercise can be a moderating factor for the frequency, duration, and/or intensity of BFRBs as well. You don't need to be an athlete or go to a gym for hours per week, although that is certainly an option. Just begin by examining the association between physical activity and BFRB symptoms. Do you notice a relationship? If you notice a helpful relationship, consider making some small changes to foster that pattern, creating a little more strength for BFRB symptom resistance.

If you are unsure of any relationship between physical activity and your psychological health, consider tracking this relationship for a month to examine this association further. As you do so, notice when you are active, where you exercise, and what kind of activity you do. Observe any fluctuations in emotional state, physical comfort/discomfort, and your BFRB symptoms throughout the monitoring period. For example, you might notice that there is a relationship between type of activity and intensity of symptoms.

Exercise and Psychological Health Tracker

★ On a daily basis, record your physical activity. Record your mood rating (on a scale from 0 = worst mood to 10 = best mood) and BFRB symptoms rating (on a scale from 0 = no symptoms to 10 = severe symptoms). Also record any additional observations regarding your physical activity and psychological health.

	Monday	Tuesday	Wednesday	Thursday	Friday	Saturday	Sunday
Activity							
When							
Where							
Mood Rating							
BFRB Rating							
Notes							

Strategies to Improve Exercise

- Start small—with one small goal, such as walking for 20 minutes a few days per week—and build upon that.
- If you tend to procrastinate before exercising, schedule it into your daily calendar, leave a sticky note reminder for yourself, or set a daily reminder on your smartphone.
- Keep track of your activities. Whether it is with pen and paper or with an app on your phone, seeing that daily activity documented can lead to a sense of accomplishment.
- Note how you feel after moderate exercise—those feel-good endorphins can naturally improve mood, sense of well-being, and bodily sensations. Recording this will increase your awareness of how different activities affect you.
- Reward yourself! Go ahead—indulge yourself for adhering to your plan. Take that bubble-bath break. Go have that lunch break with a friend. Go see that movie you've been wanting to see. You've earned it!
- Choose an activity that may be enjoyable for you. Exercising doesn't have to involve pushing yourself to your limits at the gym. Here are some ideas to get you started:

- Go for a walk or jog in the park, neighborhood, local school track, or mall.
- Go for a hike.
- Go for a swim.
- Go for a bike ride.
- Take the stairs.
- Turn on some of your favorite tunes and dance.
- Try a new class (in person or online), such as yoga, tai chi, martial arts, or parkour.
- Try a game of basketball, volleyball, base/softball, or golf.
- Check out a local batting cage or driving range.
- Check out a nearby tennis or racquetball court.
- Kick around a soccer/kick ball.
- Be a kid—climb a tree, play tag, skip, play a game of Twister.
- Visit your local ice- or roller-skating rink.
- Play a game of frisbee or frisbee-golf.
- Play a game of horseshoes, cornhole, or another outdoor game.
- Rent a canoe, kayak, paddle/surfboard and get out on the water.
- Play in the snow, go sledding, skiing, or do another snow activity.
- Pick up a jump rope or a hula-hoop.
- Try horseback riding.
- Try weightlifting.
- Try out a trampoline.
- Do some house cleaning.
- Tend to your garden.

There are many ways to hold yourself accountable to fitness plans. Explore smartphone apps that track exercise progress (many track nutrition too!), such as MyFitnessPal or MapMyFitness. Check out online fitness classes with built-in reward and/or community connection systems, such as Peloton or JEFIT. Invest in a fitness tracker, such as an Apple Watch, WHOOP, Garmin, or Fitbit. Or establish a plan to be active with another person, such as going for a neighborhood walk with a friend.

Substances and Addictions

The use of substances, especially those that are known to impact nervous system activation/suppression, can contribute to anxiety, mood difficulties, and physiological discomforts, not just while using the substance but also when the substance is leaving your system or has recently left your system. And, as you are learning, these psychological and physical discomforts are fodder for a BFRB.

Most adults have engaged in the "social" use of a substance, such as alcohol. The "social" use of a substance may be defined as using that substance in moderation in the context of a social setting owing to spoken or unspoken, internally or externally generated social expectation. Such use does not typically disrupt one's daily functioning or cause problems for people in their lives. However, you may find that the use of substances, even in moderation, whether they be legal substances (e.g., caffeine, alcohol, nicotine, cannabis—in some states), prescription or over-the-counter (OTC) medications (e.g., stimulants, decongestants, sedatives, benzodiazepines, methadone, or other medications that may stimulate or suppress the nervous system), or illegal substances (e.g., cocaine, heroin, hallucinogens, inhalants, methamphetamine, or cannabis—in some states) may be related to your BFRB by unknowingly setting up a vulnerability to the behavior. For example, you may find that alcohol or cannabis leads to disinhibition and increased BFRB symptoms while under the influence. Or you may find that the use of stimulant medication or decongestant medication causes you to feel nervous or jittery, which increases the likelihood you will engage in your BFRB. You may also find that even though initially smoking a cigarette or vaping feels pleasurable, it leads you to feel irritable or anxious after a period of time due to the effects of neurotransmitter changes over time.

If you believe substances create a BFRB vulnerability for you, examine the potential relationship between substances and your BFRB. Use the following chart to track your experiences. If you observe that the use of a particular substance may be impacting your BFRB symptoms, consult with your physician or pharmacist (if prescription or OTC medication), consider reducing or eliminating use (as appropriate), or plan strategies to reduce harm (e.g., plan for the implementation of a specific strategy that will make the BFRB more difficult to carry out—we will review many options in later chapters).

Substances and Psychological Health Tracker

★ On a daily basis, record your substance use, including legal, prescription, OTC, and illegal drug use. Record your mood rating (on a scale from 0 = worst mood to 10 = best mood) and BFRB symptoms rating (on a scale from 0 = no symptoms to 10 = severe symptoms). Also record any additional observations regarding your substance use and psychological health.

	Monday	Tuesday	Wednesday	Thursday	Friday	Saturday	Sunday
Substance							
When							
Mood Rating							

cont.

	Monday	Tuesday	Wednesday	Thursday	Friday	Saturday	Sunday
BFRB Rating							
Notes							

Oftentimes, substance use begins with a desire to feel better—to get rid of an unwanted internal experience (TIMES) and seek a more desirable internal experience. However, although substances may bring about these pleasurable experiences in the short term, they can also lead to substantial negative consequences for both your psychological and physical health. When these away moves are used often, they can lead to substance use disorders (SUDs). SUD is a diagnostic category used to describe a pattern of substance use that causes significant distress or impairment to one's functioning. That impairment may also include substance-related problems, such as legal charges related to possession, using in situations that would be considered dangerous, such as operating a vehicle, difficulties in maintaining responsibilities at work or at home, or causing a strain on interpersonal relationships.

If you are struggling with the use or abuse of substances, help is available. In addition to outpatient treatment providers and treatment facilities, the Substance Abuse and Mental Health Services Administration (SAMHSA) operates a 24/7 helpline with support available in both English and Spanish at 1-800-622-HELP (4357).

Psychological Factors and Co-Occurring Mental Health Conditions

From anxiety and other obsessive-compulsive and related disorders to mood disorders and a range of other psychiatric struggles, co-occurring mental health disorders are common for those living with a BFRB. And these difficulties can, and often do, impact one another. For example, heightened anxiety may lead to an increase in hair pulling, and an increase in hair pulling may lead to heightened anxiety. Moderate to severe skin-picking behavior can lead to shame, isolation, and depressed mood, which can lead to further skin-picking behavior. Therefore, neither is likely to improve without adequately addressing both.

It is essential to understand the interplay between psychological symptoms in order to effectively address your BFRB. If you are experiencing the significant symptoms of a co-occurring mental health disorder, it is important to see a mental health professional who can provide a comprehensive mental health assessment and appropriate treatment (psychological, psychopharmacological, or combination treatment), as warranted. Left undiagnosed and unaddressed, co-occurring disorders have the potential to perpetuate the BFRB cycle and thwart any efforts to improve your BFRB, with or without professional help.

Are you experiencing any other mental health symptoms, such as anxiety, depression, tic disorder, ADHD, etc.?

....

....

How might these co-occurring symptoms be related to your BFRB? And how might you effectively address these additional symptoms?

....

....

Are there any areas of your life that feel stressful and could use some attention? Is work or school too stressful? Do you have a tendency to take on too much? Are you experiencing financial pressure? Are any of your relationships strained?

....

....

If so, what are ways in which you might reduce any unnecessary stressors that are present? Or how might you better manage the stress in your life on a regular basis?

....

....

Research suggests that some individuals, including those who struggle with anxiety-related and OCD-related disorders, may have a tendency toward emotional sensitivity and over-responsivity to stimuli. In other words, there are people who find themselves more easily emotionally activated and who experience emotions more intensely. This may be a characteristic of temperament or a tendency that has developed over time as the result of life experiences. How you experience and manage emotions is an important aspect of psychological well-being.

Are you someone who considers themself to be emotionally sensitive?

....

....

Would you consider yourself to be someone who has always had "big feelings" (e.g., cries easily when happy or upset, feels overwhelmed by stressors, has difficulty with self-soothing/relaxing/coping/calming when distressed, or has an exaggerated startle response)?

....

....

If you are emotionally sensitive in this way, do you believe it may play a role in your BFRB? If so, in what way(s)?

....

....

> If you are experiencing additional psychological symptoms that cause you distress, consult with a local mental health professional or visit a professional directory to find a clinician near you, such as the American Psychological Association (http://apa.org), American Board of Professional Psychology (http://abpp.org/directory), American Psychiatric Association (http://psychiatry.org), International OCD Foundation (http://iocdf.org), Anxiety & Depression Association of America (http://adaa.org), Association for Behavioral and Cognitive Therapies (http://abct.org), or The TLC Foundation for Body-Focused Repetitive Behaviors (http://bfrb.org).

Acute and Chronic Stressors and Medical Conditions

Let's not overlook the importance of the impact of medical conditions on BFRBs. A growing number of researchers and clinicians are exploring the associations between autoimmune diseases, viruses, infections, and other illnesses and mental health. If you know that you have a chronic condition or have noticed changes in your BFRB during or after an illness, this may be an area of further exploration for you.

Some people with BFRBs experience skin conditions such as keratosis pilaris, acne, or eczema. Being prone to dandruff or dry skin may also be a trigger for your BFRB. Medical conditions of the hair, skin, mouth, and nails may not only be an antecedent to BFRBs but can also be the result of them. Infection, disfigurement, scarring, and permanent changes in the hair, skin, or nails can result from these behaviors.

Approach your physical and mental health with compassion and care. It is often helpful to find a dermatologist, wound-care specialist, or other physician who is familiar with BFRBs to participate in collaborative healthcare. When you are taking good care of your body though appropriate treatment, your BFRB triggers and consequences will likely decrease.

The physical and psychological effects of acute and chronic stress, illness, disease, or pain can decrease your ability to cope effectively with everyday demands and leave you vulnerable to difficult TIMES and, in turn, to BFRB symptoms. Consider these factors in the major areas of your life.

Are you living with any acute or chronic illness, disease, or pain state?

....

....

Do you "listen to your body" and respond when your mind and body need to rest? Are you currently meeting your healthcare needs (i.e., taking prescribed medication, following up with your doctors, participating in recommended therapies, etc.)?

....

....

What else might you do to support your mind and body's needs in light of these conditions?

....

....

To effectively address vulnerabilities, we turn to the Self-Assessment Summary to examine these factors. Effective strategies that address vulnerabilities aim to promote physical and mental wellness as well as minimize the impact of co-occurring behaviors and conditions in such a way that will promote a different chain of events—a chain that is less likely to lead to your BFRB. Use the planning chart below to identify strategies that may be well matched to the antecedent vulnerabilities you've identified as you consider potential changes that may decrease your triggers.

Antecedent Vulnerabilities ➔	**➔ Minimizing Vulnerabilities Strategies**
Frequently stay up late watching TV	*Practice good sleep hygiene habits—set a consistent, earlier sleep time, turn off the TV, practice a screen-free wind-down activity before bed*
Feeling ill from over-consuming alcohol	*Set a two-drink limit when going out with friends*

cont.

Antecedent Vulnerabilities ➔	➔ Minimizing Vulnerabilities Strategies

ACTION PLAN

Awareness of BFRB Vulnerabilities

What key points in this chapter really spoke to you? What are the highlights *you* most want to keep in mind that are important for you and your BFRB?

....

....

What did you learn about yourself as you **explored**?

....

....

What **practices** will you commit to working on this week to move you toward your destination?

....

....

What is your **action plan**? What steps will you take to put these practices in place?

....

....

When and how often will you engage in these practices?

....

....

As you experiment with increasing your awareness of vulnerabilities, monitor your observations in the Strategies and Skills Observation Log.

Strategies and Skills: Awareness of Vulnerabilities Observation Log

★

Date and Time	Antecedent Awareness of Vulnerabilities	Strategy/Skill	Observations
June 22, 2:10pm	*Itchy skin due to eczema rash*	*Make an appointment with a dermatologist and use prescribed medicated cream*	*Skin is soothed and scratching is deterred*

CHAPTER 7

People, Places, and Spaces

EXPLORE

The P in MA**P**—people, places, and things in your spaces—may become associated with your BFRB through a process called "conditioning." Conditioning occurs when a BFRB repeatedly occurs in a specific context. In this section, we will examine the behavioral pattern linking your BFRB to specific people, places, and things in your spaces. When your BFRB is paired routinely in this way, these people, places, and things in your spaces can become cues to behavior, signaling to your brain that the behavior (and the reward associated with the behavior) is coming. This can increase the urge in these contexts and may result in increased BFRB symptoms. The strength of reward anticipation is well documented in the addiction literature (Koob, Sanna, and Bloom 1998).

You may observe that specific people, places, and things in your spaces serve as TIMES triggers. As you interact with your environment, you will find that thoughts, images, memories, emotions, and sensations (TIMES) show up. And sometimes these experiences bring up unwanted TIMES that you may attempt to manage by engaging in a BFRB, which is then perpetuated because it brings some degree of satisfaction, pleasure, relief, or distraction. For example, if work is often a particularly stressful environment, you may find that you are more likely to engage in the behavior at work. Like settings themselves, you may also find that specific activities, being around certain people, or the presence of particular items, such as mirrors, tweezers, or other "things," may be associated with an increased likelihood of engaging in your BFRB.

To effectively change this pattern, we turn to the Self-Assessment Summary to examine your antecedent people, places, and spaces. Effective strategies that address people, places, and spaces aim to modify the environment in such a way that will promote a different chain of events—a chain that is less likely to lead to your BFRB. Use the following planning chart to identify strategies that may be well matched to the antecedents you've identified as you consider the potential interventions.

★

Antecedent People, Places, and Spaces ➔	➔ People, Places, and Spaces Strategies
Tweezers in my medicine cabinet	*Freezing my tweezers in a block of ice to reduce accessibility*
Biting my nails while alone in my office at work	*Open the door to my office or work in a common area space to decrease sense of being alone*

PRACTICE

TOOLS FOR THE TERRAIN

- Stimulus Control
- Change *Where* You Do Things
- Change *How* You Do Things
- Reduce Facilitators
- Change *Who* Is Around You
- Accommodation by Family/Others

Stimulus Control

Stimulus control strategies are efforts to modify the environment in specific ways that reduce environmental cues or reduce the ability to carry out your BFRB. The goal is to learn new patterns of behavior and create "new learning" that may supersede the previously learned pattern. These changes may not need to be maintained "forever," but they are important for learning new responses to these behavioral cues early in the process of BFRB intervention. In exploring options for stimulus control, consider changing routines that often lead to your BFRB, such as the following.

Change *Where* You Do Things

Changing your location may be helpful. If you often engage in your BFRB while in a particular location, consider changing your location. For example, if you find yourself hair pulling while doing work alone in your bedroom, consider doing work at home while sitting at the kitchen table. Or if you find yourself skin picking while reading in your bed at night, consider reading in your family-room armchair.

How might you change *where* you do things?

....

....

Change *How* You Do Things

Changing the way in which you do things may be helpful. If you find yourself in a routine that often leads to your BFRB, modify that routine in some way. For example, if you often engage in your BFRB while driving, wear driving gloves while in the car or change the way in which you sit or position your arms or hands. If you often get stuck in your BFRB pattern when looking in the bathroom mirror, install low-wattage light bulbs in the room, cover the mirror, or set a timer in the bathroom to limit the time you spend in the room. If idle time at your work desk can be problematic, keep a "toolbox" of manipulatives/fidget toys at your desk and/or wear Band-Aids on your fingers.

How might you change *how* you do things?

....

....

Reduce Facilitators

If there are "things" in your environment that you've identified as items that help you carry out your BFRB, remove or limit access to these items. For example, if you tend to engage in your BFRB while examining your reflection, remove unnecessary mirrors or other reflective items or cover them to reduce the potential for using them more often than needed. Hang Post-it note reminders or inspiring quotes on your mirror or draw messages on the mirror with dry-erase markers. If tweezers, cuticle tools, or other grooming devices or sharp objects are used to carry out your BFRB, give them to someone else for safekeeping, lock them in a cabinet, throw them away and entrust that part of your grooming routine to a professional, or freeze them in a jug of water so that defrosting the container to access the tools would be effortful.

How might you reduce BFRB facilitators?

....

....

Change *Who* Is Around You

As with where you are and what is around you, *who* is around you may also be relevant to your BFRB pattern. Noticing the who, what, when, why, and where of these patterns is important to learning about "what makes your BFRB tick" so that you can make modifications to deter the behavior. For example, maybe you find that you are more likely to engage in your BFRB when in a phone conversation with a relative whom you find stressful. Consider having that conversation in person rather than on the phone, or have that conversation in the presence of a third party. You may also work to develop effective interpersonal communication skills and learn to set appropriate limits with this individual to more effectively manage the conversation.

How might you change the context of who is around you?

....

....

Accommodation by Family/Others

Sometimes people in your life may try to help but unknowingly perpetuate your BFRB. For example, a parent notices that a child pulls their hair when they are bored. As soon as the child starts to pull, the parent gives the child an iPad to distract them. The child may make the association that if they pull their hair, they get more screen time. Any extra attention (negative or positive) that a parent/teacher/spouse/friend gives your BFRB may unintentionally increase it. This can also happen when stress is a trigger for BFRBs. For example, others may excuse you from daily tasks, responsibilities, or expectations because of fear that you will become more stressed and engage in your BFRB. While the intention is good, your BFRB is reinforced. This awareness of how other people respond to your BFRB and how that may impact you can be important to better understanding your BFRB. Others can be an amazing source of support and advocacy by learning how to respond in more effective ways—which sometimes means not over-attending to the behavior.

Do you have a relationship in your life that may be reinforcing your BFRB? If you do, what changes might be helpful? If you are unsure, we'll address interpersonal relationships further in Chapter 14.

....

....

ACTION PLAN

People, Places, and Spaces

What key points in this chapter really spoke to you? What are the highlights *you* most want to keep in mind that are important for you and your BFRB?

....

....

....

What did you learn about yourself as you **explored**?

....

....

....

What **practices** will you commit to working on this week to move you toward your destination?

....

....

....

What is your **action plan**? What steps will you take to put these practices in place?

....

....

....

When and how often will you engage in these practices?

....

....

....

As you experiment with different people, places, and spaces strategies, monitor your observations in the Strategies and Skills Observation Log.

★

Strategies and Skills: People, Places, and Spaces Observation Log

Date and Time	Antecedent People, Places, and Spaces	Strategy/Skill	Observations
December 15, 8:00am	*Getting ready for work, alone in the bathroom*	*Set a timer for preparation time in the room, place a "No pulling" reminder on the mirror*	*Didn't lean in to look in the mirror, was able to quickly engage in morning routine and leave for work on time*

STEP III

GET WITH THE TIMES

CHAPTER 8

Addressing Sensations and Urges

EXPLORE

Herein begins your road to recovery—now that you have your MAP. Before getting started, there are a few things to keep in mind: First, there will be many strategies for you to explore; some you may find useful, some you may not. That's okay and to be expected. Allow yourself to try out a few strategies at a time over the course of a week or so in order to evaluate how useful they are for you. You may decide to continue to use some, change others, or ditch some altogether. That's all fine. Refining your toolbox is key! Also, keep in mind that the strategies you will be exploring are *not* intended as ways for you to make the TIMES stop or ways to get away from your TIMES. Strategies are intended as individualized techniques and tools for you to meet the needs of your body and mind in healthier ways—ways that do not involve engaging in your BFRB or damaging your body or sense of well-being—and solidify those new patterns of behavior.

We'll begin with strategies that address sensations and urges—the S in TIME**S**. We begin here, as these strategies are often the simplest to implement and may provide an initial boost in momentum. In selecting strategies, target your specific antecedent sensations from your self-assessment in Chapter 3. This way, the strategies and skills are more likely to be tailored to your individual needs and may therefore be more likely to be effective. As you "match," pair a specific antecedent sensation with a strategy that involves the same sensation, ideally, or, if you have a preference for a particular sensory experience (e.g, the smell of flowers), you may choose to mix and match. Create a rich sensory environment, making use of multiple senses and tools, if your self-assessment involves many antecedent sensations.

Sensations and urges strategies and skills aim to replace your BFRB with an alternative sensory experience and satisfy your sensory needs. Refer to your Self-Assessment Summary for the antecedents you've identified in Chapter 3, and as you review potential strategies you may use, pair your identified antecedent with a strategy to try.

The following worksheet includes a few examples to assist in planning your strategies.

★

Antecedent Sensations and Urges →	→ Sensations and Urges Strategies
Tingling sensation on my scalp	*Brushing my hair with a nylon bristle brush*
Feeling a rough patch of skin on my face	*Washing and moisturizing my face*

PRACTICE

TOOLS FOR THE TERRAIN

- Competing Responses
- Response Prevention Tools
- Positive Self-Care
- Sensory Substitutes

Competing Responses

These are behaviors that are incompatible with picking, pulling, biting, or other BFRBs. In other words, they are activities that cannot be carried out at the same time as your BFRB, such as coloring, drawing, folding origami, shuffling cards, knitting, or playing with Silly Putty or Play-Doh.

What competing responses might be well matched to your sensations and urges?

....

....

Response Prevention Tools

Also, known as "blockers," these tools make pulling or picking harder to carry out or make the target areas less accessible, such as wearing gloves, eyebrow gel, or hats. Other examples include wearing Vaseline on eyelashes or eyebrows, braided hair, wet hair, use of barrettes, Band-Aids, liquid Band-Aids over the tips of thumbs or to cover scabs, rubber finger tips, finger cots, clothing to cover target areas, nail stickers, acrylic nails, headbands, Buff Puff, scarves, bandanas, or hairpieces/wigs.

What response prevention tools might be well matched to your sensations and urges?

....

....

Positive Self-Care

Positive self-care strategies include actions that show kindness and care toward your BFRB target areas. These may include practices such as moisturizing or applying a facial mask or lip exfoliator. You can also file your nails, paint your fingernails and toenails, massage your hands, use a face roller, or use a skin salve like Aquaphor to soothe dry skin. This is a great way to rewire your grooming response to decrease BFRBs and increase other ways to truly care for your body, mind, and soul. Keep in mind that there may be times that you need to "leave it up to the professionals" and receive spa, dermatological, or wound-care services.

What positive self-care strategies might be well matched to your sensations and urges?

....

....

Sensory Substitutes

These are items that engage the senses. Curiously observe items that stimulate the senses or that you find interesting or "satisfying." For example, if you are drawn to the wiry texture of specific hairs, explore manipulative items with similar textures, such as doll hair or long-bristle paint brushes. When exploring sensory substitutes, consider options associated with different sensations. Here is a big list of ideas to get you started:

Tactile Sensation Strategies

String, dental floss, doll hair, burlap, glue, bubble wrap, nail polish, brushes, velvet, Koosh ball, Tangle, Calm Strips, Velcro, beads, jewelry, feather, pipe cleaner, Silly Putty, squishy or stretchy items, paperclip, rubber band, kinetic sand, yarn, Buff, stress ball, ice cube, Play-Doh, finger trap, Thera-Band, puzzle ring, origami, petting a family pet, warm bath, loofah, massage, facial mask, astringent, lotion, cortisone cream, Lacri-Lube ointment, Aspercreme with Lidocaine, Icy Hot, eyebrow gel, mascara brush on the eyebrows, weighted blanket, silk ribbon, pen topper, body brush, or massage tools.

What tactile sensation strategies might be well matched to your sensations and urges?

....

....

Visual Sensation Strategies

YouTube videos, video games/apps, coloring, drawing, painting, looking at photos, visual puzzles, reading, writing, creating crafts, gears, Rubik's Cube, pimple popping/squeezing toys, or spending time in a beautiful, peaceful space.

What visual sensation strategies might be well matched to your sensations and urges?

....

....

Auditory Sensation Strategies

YouTube videos, autonomous sensory meridian response (ASMR) audio files/videos, video games/apps, music, talking to friends/loved ones, mindful listening meditation, manipulatives that generate sound, popping bubble wrap, cracking seeds, or breaking spaghetti.

What auditory sensation strategies might be well-matched to your sensations and urges?

....

....

Oral Sensation Strategies

Chewing sunflower/pumpkin/sesame/poppy seeds, eating dry spaghetti, mints, pulling/manipulating/eating celery stalk strands, chewing gum, bubblegum, gummy candy, dental floss, toothpick, coffee stirrer, straw, chewable jewelry, tingly lip balm, or hot or cold drinks.

What oral sensation strategies might be well matched to your sensations and urges?

....

....

Olfactory Sensation Strategies

Scented lotions, bath salts, candles, incense, oils, perfume, sprays, peel a citrus fruit, or bake cookies.

What olfactory sensation strategies might be well matched to your sensations and urges?

....

....

> **TOP TIP**
>
> Get creative! Keep your "Trich Tools," "Fidget Funds," "BFRB Boxes," or "Sensory Stations" in the setting(s) you are more likely to engage in the behavior.

Be Prepared

Now that you are learning about your BFRB through your TIMES MAP, you have a better understanding of when, where, and why your BFRB may show up. This awareness is key to helping you become better equipped to meet your needs in other ways. Of course, the tools that you discover are only helpful if you use them.

In order to increase the likelihood of success in using the sensory tools, do a little preparation. Search your home for items that you may already have. You can also purchase what you need to stock up your "sensory stations." It can be fun to shop for these sensory supplies. It is great to try things out in a store, but don't be afraid to explore the vast world of sensory tools you can find online. It can be fun to rotate strategies to keep your toolbox fresh and interesting. Keep your strategies accessible. It has to be just as easy to reach over and grab a hat or fiddle toy as it is to engage in your BFRB. You will likely need to set up several stations around your home, school, workplace, car, etc.

EXPLORE

The Urge Sensation

Have you ever had a staring contest? Have you noticed the increasing sense of discomfort that eventually prompts you to blink? How about noticing the sensation of an itch without scratching? What happens to the sensation over time?

What is an urge? An urge is that difficult-to-describe rising sense of tension, pressure, or discomfort that sometimes precedes your BFRB. This urge sensation is sometimes relieved by carrying out the BFRB, which provides short-term relief but long-term distress and maintenance of the behavior cycle. Research demonstrates that many, although not all, individuals with a BFRB experience some sense of urge at some point in their BFRB cycle. And this urge can be a very powerful factor that keeps that BFRB cycle going. For some, this urge can feel like an intense wave of the ocean, rising up and trying to pull them toward their BFRB. Sometimes, urges and other bodily sensations feel uncomfortable and a BFRB's function has become the means by which these sensations are regulated.

You don't have to shudder at the thought of an urge, and you don't have to struggle with the urge if it shows up. Trying to control it in this way is often a futile struggle. Instead, learning to respond differently to the urge can be an important strategy for effectively managing a BFRB. Rather than struggling with it, you can become an expert surfer, learning to ride the waves all the way out from the crests to the troughs.

PRACTICE

TOOLS FOR THE TERRAIN

- Learning to Surf

Learning to Surf

Surfing is an activity that involves the body as much as it involves the mind. It involves learning to be fully present in the moment—to feel the rising and falling of the water beneath you and to move along with it. Even if you've never surfed, we can all agree that surfing takes practice. But, once you've gotten the hang of it, riding the waves becomes easier and less effortful. Why does that happen? In part, you become a more skilled surfer when you are less fearful of surfing and learn to welcome the waves, becoming more relaxed, less rigid, and more flexible in your mind and body.

Urge surfing is similar (Ostafin and Marlatt 2008). Urge surfing is a mindfulness practice that may be useful for those who experience urges or other strong emotions that lead to BFRBs.

If you experience an urge or a strong sensation that precedes your BFRB, chances are you have felt like you are struggling to move against the tide when that urge or emotion shows up. And the more you struggle to swim to shore, the more likely it seems you will inevitably get swept up in the current. Through repeated experiences like this, you've likely learned to become resistant and avoid that strong feeling because you know where it typically leads... and you don't want that. The very sensation can cause distress and an immediate desire to push it away, even if it has not yet led to the behavior you'd like to reduce.

Instead of responding to your emotions and bodily sensations with this willfulness and rejection—struggling against them with all of your effort to try to make them stop—becoming willing to have these internal experiences—even welcoming them as normal ways in which your body and mind operate—can help to reduce the discomfort you experience. And learning to ride the comings and goings of these internal experiences in whatever changing dynamic of intensity and duration they arrive and dissipate is a helpful tool to use when you have a BFRB. You, too, can learn to surf.

> Initially, practice urge surfing to a bodily sensation with which you are somewhat more comfortable than your BFRB, such as an itch or tickle sensation. Give yourself the opportunity to practice and get accustomed to the experience before approaching your BFRB in this way. We'll revisit urge surfing and apply it to the BFRB urge once we've gathered some additional skills.

How to Surf

Preparing to surf: Remember that surfing is a skill that takes practice to develop. Keep in mind that thoughts, emotions, and bodily sensations come and go naturally whether or not you struggle with them. Urges are temporary. Psych yourself up by reminding yourself that urges are like ocean waves that arrive, crest, and subside. Practicing daily mindfulness will also help to develop this skill.

Step 1: Close your eyes and take a few relaxing breaths. Bring mindfulness to the moment, being fully present and aware of your breath as you breathe comfortably. It's okay to notice your thoughts without judging them and if they wander, bring them back to your breath.

Step 2: Locate a specific sensation in your body. Pay close attention to it with curiosity. Notice what happens to that sensation over time. Notice the quality of the sensation, its position, boundaries, and intensity. Notice how it changes as you inhale and exhale. Notice how the sensation intensifies, diminishes, or moves around. If your attention to the sensation wanders, gently bring your attention back to the sensation.

Step 3: Acknowledge that this can be uncomfortable and even difficult. If you get distracted by difficult thoughts or emotions, that's okay. Just return to your breath, inhaling and exhaling as you ride the ebbs and flows. Stay curious and observant as your moment-to-moment experiences unfold and change over time.

ACTION PLAN

Addressing Sensations and Urges

What key points in this chapter really spoke to you? What are the highlights *you* most want to keep in mind that are important for you and your BFRB?

....

....

What did you learn about yourself as you **explored**?

....

....

What **practices** will you commit to working on this week to move you toward your destination?

....

....

What is your **action plan**? What steps will you take to put these practices in place?

....

....

When and how often will you engage in these practices?

....

....

As you experiment with sensations and urges tools, monitor your observations in the Strategies and Skills Observation Log.

Strategies and Skills: Sensations and Urges Observation Log

Date and Time	Antecedent People, Places, and Spaces	Strategy/Skill	Observations
February 8, 3:25pm	*Feeling fidgety and the urge to engage in the BFRB*	*Grab a paperclip to manipulate*	*Kept attention on bending paperclip and refrained from picking cuticles*

CHAPTER 9

Habit Reversal Training

EXPLORE

Habit Reversal Training (HRT) is an evidence-based behavioral procedure used to reduce the occurrence of BFRBs. It is also the first behavioral treatment to address unwanted repetitive behaviors, such as Tourette's disorder and other tic disorders. There are four essential components of HRT:

- Psychoeducation and functional analysis: As you've explored in earlier chapters, these elements help you to understand your BFRB and the patterns in which it is carried out, including all of those antecedent cues you've identified that make it more likely to occur, as well as those consequences of the behavior.
- Awareness training: These are the strategies for acknowledging and increasing your awareness of the behavior chain, including self-monitoring, using awareness training devices, self-check-ins, and response prevention strategies. Self-monitoring is an important component in increasing your recognition of any BFRB urges and further identifying the behavior pattern.
- Stimulus control: The goal of stimulus control is to manipulate the environment to avoid behavioral cues and divert the learned pattern of behavior.
- Competing response training: Competing response training is center stage in HRT. Yes, you've considered competing responses previously in this workbook as well, but in HRT, you will practice competing responses in a specific manner.

Competing responses are those simple behaviors that are selected to replace the BFRB in response to the antecedent cues; thus, it is preferable that the competing response selected is a behavior that is incompatible with the BFRB. In other words, you should not be able to engage in the BFRB at the same time as engaging in the competing response, such as clasping your hands together. Choose a competing response that is discrete and unlikely to be noticed by others. If a competing response is discrete, it will not draw attention in public settings, so you will be more likely to feel comfortable using the strategy regardless of where you are or what you are doing. For example, gently placing your hands down—on your lap when sitting, or by your sides when standing—is a discrete competing response you may choose to use. It is also recommended you choose a competing response that may be used flexibly across different contexts so that it is always possible, such as touching the tips of your fingers together. A competing response that may be applied in most if not all situations throughout your daily activities is likely to be more useful. Therefore, an ideal competing response may be something like clenching your fists or folding your arms.

To choose an effective competing response, choose a response that:

- ✓ is incompatible with the BFRB
- ✓ is discrete
- ✓ may be used across different situations
- ✓ can be carried out for at least one minute.

Identify a competing response to your BFRB(s):

✱

What Is My BFRB?	What Are My BFRB cues?	What Is My Competing Response?
Hair pulling	*Stroking the hair, visually searching for split ends*	*Fist clenching*

PRACTICE

TOOLS FOR THE TERRAIN

- Habit Reversal Training

Habit Reversal Training

Begin by practicing the chosen competing response in the absence of urges or BFRB cues frequently and for varied lengths of time so that you become comfortable using it. Try it out for brief intervals of at least 60 seconds. When you are ready to begin to use a competing response as a behavioral redirection strategy, carry out the competing response for 60 seconds whenever you notice an antecedent cue or when you notice the behavior itself. If the urge persists after 60 seconds, repeat the competing response for an additional 60 seconds, and repeat, if needed, until the urge subsides and you are able to refrain from the BFRB. Below are examples of competing responses:

BFRB	Competing Response
Hair pulling	*Hand clasping* *Interlocking fingers*
Skin picking	*Placing hands down at sides* *Placing hands on lap*
Nail biting	*Touching fingertips together* *Fist clenching*
Cuticle biting	*Folding arms across chest* *Pressing tongue against front teeth*
Cheek biting	*Pressing tongue against roof of mouth* *Letting jaw and tongue sit loosely apart*
Lip biting	*Gently clenching teeth and breathing deeply* *Pursing lips together*

Note that it is "normal" and to be expected that using HRT may initially result in a short-term increase in unpleasant internal BFRB cues (TIMES), including frustration. That's okay. The more you practice, the easier riding out the urge and using the competing response is likely to become. So, keep it up! Using HRT is not only a great strategy to redirect the BFRB to a behavior that is more aligned with what you want for yourself, it is also one of the helpful ways to learn that you can ride out your uncomfortable TIMES without the BFRB.

ACTION PLAN

Habit Reversal Training

What key points in this chapter really spoke to you? What are the highlights *you* most want to keep in mind that are important for you and your BFRB?

....

....

What did you learn about yourself as you **explored**?

....

....

What **practices** will you commit to working on this week to move you toward your destination?

....

....

What is your **action plan**? What steps will you take to put these practices in place?

....

....

When and how often will you engage in these practices?

....

....

As you experiment with HRT, monitor your observations in the Strategies and Skills Observation Log.

Strategies and Skills: HRT Observation Log

Date and Time	Antecedent	Strategy/Skill	Observations
January 4, 7:28pm	*Watching TV, sitting on the sofa*	*Clasping hands together*	*Practiced for two 60-second periods in response to the urge and was then able to refrain from my BFRB after clasping my hands*

CHAPTER 10

Minding Your Mind

EXPLORE

Let's take a deep dive into the mind and focus on the TIM in **TIM**ES. The concepts and strategies related to the thoughts, images, and memories you experience are intended to help you practice noticing the cognitive processes that influence your emotions and behaviors, including your BFRB. In order to do this, it's important to understand the relationship between the fundamental processes in your mind and body. After all, we humans are pretty complex. Fortunately, we are able to think about our own experiences, both internal and external, so that we may better understand them, which better enables us to influence and/or change them.

CBT is based upon the principle that thoughts, emotions, and behaviors are interrelated. Let's look at automatic thoughts. Automatic thoughts include that naturally occurring, non-effortful, internal voice you have—your narrator. Examples of such thoughts are:

- "I'd like to start reading my new book today."
- "I want to try some of these strategies."
- "This seems like it could be helpful."

Thoughts influence emotions:

- Thought: "I'd like to start reading my new book today." ➔ Emotion: Excited.
- Thought: "I want to try some of these strategies." ➔ Emotion: Interest.
- Thought "This seems like it could be helpful." ➔ Emotion: Hopeful.

Emotions directly influence behavior:

- Thought: "I'd like to start reading my new book today." ➔ Emotion: Excited ➔ Behavior: Set aside time and sit down in a comfortable, quiet place with my new book.
- Thought: "I want to try some of these strategies." ➔ Emotion: Interested ➔ Behavior: Choose three strategies and practice throughout the week.

- Thought: "This seems like it could be helpful." ➔ Emotion: Hopeful ➔ Behavior: Set reminders on my phone to practice strategies twice daily.

Thoughts, emotions, and behaviors influence one another and are influenced by one another. When we have a thought, we experience associated emotion(s), and these experiences influence behavior(s).

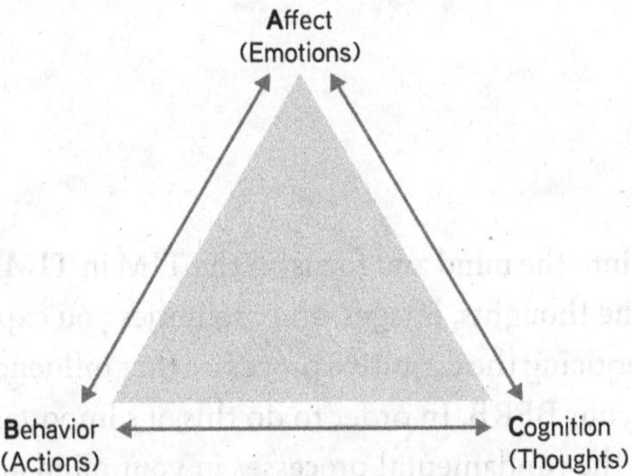

Let's take a look at this in action. What happens when you notice an activating thought? Let's use the example, "I can't control this BFRB." This is a commonly experienced thought for individuals living with a BFRB due to the chronic waxing-and-waning pattern of symptoms. When the thought "I can't control this BFRB," shows up in your mind, what emotion(s) do you notice? You may notice, for example, feelings of frustration or sadness. Maybe you've been struggling with your BFRB for a long time or maybe you've been caught up in an expectation that you will make this behavior stop immediately. If you are thinking, "I can't control this BFRB," and are feeling frustration or sadness, what bodily sensation(s) do you notice? How is your body feeling? Maybe you notice rising tension or discomfort. Maybe you feel fidgety or on edge. If you do, chances are you want to try to make this discomfort stop or just make yourself feel better. And, you may do that by pulling, picking, biting, or otherwise carrying out a behavior that ultimately makes you feel worse, not better. You may even choose to opt out of activities and isolate yourself in response to feeling this way.

Thought ➔	**➔ Emotion(s) ➔**	**➔ Behavior(s)**
"I can't control this"	*Frustrated, sad*	*Pull, pick, avoid*

TOP TIP

Learn to identify the relationships between your thoughts, emotions, and behaviors, and you can become an expert on the fundamentals of behavior change.

If you can identify the patterns between your thoughts, emotions, and behaviors, you are on your way to discovering some of the answers to, "Why do I do this?" and "How do I deal with this?"—*the* most common questions asked by those who are living with a BFRB.

Learning About Your Thinking Patterns

Can you identify the relationship between your thoughts, emotions, and behaviors? To do so, get curious about the impact of your thoughts. When you notice a thought show up, ask yourself:

- "What emotions do I notice?"
- "Do I notice the urge to respond?"
- "What behavior follows when I'm thinking and feeling this way?"
- Jot down these observations below:

★

Thought	Emotion(s)	Behavior(s)
"I can't control this"	*Frustrated, sad, helpless, distressed*	*Pull/pick, avoid activities, keep to oneself*

If you take a magnifying glass to these thoughts and look closely, you will find that not all thoughts are helpful to you. Furthermore, thinking tends to fall into specific patterns—patterns that can unintentionally enable or maintain a BFRB. We'll call these unhelpful thoughts cognitive distortions because they pull us away from who and how we want to be. (And they're not always accurate!)

Ask yourself, "How might my internal narrator/advisor be off track?" In order to easily call out these unhelpful patterns, let's look at the common ways in which BFRB-triggering thoughts can show up.

Common Cognitive Distortions in BFRBs

What Is a Cognitive Distortion?

A cognitive distortion is an inaccuracy in thinking that can cause unpleasant feelings and can influence behavior in undesirable ways. The good news is that you can change this pattern to one that is more helpful to your well-being. Here are a few common distortions in BFRBs of which to be aware:

Perfectionism: An expectation and effort to achieve perfection. ("I can't have any stubble or rough spots." "My eyebrows must be nicely arched and exactly even.")

Permissiveness: Giving yourself permission to engage in a behavior that is not consistent with your goals, feelings, or beliefs. ("I will start my efforts to stop tomorrow, not now." "I'll only pull for a minute." "I'll just pick this one scab.")

Can'ting: Telling yourself that you cannot do something that is within the realm of possibilities. ("I can't stop." "I can't control this.")

Unrealistic expectations: Having unrealistic goals for yourself that are unlikely to be obtained. ("As soon as I begin therapy, I will never pull/pick again." "This medication will make my urges disappear.")

Mind reading: Assuming you know another person's thoughts without having sufficient evidence for this assumption. ("They think I'm strange." "They don't want to be my friend.")

Fortune telling: Predicting the future without sufficient evidence for this prediction. ("I'm not going to be able to stop pulling." "No one will want to date me if they know I pull/pick.")

Catastrophizing: Magnifying a problem such that it is or would be extremely distressing or intolerable. ("If someone at school/work finds out I have a bald spot, everyone will talk about me behind my back and alienate me. I'll never be able to go back there.")

Negative filtering: Overlooking or discounting positive attributes and magnifying or over-attending to what you perceive to be negative attributes. ("I look terrible today; my eyelashes are almost completely gone." "These scars on my face make me look ugly.")

What if?: Asking yourself a series of worrisome "what if?" questions that cannot be satisfied or resolved with the responses. ("What if someone notices my hair?" "What if my makeup comes off?" "What if I can never stop picking/pulling?")

Overgeneralization: Seeing an event as a never-ending pattern. ("I pulled/picked so much today, I will always have this problem." "I have a new bald spot, I will never be able to control this behavior.")

Emotional reasoning: Assuming that negative emotions are a reflection of the way things actually are. ("I feel embarrassed and everyone is judging me because of my BFRB." "These urges are making me do it.")

Should statements: Assuming that your experience and response must match those of other people. When "shoulding on ourselves," people typically feel guilt, resentment, frustration, and anger. ("I shouldn't have this problem." "I should be able to just stop.")

All or nothing: Seeing a situation in a dichotomous, black-and-white manner while dismissing other possibilities. ("I already picked/pulled today, so I am a total failure." "I bit off one nail, so I need to bite off the rest."

PRACTICE

TOOLS FOR THE TERRAIN

- Reframing Unhelpful Thoughts
- Examine the Evidence
- Test Your Beliefs
- Soften Your Words
- Rewrite the Narrative
- Change the Scene
- Write a Fast Forward for Inspiration
- Create Coping Cards

Some (or all) of these cognitive distortions are familiar, aren't they? And they lead to BFRBs or avoidance behaviors that ultimately cause you to feel worse, don't they? Let's call them out! You don't have to be pushed around by these thoughts! You don't have to believe everything you think. First and foremost, remember this is your mind trying to look out for you, trying to help you to feel better in some way or avoid what it thinks will make you feel worse. You don't have to take that bait. There are many different strategies you can use. Some strategies aim to shift perspective on your thoughts and develop healthier, more accurate thoughts in response, while others identify those thoughts as unhelpful to you and aim to give you some distance from unhelpful thoughts and refrain from responding to them. We'll cover a wide range of these strategies, from those originating from traditional cognitive therapy to those that are based in more contemporary mindfulness- and acceptance-based approaches, because we want to give you a wide range of tools for your toolbox. You choose the tools that work best for you.

Reframing Unhelpful Thoughts

Most of the time, you probably have a sense that you don't want to get caught up in a particular thought; you see the rabbit hole before you go down it. However, sometimes, thoughts can really catch us off guard. Maybe, unbeknownst to you, you get caught up in the thought and you really believe it. Maybe you stray from the ability to see it for what it is—just an unhelpful thought. For example, maybe you are having a movie night at home with your family when you need to briefly excuse yourself to use the bathroom (during a lull in the movie's action, of course). In the bathroom, you glance in the mirror as you are washing your hands and notice a few stray eyebrow hairs. Perhaps you think, "I need to get rid of those stray hairs. There are some tweezers in the cabinet. It will only take a minute." In this example, the antecedent thoughts included, "I need to get rid of those stray hairs. There are some tweezers in the cabinet. It will only take a minute."

Whereas some individuals practice allowing unhelpful thoughts to come and go, others find it useful to develop healthy responses to negative self-talk. Learning to talk back from a reasonable, flexible, compassionate stance can be a helpful way of supporting yourself when your analytical mind begins to chatter. A strategy from cognitive therapy known as cognitive restructuring aims to recognize and replace irrational or unhelpful cognitions with more helpful thoughts. This can be done with a simple two-column thought chart, such as:

Unhelpful Thought	Helpful Thought
"I'll just pull for a minute"	*"It's harder to stop once I've started. Giving myself permission to pull for just a little while is self-defeating and not aligned with what I want for myself."*
"Nobody understands"	*"If I feel alone and misunderstood, I can attend a support group or talk to a friend. Remember, BFRBs are common, so I'm not alone."*

Your job here is to call out an unhelpful thought and to ask yourself, "How might I think about this differently?" "What might be another perspective?"

Give it a try:

★

Unhelpful Thought	Helpful Thought

You can also take a closer look at this thought process and tell yourself, "I CAN."

I CAN Develop Healthy, Flexible, Self-Talk

1. **C**atch an unhelpful thought and the way it influences your emotions and behaviors.
   - What thoughts are showing up in my mind just now? What emotion(s) am I feeling? How do these thoughts and emotion(s) make me want to behave? In what way do I feel an urge to act?
2. **A**sk yourself if this thought is helpful or unhelpful and spot the distortion.
   - Is this thought helpful or unhelpful? In what way might it be distorted, inaccurate, unreasonable, or unhelpful?
3. **N**ame alternative thoughts and proceed toward what matters most to you.
   - How likely is this to happen? Is there some part of this thought or feeling that I can't have and must get rid of? Could I tolerate this thought? How might I think about this differently? What might I tell a friend if they voiced this thought to me? Construct alternative perspectives or responses to the unhelpful thought.
   - Notice how this influences your thought(s), emotion(s), and the urge to behave/act. What emotion(s) am I feeling? How do these thoughts and emotion(s) make me want to behave? Is this new thought more helpful?

You can practice the process of developing healthier self-talk. It may be challenging at first, but with practice, you can learn to respond to difficult thoughts in a healthier, more flexible way, which may positively impact your emotions (and your BFRB, too!).

The following exercise will lead you through the process of (re)thinking about your thinking:

(Re)Thinking About Thinking

Thought	Associated Emotion(s) and Behavior(s)	Is This a Helpful or Unhelpful Thought?	How Is This Thought Distorted?	Realistic Response	Associated Emotion(s) and Behavior(s)?	Is This a Helpful or Unhelpful Thought?
"I can't control this"	*Distressed, frustrated; pull/pick, avoidant*	*Unhelpful*	*Can'ting*	*"I may be able to control this if I use my log and use my strategies"* *"If I'm feeling overwhelmed, I may think this way. Perhaps I'll think differently if I use a strategy to address this feeling"*	*Hopeful, motivated; use log and strategies*	*Helpful*

Examine the Evidence

When you get stuck on a difficult, judgmental thought, ask yourself for the evidence. First, identify the difficult thought. For example, "I'm a failure."

Then ask yourself, "Is this 100 percent accurate?" "Is this a reasonable conclusion?" What evidence do I have to demonstrate that this thought is true?" "Do I have any evidence to the contrary that brings the accuracy of this thought into question?" If there is some wiggle room here, "How might my thoughts reflect a more reasonable perspective on this?" "Might there be a more accurate statement?" For example, "I didn't pass my exam today, but that doesn't necessarily mean I am a failure. This is one test. Failing one test does not make me a failure. I've done well on other tests. And, there are a number of things at which I have excelled, such as getting that promotion last year and finishing that 5k. Perhaps I can determine what was most challenging for me about the exam and prepare to take it again."

Now, it's your turn. Examine the evidence for your thoughts. These thoughts may be directly or indirectly BFRB related.

★

Thought	Evidence	Conclusion and Response

Test Your Beliefs

Conduct experiments to test whether your beliefs are accurate. For example, let's say you find yourself stuck, time and time again, in a pattern of picking at scabs in response to the thought, "If I pick this scab off, it will heal faster." Conduct a behavioral experiment. Test this belief.

Next time you notice a scab that you feel the urge to pick, decide to refrain from picking it in order to test your hypothesis. Record your observations:

- If you don't pick this scab, will it still heal?
- How long does it take?
- Does it heal faster?
- Does it heal more slowly?
- What are your observations of the uninterrupted healing process?

....

....

Soften Your Words

Words have power. When we speak harshly to ourselves, not only is it often painful and self-defeating, but it also takes the wind out of our sails, making it that much more difficult to move forward toward our destination. Try changing your words to less emotionally evocative terms. Soften the words you use, removing judgment and sticking to the facts, as if you are an observer, looking in. For example, if you think, "I'll never be able to feel good about myself," you might revise that sentence to say, "I'm feeling discouraged at the moment because my BFRB has been a struggle; but, there are times when I feel good about myself. I am so much more than my hair, skin, and nails."

Try it. Take a judgmental sentence and soften the words:

★

Judgment	Softened Observation

Rewrite the Narrative

Have you ever noticed a narrative in your mind about your BFRB? Not just a single thought but a collection of thoughts that are connected to a history and perhaps project a grim future? Maybe you notice a narrative that's something like this, "I can't win. I was doing so well. I was pull-free for a week and now I'm back to square one. This always happens. I get so excited about using my strategies and feel motivated to keep going, but then I always mess up. I'll never be able to stop pulling or feel good about myself. What's the use in even trying?"

Oof! That's quite a blow to your motivation to keep going, isn't it? It's going to be more difficult to get back on track with that narrative taking center stage. You have the ability to rewrite that narrative. Think about that cognitive restructuring exercise. How is this narrative inaccurate or unhelpful? What might you say to yourself to rewrite and override this narrative? How do you respond to yourself with more kindness and understanding, with more flexibility and an openness to the possibility that you have the ability to adapt and change? Rewrite your narrative and practice reading it to yourself when your self-defeating narrative shows up.

Change the Scene

Have you ever had an unpleasant image, either imagined or from memory, that you cannot get out of your mind? Perhaps it's a short snippet of memory, like a video that plays in your mind. Maybe you can't stop thinking about a time when you were teased for playing with your hair. Or a time you felt ashamed looking in the mirror at some skin damage you unintentionally caused by engaging in your BFRB. You can change the scene. Just like it's a movie. You can add parts, delete parts, change parts, or transition to a whole new scene altogether. For example, maybe embarrassment turns to joy as you imagine someone entering the room and telling you how beautiful you are. What's your scene and how might you change it?

....

....

Write a Fast Forward for Inspiration

A fast forward is an imagined narrative about the future in which you've met your goals and feel good about your place in life. What is life like for you? How are things different? How do you feel? What do you want your younger self to know about your future?

....

....

Save this fast forward and tuck it away for safekeeping—somewhere within reach. Read it several times each day and when you are having a difficult moment to remind yourself of where you want to be and the direction in which you are heading with every choice you make, big or small.

Create Coping Cards

Create a deck of cards, with each card having a problematic thought on one side and a list of alternative, adaptive responses on the other side. You might also add other strategies to the list of responses. Practice reading this list when the thought arises and try out an alternative response or two. Below, you'll find an example of what a coping card might look. Try some on your own.

(Front)	(Back)
"I just need to even up my eyebrows."	*"I'm having the thought that I need to even up my eyebrows, but this is just a thought, not anything I actually need to do."* *"If I start to pluck my brows, I may get carried away and pluck too much. I can use my strategies to ride out this urge."* *"This thought is uncomfortable, but I can walk away and manage this discomfort until it subsides."* *"I can make an appointment with an aesthetician to have my eyebrows professionally groomed. I don't need to take responsibility for grooming them myself."* *"Let's see if I can tolerate this uncomfortable feeling and notice how this urge changes over time if I walk away."*

★ Thoughts, Images, Memories (T-I-M)

Everyone engages in unhelpful thinking from time to time. And, for many individuals living with a BFRB, thoughts about themselves, their hair, skin, or nails, thoughts about others, and thoughts about their ability or inability to control the behavior can serve as a trigger for BFRBs. Glance back at the Self-Assessment Summary you completed in Chapter 3. What antecedent thoughts, images, and/or memories did you identify as triggers for your BFRB? What thoughts, images, and/or memories strategies might you try in response to each trigger you identified?

Antecedent Thoughts, Images, Memories ➔	**➔ Thoughts, Images, Memories Strategies**
"Picking the scab will help this heal"	*I CAN strategy, test your beliefs*
"I can't believe I pulled so much and I'm back to square one!"	*Soften your words, coping cards*

It's time to implement and observe. Try a few (two or three) strategies this week that you've identified and record the results. After approximately one week, review your Strategies and Skills Observation Log and evaluate how helpful each strategy was. If you liked them and they were helpful, great! They're keepers! If they were not helpful, you can refine the strategies or simply try others. Remember—not every strategy will be effective for you, and often you will need to use several strategies to maximize your outcome. Everyone's needs are different, so be curious, be observant, and be committed to what matters most to you.

ACTION PLAN

Minding Your Mind

What key points in this chapter really spoke to you? What are the highlights *you* most want to keep in mind that are important for you and your BFRB?

....

....

What did you learn about yourself as you **explored**?

....

....

What **practices** will you commit to working on this week to move you toward your destination?

....

....

What is your **action plan**? What steps will you take to put these practices in place?

....

....

When and how often will you engage in these practices?

....

....

As you experiment with these strategies, monitor your observations in the Strategies and Skills Observation Log.

Strategies and Skills: T-I-M Observation Log

★

Date and Time	Antecedent Thoughts, Images, and Memories	Strategy/Skill	Observations
February 8, 3:25pm	*Remembering a satisfying pimple pop and thinking, "This going to heal so much faster if I pick at it"*	*Examine the evidence, healthy, flexible self-talk*	*Was able to walk away without picking, noticed that the pimple formed into a scab and healed more quickly without having picked at it*

CHAPTER 11

Embarking on a Healthy Relationship with Yourself

EXPLORE

In Chapter 10, we examined the relationship between thoughts, feelings, and behaviors, and we approached the thoughts from a traditional cognitive lens—examining unhelpful, maladaptive thoughts and initiating change to the sequence by practicing the generation of more helpful, more accurate, more reasonable thoughts. But sometimes, people find that this is insufficient. Sometimes, people learn to "talk back" to their thoughts in healthier ways, only to find themselves getting caught up in a debate with that maladaptive voice in their minds, becoming exhausted, and just not feeling any better or seeing any behavioral change. Sometimes we hear, "I know what to say, but I still feel stuck." Here, we'll discuss a different perspective on working on those sticky thoughts.

More contemporary cognitive-behavioral approaches utilize mindfulness as a foundation for approaching cognitive processes. Drawn from eastern philosophies, such as Buddhism, mindfulness-based therapies aim to increase awareness of cognitive processes and enable someone to learn to observe them from a distance rather than engage with them or try to change them in any way. In other words, mindfulness practices can help you become less drawn in by unwanted TIMES, less rattled by them, and less likely to react or respond in ways that are not aligned with who you want to be and what you want for yourself. Mindfulness skills are a path to behavioral change, as the ability to have full contact with the moment, including all of your thoughts, emotions, and bodily sensations as they naturally occur, leads to psychological flexibility. Psychological flexibility is the ability to accept your experiences, both those that are wanted as well as those that are unwanted, while continuing to pursue your values and goals, despite those experiences.

In ACT, the intention is not to change your thoughts but, rather, to be fully present, noticing your internal and external experiences with curiosity, openness, and self-compassion, while moving toward your values. Think of this approach as developing the ability to get a little distance from your thoughts, watching them as an observer, getting curious about them, without reacting or responding to them, like watching actors on a stage.

PRACTICE

TOOLS FOR THE TERRAIN

- Leaves on a Stream
- Your Mind as a Protector
- Passengers on the Bus
- Words Are Powerful
- An Adventure in Cognitive Defusion
- Carry It with You
- Practice Perspective Taking
- Thank You, but No Thank You
- Anchor Yourself to What Matters: The Choice Point
- STOP
- Developing a Healthy Relationship

Leaves on a Stream

Leaves on a stream is a mindfulness exercise commonly practiced in ACT. Like other mindfulness exercises, the intention is to practice becoming an observer of your own experience from the vessel that is your body.

The purpose of this mindfulness exercise is to practice noticing your thoughts and looking at your thoughts rather than from your thoughts—to practice watching your thoughts rather than getting caught up in them. And, as you look at your thoughts, notice that there's no need to control your thoughts in any way, but, rather, you can let them come in and flow out naturally without engaging with them or trying to move them around.

> *We invite you to sit comfortably in your chair, with both feet on the floor, and allow your eyes to close if you are comfortable or maintain a soft, downward-cast gaze. Take a few slow, gentle breaths, in and out. With each inhale, notice the cool air as you breathe in, and notice the warmth of your breath as you exhale. Notice your breath softly expanding.*
>
> *Imagine in your mind's eye that you are sitting at the base of an old tree, by the banks of a beautiful, gently flowing stream. The water softly flows over rocks and around green plants and tall trees, slowly descending downstream. Feel the ground beneath you and the warmth of the sun above you. Notice the sounds of the water flowing past you as you admire the beauty and simplicity of nature. You notice that every so often, a leaf drifts down from above you as it drops into the stream and is gently carried away by the water. Become aware of your thoughts. Each time a thought comes into your mind, imagine that it is written on one of these leaves drifting down into the water. If you think in images, imagine those images on these leaves. Your goal is to sit beside the stream and allow the leaves to float by. Don't try to make the water flow faster or slower. Don't try to change what shows up on the leaves in any way. Just observe them. Maybe you notice the thought, "This is really nice,"*

or, "I don't know if I'm doing this correctly;" put those thoughts on leaves. If your mind wanders or you notice the leaves have stopped falling, just acknowledge that this has happened and return to the stream. Observe a thought come into your mind, put that thought on a leaf, and allow it to float away downstream. Take a few minutes to watch this peaceful moment in time.

Notice that it's effortless to watch your thoughts in this way, allowing them to come and go, without getting caught up in them or struggling with them. Notice what it feels like to watch your thoughts from this more distanced perspective, looking at your thoughts rather than from your thoughts. Notice what it feels like to sit by the banks of the stream, the warmth of the sun shining down on you. Bring your awareness back to your breath, taking a few expanding breaths. Bring your awareness back into the room. And, when you are ready, open your eyes.

What kind of thoughts showed up?

....

....

Did you notice any thoughts that took your mind away from placing those thoughts on the leaves?

....

....

Did you notice that the water stopped flowing at any point?

....

....

Were there any thoughts that took your mind away from being at the banks of the water?

....

....

What was it like to redirect your attention—to return your mind to the leaves and the flow of the stream?

....

....

When your mind is distracted from the exercise, you are interacting with your thoughts rather than being an observer of your thoughts. Your job is to practice becoming an expert observer—to watch your thoughts come and go, allowing them to come into your mind and flow away from your mind, naturally, in their own time.

There is no need to interact with them or get caught up in them by analyzing them or judging them in any way. Even if the thoughts that show up are unpleasant, there is no need to push them around or try to make them go away more quickly. Instead, try to make space for whatever thoughts show up, allowing them to perhaps even stay for a while and to move around freely so that they are able to more easily come and go at their own pace.

> There are many useful mindfulness exercises and metaphors to provide a guide for the development of this skill. With a quick internet search or the download of a mindfulness app, such as Headspace, Ten Percent Happier, or Insight Timer, you'll have great opportunities to practice this skill set.

Your Mind as a Protector

Your mind has many jobs, one of which is to protect you at all costs. During the Stone Age, early humans ensured their own survival in many of the same ways we do now—by relying on their nervous systems to alert them to danger, compare their own behavior to others to ensure they'd be accepted by a group and not left alone, which would increase their vulnerability to aggressors, and use their superior thinking and reasoning ability to ensure their survival. It makes sense that the human mind and body functioned in this way; in many ways, it was a much more dangerous existence.

It can be immeasurably helpful to have a mind that has the ability to think about thinking and constantly analyze, judge, and compare; however, as you know, it can also be a hindrance when we get too caught up in those thoughts and when those thoughts are unnecessarily harsh or judgmental. No longer faced with the danger of being hunted by a saber-toothed tiger as we sleep in our huts, our minds may not need to be protective in that same way, all the time. But, it's how we're built. The design was good, but the ways in which these processes operate in modern times are not always in our best interest.

Consider how your mind attempts to protect you.

What does your protective mind tell you about yourself, your BFRB, about others, and about the world around you?

....

....

Is your mind sometimes an unhelpful advisor?

....

....

What happens when your mind gives you unwanted thoughts that cause you to experience distress?

....

....

How do you typically respond when your mind does this? Do you argue with it, buy into the thoughts, or get caught up in what it's saying?

....

....

What happens if and when you do? What do you notice you are thinking, feeling, and doing?

....

....

Passengers on the Bus

You may not need to be directed to run away from the danger of saber-toothed tigers, but your mind continues to analyze, judge, and give you feedback in similar ways, much of the time. Passengers on the bus is a common ACT metaphor (Hayes, Strosahl, and Wilson 1999) that illustrates the mind's activities.

Imagine that your life is a journey and you are the bus driver on your life's road. You have many different places you'd like to go on your journey that are important to you, and you look forward to these destinations. Throughout your journey, passengers board your bus. These passengers embody the thoughts, feelings, and experiences you've had in your life. Some, you feel positively about and welcome on board, and others, you don't like and prefer would exit the bus. These less-preferred passengers are unpleasant to have on board. They can distract you from the road, giving you unwanted feedback and criticism, like saying, "You don't know what you're doing! You can't be trusted to make decisions here! Let us take the wheel!" They may try to divert you with comments like, "Don't go that way! Go this way!" They may scare you, anger you, overwhelm you, or make you feel terrible about yourself. They may bring up unpleasant memories, yell directions at you, and get pretty rowdy.

Eventually, you've had enough of these troublemakers, so you stop the bus, pull over, and begin to argue and fight with them, but you are unable to force them off the bus—after all, they are parts of your life experiences. In the meantime, your bus is stopped. You are caught up in struggling and you are not moving toward your desired destinations. So now you've got a bigger problem. When you notice this, you try to negotiate with them; maybe you'll do what they say if they'll just quiet down. If you do what they say, this may quiet the bus for a while and bring you some relief, but you won't be going where you want to go. You'll be giving them control of your bus journey. Whether you struggle with these unwanted passengers or you give in to these passengers, you're probably not driving the bus in the direction you'd like to go.

What if, even if these passengers are loud and unruly, they could not take control of your path unless you allowed them to do so? What if you stayed in the driver's seat, heading in your desired direction, no matter what they say or do? The passengers may be loud or they may be quiet. They may come and they may go. But, you—you are in control of how you respond to them and what you do with the wheel.

Can you relate to this bus driver? How does this metaphor relate to your experience of having a BFRB?

....

....

Are you always driving your bus or are there times when you get distracted by the unruly passengers?

....

....

What happens when you do get caught up in responding to the passengers? How do you feel? What do you do?

....

....

How do you get yourself back in the driver's seat when the passengers are so loud and disruptive, and cause so much distress?

....

....

What do you think would happen if you stopped responding to them and just let them do whatever it is they are going to do? How might their behavior change over time? How might your experience of the road to your destination be?

....

....

Words Are Powerful

Resistance sometimes creeps in—that willfulness that can result from struggle and frustration. Perhaps you are thinking, "But, the thoughts feel so powerful. I get so upset that I can't help but respond by engaging in my BFRB." This is the continued struggle. Yes, words can elicit very strong emotions and that can drive behavior, but words in and of themselves hold no power. They are just words. Words are representations of meaning. They are not the meaning. They are just letters and sounds. And you can change how impactful words are.

Let's do an experiment. Imagine that fruit that is a large, oval melon. It is striped shades of green on the outside and pink with black spots on the inside. The word "watermelon" came to mind, right? And, you probably pictured a watermelon in your mind. You may have also imagined the taste of the watermelon, the texture of the outside and the inside of the watermelon, the smell, and the feeling of touching the watermelon. And, when you hear the word, "watermelon," this mental experience of what that word means comes to mind.

Now, let's see if we can change the way you experience the word "watermelon." Set a timer for 30 seconds, and quickly repeat the word, "watermelon" aloud, over and over, until the time is up. Ready? Set? Go.

What was that like for you? Did your mental experience of the word change over time? Did the image disappear? Did you wind up focusing on just getting the parts of the word out of your mouth? Did it start to sound like a strange, garbled-up stream of sounds?

....

....

Your inside experience of the word changed, didn't it? It lost its meaning. It lost its representation, its power. Language is a funny thing. You can use this to your advantage when you get too caught up in words.

An Adventure in Cognitive Defusion

Words are just words. We can learn to observe them, play with them, experiment with them, or back up from them. Try this:

1. Imagine your most difficult, negative self-judgment and put that into a single sentence. "I am ...."
2. Try to believe it. Say whatever comes to mind to convince yourself for 15 seconds. Believe it as much as you can. Notice what that's like for you.
3. Replay that thought beginning with this phrase, "I'm having the thought that I am ...." Notice what that's like for you.

4. Replay the thought with this phrase: "I'm noticing I'm having the thought that I am ...." Notice what that's like for you.

What happened? What did you notice? What other thoughts came to mind? What emotions did you notice and at what intensity? What bodily sensations did you notice and at what intensity?

....

....

Have you ever used an augmented reality animation, one of those silly smartphone apps that changes the way you look or sound when you look and speak into your camera? This could be something like iPhone Memojis or an app like Snapchat. What if you took that difficult thought and said it aloud while looking into one of those filters? What if you recorded that and played it back to watch? Give it a try.

What happened? What did you notice? What other thoughts came to mind? What emotions did you notice and at what intensity? What bodily sensations did you notice and at what intensity?

....

....

What if you captured the meaning of that thought in one single word and drew that word in rainbow-colored bubble letters? Give that a try. What do you notice about the thoughts as you get some distance from them?

....

....

You can change the way thoughts feel. You can lighten their weight so that they are easier to make space for and allow them to be there. They don't have to be a burden.

The Many Ways of Cognitive Defusion

There are many more ways to get some distance from your thoughts. Try some of these playful strategies as well. You might just find that the words that weigh you down are not so heavy after all.

- Say the words very slowly or very quickly, repeatedly.
- Say it in a silly voice or as an impersonation, like Donald Duck.
- Sing it to a familiar tune, such as happy birthday.
- Draw the words in colorful flourishes.

- Imagine the thought on a computer screen. Change the color, font, formatting. Add animation.
- Imagine thoughts as actors on a stage, entering, saying their lines, and exiting stage left.
- Imagine putting your thoughts on clouds and imagine those clouds rolling by.
- Name the story, as if the thought were a snippet of a TV show or a book you know well. Identify the story according to the identified theme you recognize in your thought, such as, "Oh, there's that 'I'm not good enough story' again."

Carry It with You

Thoughts show up in your mind to bring your attention to something, regardless of the judgments you may have about them or whether they are wanted or unwanted. Try carrying the thought with you. In other words, when a difficult thought comes to mind, rather than struggle with it, write it down on an index card or on a notes page on your smartphone and carry it with you throughout your day. If that thought shows up again, acknowledge it and remind yourself, "Yes, I'm aware of that one and I have it with me."

Practice Perspective Taking

Instead of speaking to yourself harshly, practice speaking to yourself in the same manner you'd speak to a friend with a similar problem. Try this perspective-taking exercise to soften your self-talk.

Think about a specific time (real or imagined) a good friend confided in you that they were having a difficult time in some way and were feeling guilt or they were blaming themselves for a negative occurrence. How would you respond to that friend? What would you say to them?

....

....

Now, recall a time when you were really struggling with your BFRB and noticed difficult feelings about yourself, your appearance, your ability to control the behavior, and/or the world around you. How would you typically respond to these thoughts and feelings? What would be going through your mind? What might you be telling yourself?

....

....

Are these two responses to pain and distress different in any way? Do you tend to speak more harshly to yourself than you do to others? Why do you think that might be?

....

....

If you were to rewrite your self-talk script, how might you change the way you speak to yourself, as if you were speaking to a good friend? What might you say to yourself?

....

....

Thank You, but No Thank You

Many times, when these thoughts arise, because we've typically heard them all many times before, we can call them out as familiar, unhelpful thoughts; we can practice recalling what's important to us in this moment and refrain from getting caught up in them. For example, let's say you are watching a movie with your family and enjoying the evening together. You get up to quickly use the restroom and when you glance into the bathroom mirror, you notice the thoughts, "I need to get rid of these stray hairs. There are some tweezers in the cabinet. It will only take a minute."

Will it though? Nope. Unlikely. You've heard that one before. How is this thinking pattern distorted? Is it permission giving, limit setting, and/or perfectionistic? Unhelpful advice, isn't it?

Have you ever had an advisor, friend, or relative who wants nothing but the best for you but who doesn't always give you accurate feedback or the best advice? You might think of these thoughts as advice from *that* friend.

Learn to observe, acknowledge, and say, "Thank you, but no thank you." Thank your mind for caring about you and trying to look out for you with this thought, but decline the opportunity to get caught up in it and let it influence your behavior, sending you down a path you really don't want to go. You have the power to choose whether to interact with that thought or to just let it come and go in its own time. It's like setting that thought on a leaf and watching it go downstream.

Anchor Yourself to What Matters: The Choice Point

Remind yourself about what matters most to you. It can serve as an anchor and guide you toward behavioral choices that will be more desirable in the long run. Before you pick up those tweezers, consider, "Might I get caught up in pulling if I do this? Is it likely to be the case that I will only pull these few hairs and then be done? Or will it take me away from my family movie night for what might be a lengthy period of time?"

Ask yourself, "What's most important to me at this moment?" You now have a choice to make, right? You can choose to pull these few hairs or you can choose to walk away. Let's look at an exercise called the Choice Point (Harris 2017) to help you to closely evaluate this choice.

There are many, many moments each day in which we are faced with a decision, a choice, and those choices direct our behaviors all day long. We get up in the morning. We get ready for school or work. We eat meals. We do work tasks and take care of responsibilities at home. We exercise. We spend time with others. Each action begins with a situation that prompts a choice. As we discussed previously in the My Matrix exercise in Chapter 2, some of our actions move us toward what matters most to us in our lives, our values, and some of our actions move us away from what's important to us and the kind of people we want to be. When we choose to move away, it's often because we get hooked and pulled away by those TIMES, the uncomfortable thoughts, images, memories, emotions, and sensations that show up in our minds and bodies.

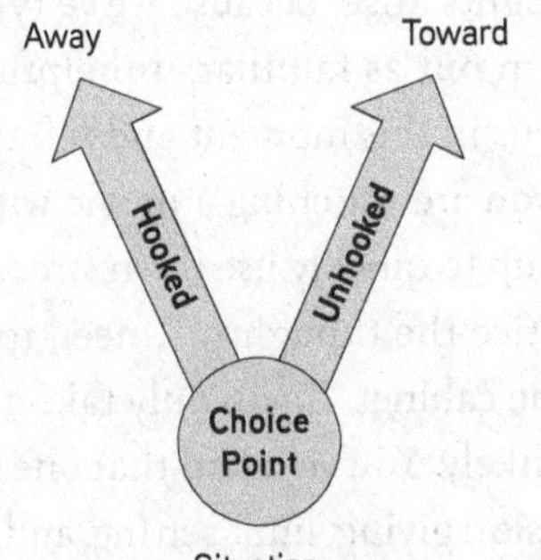

Press pause when faced with a choice. Let's look at what's important to you. What matters most in your life? What kind of person do you want to be? What kind of characteristics do you want to bring to the things that you do? What do you value? Now, in this particular situation, what might it look like if you were to act in the service of these values? What might you do that takes you toward what matters most to you?

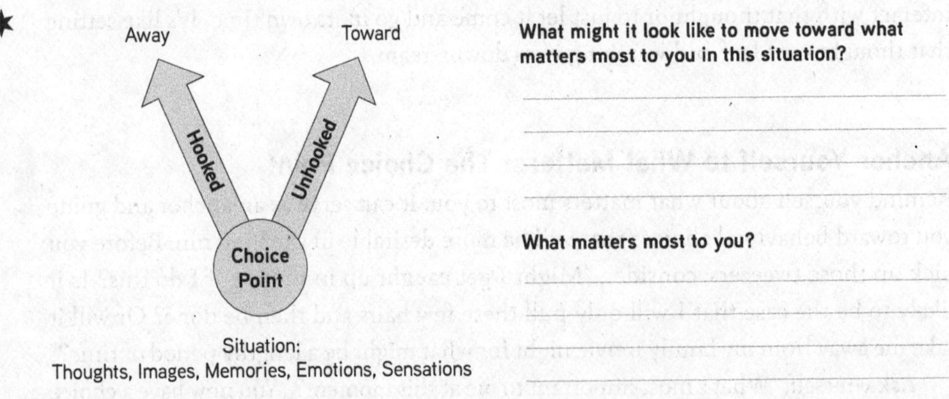

In the family movie night scenario, the right side of the Choice Point might look like this:

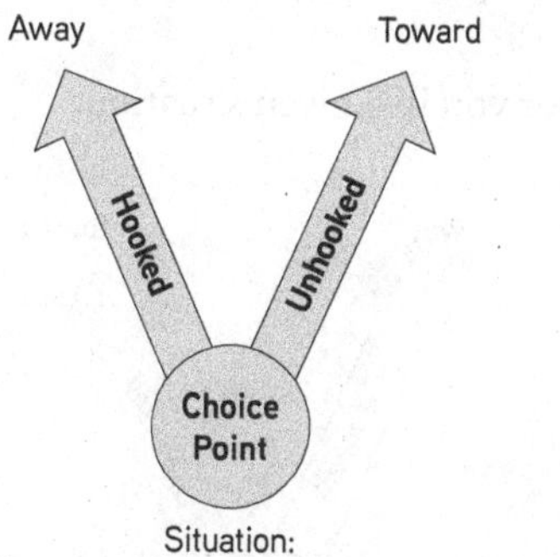

What might it look like to move toward what matters most to you in this situation?

Practicing self-compassion, using another BFRB skill, returning to family movie night

What matters most to you?

Family, friends, honesty, kindness, health, self-care, reliability, charity, dependability, sports, music, art

In this example, anchoring our behavioral choices to our values may clarify what behaviors would take us toward what's important to us in this moment. However, our TIMES can hook us and pull us away.

Sometimes, our TIMES interfere with what we might call meaningful action, the moves that take us in the direction of what matters most to us. Remember those TIMES from the My Matrix exercise in Chapter 2? Uncomfortable thoughts, images, memories, emotions, and sensations show up on the inside, in our minds and in our bodies, and they can distract us from what's important to us, like the thoughts, "I need to get rid of those stray hairs. There are some tweezers in the cabinet. It will only take a minute." These thoughts evoke concern, perhaps anxiety, and maybe even an urge to pull the hairs. These thoughts and feelings don't feel good. And, being the smart problem solver that you are, your mind focuses on this discomfort and aims to make you feel better again. The quickest way to do that, according to your mind, is to pull these stray hairs. But, even though this may serve to relieve you of these thoughts and emotional discomforts, it would also take you away from what's important to you in this moment—spending time with your family.

In the family movie night scenario, the left side of the Choice Point might look like this:

When you're hooked, what do you do that moves you away from what's important to you?

Pulling the stray hairs, searching for additional out-of-place hairs, pulling additional hairs, continuing until a feeling of relief or satisfaction

What shows up in your mind and body that gets in the way of what's important to you—those TIMES (thoughts, images, memories, emotions, sensations)?

"I need to get rid of those stray hairs."

"There are some tweezers in the cabinet."

"It will only take a minute."

Anxious, imagining relief

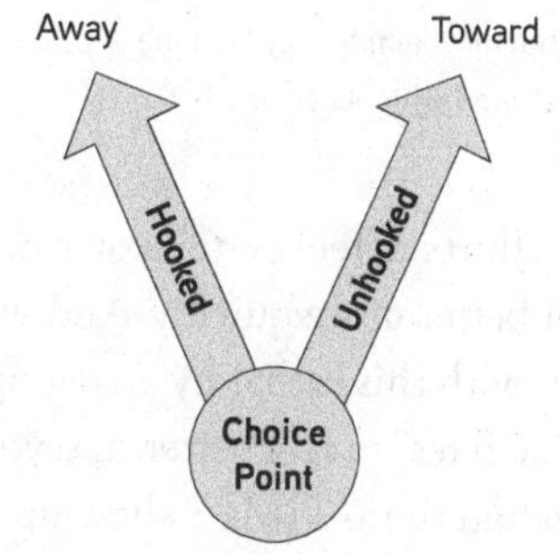

In this example, the TIMES that get in the way are thoughts that cause you to feel anxious and imagining a situation in which pulling relieves your distress. Tempting, isn't it?

Let's examine what TIMES get in the way for you in a given situation:

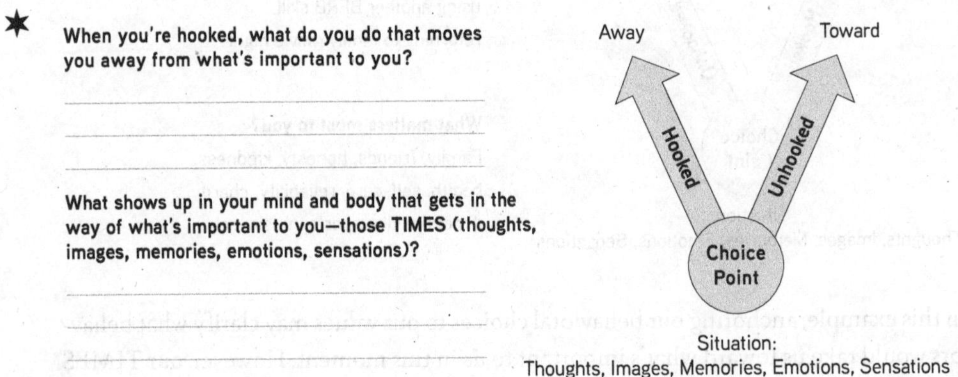

This is where things get sticky. There's a "not so simple" choice to be made. Why? Because there are both potential pay-offs and potential costs to every choice. And this choice is a tough one. Let's look at the potential pay-offs and potential costs in the family movie night scenario.

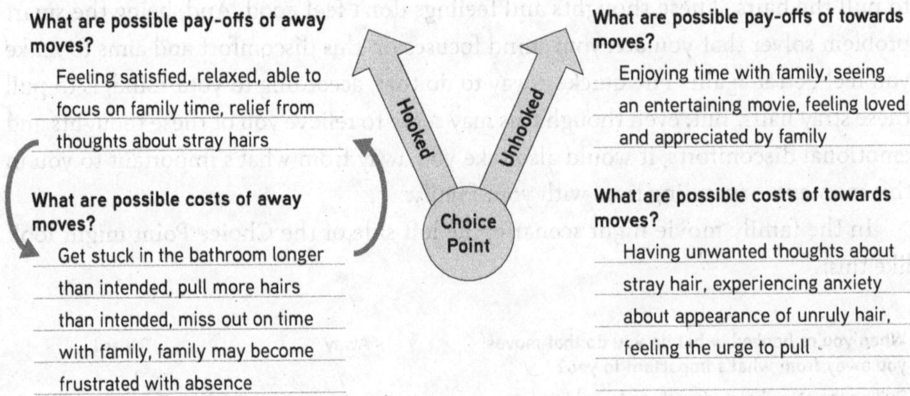

In your efforts to feel better, you can get stuck in these away moves because they make you feel better more quickly. And who doesn't want to feel better more quickly? The problem with this is that by engaging in away moves, you've taught yourself that there are "quick fixes" to feel better, and you'll be more likely to carry out these actions in the future when these TIMES show up again. And they will, if not now, then later. What seems like a good solution in the short term maintains the problem in the long term.

LET'S EXAMINE THESE POSSIBLE "MOVES." WHAT WILL YOU CHOOSE?

★ **What are possible pay-offs of away moves?**

What are possible pay-offs of towards moves?

Hooked

Unhooked

Choice Point

What are possible costs of away moves?

What are possible costs of towards moves?

You will always have a choice to engage and respond to thoughts or to refrain from doing so and turn your attention elsewhere. The Choice Point can be a useful exercise to help you to look at these individual situations as they arise. Other briefer strategies may also be useful in helping you to pivot away from these unhelpful thoughts and toward meaning and value.

STOP

When faced with the choice of engaging in your BFRB or refraining from your BFRB, try doing this:

- Slow your breathing and press pause.
- Tune into your TIMES—the thoughts, images, memories, emotions, sensations, and urges in this moment that are triggers for your BFRB.
- Observe the TIMES with curiosity and open up around them. Breathe into them and see if you can allow them to be there and move around without reacting to them.
- Proceed with what matters most to you at this moment and practice willingness to allow the TIMES to come and go on their own.

As you STOP and observe, you can practice your own Choice Point or utilize another strategy or skill to enable you to proceed.

When the "TIMES get tough," press pause. Take a look at your inner experiences, your TIMES. Acknowledge them, make space for them, allow them to be there even if they are unwanted or uncomfortable. Ask yourself, "What is really important to me here?" You might, for example, conjure up an image of your partner and recall that you'd like to have a comfortable, intimate relationship. Ask yourself, "Instead of pulling, how might I use a strategy in the service of that which is important to me?" (move toward what matters most).

Developing a Healthy Relationship

Throughout Chapters 10 and 11, you've examined how your thoughts can interfere with your life and may even drive your BFRB. Developing a healthy relationship to your thoughts—even those that aren't wanted—is an important skill set for managing your BFRB effectively. Ask yourself:

Are you willing to have uncomfortable thoughts? Do you get caught up in and struggle with your unwanted thoughts? Is this helpful to you or does it hinder you and take you away from what matters most to you? Is there really any part of that thought that you need to get rid of—or that you can't allow yourself to have? Or is it okay to make space for your thoughts, thank your mind for trying to protect you, and just let your thoughts come and go in their own time?

....

....

Thoughts, Images, Memories (T-I-M)

There are many strategies for approaching thoughts, images, and memories—those mental experiences that show up in your mind. What thoughts, images, and/or memories skills or strategies might you try in response to each trigger you identified? How might you work toward a healthier relationship with yourself?

Antecedent Thoughts, Images, Memories →	→ Thoughts, Images, Memories Strategies
"I hate the way I look"	*Soften my words. "I am unhappy with my appearance right now because of my scabs. It's understandable. Many people would feel this way. I'm working on this and I deserve to be kind to myself in this effort."*
"If they find out I pull, they'll think I'm weird"	*Say this into a Snapchat filter. Notice the thought: "I'm noticing I'm having the thought that they'll think I'm weird if they find out I pull my hair."*

ACTION PLAN

Minding Your Mind

It's time to implement a few strategies and observe the outcome. Try two or three strategies this week and record the results. Review your Strategies and Skills Observation Log and evaluate how helpful each strategy was. See what happens. Be curious. Be playful, even with the heaviest of mental experiences, and see if you can change the way those thoughts, images, and memories are experienced.

What key points in this chapter really spoke to you? What are the highlights *you* most want to keep in mind that are important for you and your BFRB?

What did you learn about yourself as you **explored**?

What **practices** will you commit to working on this week to move you toward your destination?

....

....

What is your **action plan**? What steps will you take to put these practices in place?

....

....

When and how often will you engage in these practices?

....

....

As you experiment with these strategies, monitor your observations in the Strategies and Skills Observation Log.

★ Strategies and Skills: T-I-M Observation Log

Date and Time	Antecedent Thoughts, Images, Memories	Strategy	Observations

CHAPTER 12

Examining Shame and Other Difficult Emotions

EXPLORE

From the joy that brings us satisfaction and fulfillment to the depths of despair, emotions are undeniably a dominant part of the human experience. When we struggle, this is some of the tough stuff, the stuff that is painful, that we most want to avoid. It's also the stuff that maintains our suffering. And it's often un- or under-addressed in BFRBs. Yes, we're talking about the emotions in your TIMES.

Everyone experiences emotions. Sometimes, those emotions are big and they are difficult to manage effectively. For many individuals, one of the functions of a BFRB is to regulate strong emotions. It is believed that some individuals have a lower threshold of emotional vulnerability. If you are someone who is easily brought to intense emotions or impacted by the emotions of others, this BFRB cue may be particularly relevant.

Having a BFRB can be emotionally painful. The feelings of embarrassment, self-consciousness, anxiety, fear, sadness, frustration, anger, and a wide range of other emotions are connected to living with a BFRB. Difficult emotions show up with depth and breadth, and are associated with thoughts and mental images, memories, and bodily sensations resulting from the ways in which you interact with the world around you.

Our experiences within the various cultural groups in which we spend time send us messages about what is acceptable, what is not acceptable, and all of the attitudes in between. We learn the meaning and values our cultural groups assign through our encounters in a range of cultural contexts, including gender, sexual orientation, nationality, ethnicity, religion, community, and family, among others. These associations may come from:

- messages about beauty, attractiveness, femininity/masculinity
- messages about what is "right" vs. "wrong"
- messages about what it means to have a "habit" behavior
- messages about what it means to have a "mental health" disorder
- attitudes and acceptance of help-seeking behaviors for psychological well-being

- accessibility to evidence-based healthcare and appropriate support
- negative feedback from others or more subtle interactions about BFRBs, the overt and covert consequences of BFRBs, and any misunderstandings others may have about the behavior
- self-judgment and negative self-talk resulting from difficult thoughts, emotions, or unwanted behaviors
- the reinforcing nature of avoidance and isolation in an attempt to protect oneself from pain.

Shame is a Normal Human Emotion with Purpose

Every emotion has a purpose—even shame. Shame is an emotion that may bring to your attention the possibility that you've done something wrong, unacceptable, or inconsistent with your values. It may alert you to the possibility of disapproval by others. Its intended purpose is to inform you of something that may be problematic for you and influence your behavior to take action in the service of self-protection. Sometimes this warning is warranted and sometimes it is not. However, regardless of whether it is helpful or unhelpful, shame is uncomfortable. This discomfort is not merely a feeling; it may also involve bodily sensations, such as muscle tension, nausea, headache, or uncomfortable sensations in the chest. Furthermore, negative thoughts and judgments come to mind in the form of critical self-talk, which may add to the pain you are experiencing. And this emotion, coupled with upsetting thoughts and uncomfortable bodily sensations, leads to behavior carried out in an attempt to feel better. This behavior may be helpful and adaptive, such as taking a walk or talking to a friend, or it may be unhelpful and maladaptive, such as pulling, picking, biting, isolating, or otherwise avoiding or trying to push away these discomforts.

The cyclical nature of these patterns can leave you feeling stuck in your distress. For example, maybe you've experienced shame about visible hair loss that has resulted from hair pulling, noticing tension in your shoulders and an uncomfortable feeling in your chest. Perhaps you've thought, "I'm so ugly. There's something really wrong with me. Just look at me! No one would want to be close to me if they knew my secret." As a result, you decide to decline that party invitation and stay home in an effort to avoid "being discovered" and intensifying the experience of shame. But this may be fodder for feelings of sadness, isolation, and further picking, pulling, biting, or other BFRBs.

Where Is Your Shame?

Let's explore some of the difficult feelings you experience. These feelings may have a direct relationship to your BFRB or they may be more generally related to your self-concept or overall sense of self-worth.

What are aspects about yourself that you do not like? What do you think are your greatest weaknesses or inadequacies?

....

....

In what situations do you most feel like a failure?

....

....

Do you notice thoughts related to shame? What do they say?

....

....

When do you most often notice this pain? Where are you? What are you doing? Who are you with?

....

....

How do you experience the feeling of shame in your body?

....

....

How do you tend to sit with yourself during these painful moments? Are you curious and open to the experience? Are you cruel or critical of yourself? Are you kind and compassionate with yourself?

....

....

If there are times when you are cruel or overly critical of yourself, what are those times like? In what types of situations does this occur?

....

....

If there are times when you are kind and compassionate with yourself, what are those times like? In what types of situations does this occur?

....

....

In these most painful of times, do you feel alone in this experience of painful emotion or do you acknowledge that others understand what it feels like to struggle like this?

....

....

In moments of pain, what types of behaviors/actions do you typically carry out? For example, do you blame others, cry, lash out, isolate, or engage in your BFRB? Or do you sleep, meditate, exercise, or snack?

....

....

Does shame ever get in the way of developing or maintaining close connections with other people?

....

....

Does shame ever leave you more vulnerable to carrying out your BFRB and/or does your BFRB ever lead to shame?

....

....

How might things be different for you if you did not experience shame?

....

....

When others in your life are experiencing shame, how do you typically respond? Do you feel drawn to respond with criticism? Do you ever think their shame is justified? Do you feel drawn to respond with kindness and compassion?

....

....

Is there a discrepancy between how you treat yourself and how you are drawn to respond to others who express emotional pain? Why or why not?

....

....

What are the barriers to treating yourself with greater compassion and understanding? What do you think may happen if you do?

....

....

The Paradox of Struggling with Emotional Pain

Many people struggle with self-compassion because they are trying to push away pain; however, they inadvertently cause or maintain their pain in doing so. But it is impossible to avail yourself to the joys of life without risking the possibility that you may experience pain. For example, you could never experience love without allowing yourself to be vulnerable to the experience of loss. You could never experience pride without allowing yourself to be vulnerable to shame. We make choices in our lives every day; this one is the choice to feel. Are you willing to experience painful emotions from time to time in order to experience greater joy and self-satisfaction? If strong emotions sometimes lead to BFRB symptoms, are you willing to try to respond to these antecedent emotions differently?

....

....

....

PRACTICE

TOOLS FOR THE TERRAIN

- Physicalizing Emotional Pain
- Being "Your Best You"
- Gently Hold Difficult Feelings
- Lend a Helping Hand
- Self-Compassion: Being There for Yourself
- Keep a Self-Compassion Journal
- Self-Compassion Meditations: Loving Kindness Meditation
- Changing Your Response to Shame and Other Difficult Emotions

Physicalizing Emotional Pain

Everyone experiences difficult emotions. And, although emotional pain is a normal part of the human experience, we can get stuck on the feeling and in our struggle to push it away. The goal of physicalizing (adapted from Hayes and Smith 2005) is to manage this discomfort more effectively by imagining it as something outside of yourself so that you may more easily accept it and allow it to come and go in its own time. You may find that this exercise is more easily done with your eyes closed so that you may imagine more clearly, but you may choose to fix your gaze downward, if you prefer.

> *First, settle into your seat and bring to mind something with which you are struggling. Scan your body for this feeling. Where is it located? When you've located it, imagine this feeling is an object. And see if you can move it outside of yourself so that it is sitting on your lap in front of you. You are not pushing it away or getting rid of it. You will be taking it back inside, but, for now, let's imagine it is in front of you so that you can more easily observe it.*

What shape and size is it? Describe it.

....

....

Is it a solid object or is it in another form, like a gas or a liquid?

....

....

Does the object have color(s)? If it does, describe what it looks like.

....

....

Does it appear to have texture? If so, describe that.

....

....

Does it have movement? If so, how is it moving?

....

....

Does it make sound? If so, what does it sound like?

....

....

Does it have a smell? If so, what does it smell like?

....

....

Can you imagine what it would feel like if you were to touch it? What would it feel like?

....

....

If you reach out to touch it, how does it respond? Does it change or move in any way?

....

....

What did you notice when you tried to touch it? Do you notice your response to it? Do you notice any thoughts, feelings, or bodily sensations show up when you try to interact with it?

....

....

Allow it to sit in front of you. Acknowledge your response to it. And focus on that response. Where is that located in your body? What is that feeling like? What thoughts show up as you attend to that feeling? Describe that.

....

....

Notice that this reaction on the inside is separate from the object on your lap. Take a deep breath, breathing into this internal experience, creating space for any emotions you are feeling, making room for them and making room for the thoughts that show up in relation to them. Acknowledge that this experience is difficult. Acknowledge that others have similar experiences and understand this. Acknowledge that this experience deserves kindness from you and from others.

Ask yourself, "Is there any part of this internal experience that I can't have?" You don't have to want it or like it, but are you willing to allow it to be there for a period of time? If you notice resistance, sit with this question, observing your internal experience until you feel a loosening and a sense of willingness come forward.

....

....

Now return your attention to the object on your lap—does it appear to be any different? Has it changed in any way? If so, how?

....

....

Would you be willing to consider returning this object to your private experience, bringing it back inside? Ask yourself, "Am I willing to make room for this object so that I may move more freely toward what matters most to me?" You don't have to want it or like it, but are you willing to allow it to be there for a period of time? If you notice resistance on your part or on the part of the object, sit with this question, observing the object and your response to it, until you feel a loosening and a sense of willingness come forward. Bring the object back inside.

How do you feel? Do you notice any difference between how you feel now and how you felt when you were first imagining this painful emotion within you?

....

....

Sometimes, the resistance to emotional pain is far more difficult to experience than the pain itself. Self-compassion and the willingness to have and accept one's full experience can make a significant difference in the ability to live a valued life and move past your distress.

Being "Your Best You"

Imagine you have a loved one who is very ill and is being cared for in a hospital. They have been in a great deal of pain, have lost a significant amount of weight, appear pale, and are being treated with intravenous medications which sit atop IV poles at their bedside. Their health has recently begun to improve slowly, and they call you to say hello from their hospital room. During the call, they tell you that they would really enjoy some company, and they ask if you'd be willing to pay them a visit. How do you respond? Do you agree to go? If so, what might that experience be like for you (imagine with your five senses)? What might you be thinking and feeling during the visit? If you choose not to go, why might that be? What are your thoughts and feelings about this decision?

....

....

If you are hesitant or choose not to go to visit your friend, this may be because you imagine this will be stressful or emotionally painful, which you may want to avoid at all costs. Perhaps you think you couldn't "handle it" or that it would be "too hard." Maybe you think you lack the strategies to be able to effectively manage this difficult experience. That's okay. You're here to learn new skills, including skills to manage strong emotions more effectively.

If you choose to go, you will likely be doing so as it aligns with what is important to you (e.g., friendship, caring for those in need, etc.); however, it does not come without cost. This choice comes with a willingness to endure what is likely to be some unpleasant internal experiences, including sadness, sympathy, concern for their well-being, and thoughts about how sick they appear to be. You've chosen to be willing to hold those thoughts and feelings of your own as well as show up for your loved one in such a way that is pleasant, positive, and supportive. There is a gentle strength that shows up, a sense of kindness, compassion, and resolve. In this case, you show up for your friend as "your best you."

Similarly, if you are a parent or if you have ever provided care for a young child, you have had to soothe a crying child who may have been hungry, overtired, hurt, or otherwise in need of comfort. It can be distressing to hear a child cry out in pain—we are inherently pulled to sit with the distress we may be experiencing and respond to these cries to help. As a parent of an infant, even in the middle of the night, when we, ourselves, are exhausted, we manage to get out of bed, despite feeling this way, in order to feed, change, and soothe our little ones. We have the capacity to make space for our own unwanted internal experiences in the service of who and what matters most to us.

In your daily life, when difficult emotions arise, imagine being "your best you" for *yourself*. Can you show up for yourself in this way—cultivating kindness and holding this experience gently during your time of need as you would for your sick loved one or crying child?

Gently Hold Difficult Feelings

When difficult feelings arise, you may find yourself doubling down on your harsh efforts to push them away. You may criticize yourself, order yourself to stop, invalidate your experiences, or otherwise unintentionally intensify the negative emotions or the sense of being stuck in your distress. You essentially beat yourself up.

Bring to mind a time when you experienced a physical injury. How did you respond to feeling sore and physically uncomfortable? Maybe you wore a brace, protected the injury with a bandage, or supported that part of your body with a pillow in order to allow it to heal.

Instead of responding to your emotional pain in ways that increase and prolong your distress, see if you can imagine yourself softening around this feeling inside. Make space around the emotion to cushion and support it during its time with you to promote healing.

Lend a Helping Hand

If you can locate where in your body you feel emotional pain most intensely—perhaps there is a sense of emotional discomfort in your chest or your belly, for example—gently place your hand on that location. Envision sending warmth and comfort into that area to provide it with the support and compassion it needs for healing. Take a few slow, deep breaths, breathing into this area, holding it gently. Be still and allow yourself to be there to support yourself in this moment.

Self-Compassion

Self-compassion is the ability to show kindness toward yourself. It is the act of being warm and understanding toward yourself, as you would be toward others, especially in instances of perceived inadequacy, failure, or suffering. This is particularly important in times of emotional pain. It is a skill that does not come easily to everyone, but, if developed, it is a tool that is very effective in reducing rumination, stress, anxiety, depression, and self-criticism. It consists of three components: self-kindness; a sense of common humanity; mindfulness of experience (Neff and Germer 2022). There are many ways in which one may practice developing self-compassion. It may not feel natural at first, but with practice, you may find it to be comforting and useful in helping to manage difficult emotions when they show up.

Being There for Yourself

Begin by noticing when critical or harsh self-talk shows up. What was the comment you noticed?

....

....

What was the situation that preceded this self-talk? Does critical self-talk of this nature show up in similar circumstances? Can you expect this type of commentary in specific contexts?

....

....

Are there any experiences with others that may have taught you to respond to yourself in this way?

....

....

Ask yourself, "What might I say to a friend in this situation?"

....

....

Ask yourself, "How might I respond to a friend if they told me they were suffering in this way?"

....

....

Notice critical or harsh thoughts about your BFRB and consider how you might respond to a friend who revealed having such thoughts. What might you say to them?

....

....

How can you direct this compassion toward yourself? Consider writing this kinder response down on a sheet of paper or on a notes page on your mobile device and read it when you notice these thoughts showing up. Practice replacing your criticism with gentle understanding and support.

....

....

Keep a Self-Compassion Journal

Journaling can be a tool to practice self-compassion skills. Consider keeping a self-compassion journal wherein you write to yourself in a compassionate tone, taking care to provide yourself with the following.

EXPRESSIONS OF KINDNESS

Negative self-judgment is often unhelpful, leading to further negative self-talk and intensifying difficult feelings. Instead, acknowledge that this is a moment of suffering and it is painful. Remind yourself that the experience of failure is to be expected in life. We do not always get or sustain what we want. Humans are fallible. We are dynamic. Our experiences ebb and flow. Yes, we all have successes, but we also make mistakes. We, at times, knowingly or unknowingly, make poor choices. And, in an effort to strive to be the best people we can be, we sometimes find ourselves disappointed, unhappy, or upset with ourselves. Expressing kindness toward yourself includes the understanding that you are, in fact, imperfect and that in such times, you are gentle with yourself.

A SENSE THAT OTHERS WOULD UNDERSTAND AND FEEL SIMILAR

Self-criticism tends to be associated with thoughts of "singling oneself out," treating yourself as though you are the only person who would ever be in this situation or would ever feel this way. Not only is this unhelpful, it is also most often inaccurate. Thus, in supporting yourself in times of distress, it is important to acknowledge that all people suffer and experience times of feeling inadequate, like "a failure," or "not good enough." Remind yourself that you are not alone in your experience. It is part of our shared humanity to feel as though you are alone.

A BELIEF THAT YOU ARE DESERVING OF KINDNESS DURING TIMES OF SUFFERING

It is natural to want to push away or rid ourselves of negative thoughts and feelings. However, these efforts are often ineffective and can lead to further suffering. To successfully practice self-compassion, it is important to recognize, without judgment, these difficult thoughts and feelings, allow them to be there, and acknowledge that you are deserving of kindness in this experience. This involves an openness to the experience and a willingness to be there to support it while it is present, taking care not to get caught up in it or struggle with it but simply acknowledge and allow it to be.

Let's practice! We'll go first as an example for you:

> This is a difficult situation. I'm doing the best I can, given the circumstances. Other people would also find this situation difficult and would feel upset, frustrated, and alone, like me. I deserve respect, kindness, and support, especially during these difficult moments. May I be kind to myself in this moment. Moments like these are hard, but they do pass with time.

Okay, now it's your turn. You can include the details of your situation or simply provide yourself with compassionate statements to which you relate and with which you feel supported. Give it a try:

....

....

Self-Compassion Meditations

The practice of self-compassion meditation exercises may help you to become mindful of this self-talk, increase openness to experience, and give you the language to reflect self-compassion, particularly if you find it difficult to show kindness toward yourself in these difficult times. There are many resources for self-compassion meditations on the internet, including YouTube videos, MP3 audio recordings, and exercises available in a wide range of mobile apps. Take some time to explore self-compassion meditations. These meditations may be called "acceptance," "witness," "self-compassion," or "loving kindness meditations." Below, you will find a loving kindness meditation script to try. Read and reflect on the meditation. Consider recording and listening to it as a regular practice to build self-compassion skills or to listen to in times of need when you notice self-judgment. Understand that this is a skill and it takes practice.

Loving Kindness Meditation

Get into a comfortable upright position in which your body feels supported, awake, and safe. Close your eyes or hold them in a soft gaze. Notice your breath and where you feel it in your body. If you'd like, you can place your hands over your heart, in prayer position, or wherever you feel like your body needs that touch of compassion. Your focus is to bring loving awareness to yourself as you open up to kindness and a deep feeling of acceptance.

Now take a few deep, relaxing breaths and feel your body breathe in and breathe out. Notice when your mind wanders and bring your awareness gently back to your breath, the healing touch of your hands, and the well wishes you make toward yourself and others. Imagine offering yourself a gift of kindness, warmth, and untethered self-love. Embrace your compassion without being embarrassed by it or attempting to suppress it. Open your heart widely as you do this important practice of healing and inner resource. Repeat the following phrases or choose phrases like these with pause and meaning:

May I be filled with loving kindness.
May I be safe.
May I let go of struggle.
May I be well in body and mind.

Compassion for others begins with compassion for ourselves. Now bring to mind another person or animal with whom you share a bond, friendship, or positive presence. Keep them in mind as you offer them these wishes:

May you be filled with loving kindness.
May you be safe.
May you let go of struggle.
May you be well in body and mind.

Next, you can invite in anyone who may be struggling in some way and send loving kindness. It may be a friend going through a tough time, an acquaintance, a person with whom you hold tension, or a complete stranger—whoever comes to mind. Send them wishes for their well-being:

May you be filled with loving kindness.
May you be safe.
May you let go of struggle.
May you be well in body and mind.

Now call to mind all people, all beings everywhere known and unknown, close to you and far away:

> May all beings be filled with loving kindness.
> May all beings be safe.
> May all beings let go of struggle.
> May all beings be well in body and mind.

When you are ready, you can raise your gaze with the intention of bringing this sense of compassion and connection into your day.

> Take a few minutes out of your day to practice self-compassion. Build your ability to treat yourself kindly in order to find greater joy and less suffering. If you'd like additional guided exercises, check out these audio recordings from compassion-focused therapy psychologist, Dr. Dennis Tirch: https://mindful-compassion.com/meditations, and the self-compassion work of Dr. Kristin Neff: https://self-compassion.org.

Changing Your Response to Shame and Other Difficult Emotions

Now that you've looked at when and how shame and other difficult emotions show up, how will you respond differently when they do? What strategies might you try out and practice to build your BFRB toolbox? Take a few moments to plan a few new practices and chart your experiments below.

★

Antecedent Emotions →	→ Emotions Strategies
Shame	*Ask myself, "What would I say to a friend who told me they are feeling this way?"*
Sadness	*Write a journal entry expressing self-compassion toward myself*

cont.

Antecedent Emotions ➔	➔ Emotions Strategies

ACTION PLAN

Examining Shame and Other Difficult Emotions

What key points in this chapter really spoke to you? What are the highlights *you* most want to keep in mind that are important for you and your BFRB?

....

....

What did you learn about yourself as you **explored**?

....

....

What **practices** will you commit to working on this week to move you toward your destination?

....

....

What is your **action plan**? What steps will you take to put these practices in place?

....

....

When and how often will you engage in these practices?

....

....

As you experiment with these strategies, monitor your observations in the Strategies and Skills Observation Log.

★ Strategies and Skills: Emotions Observation Log

Date and Time	Antecedent Emotions	Strategy	Observations

CHAPTER 13

Regulating Intense Emotions

EXPLORE

Emotions play an important role in our interpretation of everyday experiences, and they impact our thoughts and actions. Difficulties regulating unpleasant emotions often result in difficulties with our behaviors, which for many include BFRBs. Learning how to regulate your emotions may be an important component in better managing your picking, pulling, or biting behaviors. This starts with a non-judgmental observation of your primary emotional experiences by allowing yourself to "feel it in order to heal it."

It is important for you to be better able to identify emotions, reduce vulnerabilities, learn how they impact your BFRB, and practice more effective ways of regulating your emotions. There are a number of strategies and skills that you can use to experience both long-term and short-term benefits while also building your ability and confidence in handling challenging experiences.

Defining emotions can be much more complicated than you might expect. Researchers believe that there are around eight core emotions, which vary slightly but often include joy, fear, sadness, disgust, interest, shame, and anger. Our emotions often mix together and create new and more complex experiences. We also have secondary emotions, which are emotional reactions to our primary emotion! An example of this might be feeling embarrassed after being angry. Some speculate that this creates around 34,000 different emotional experiences that develop from our biology, learned experience, and culture.

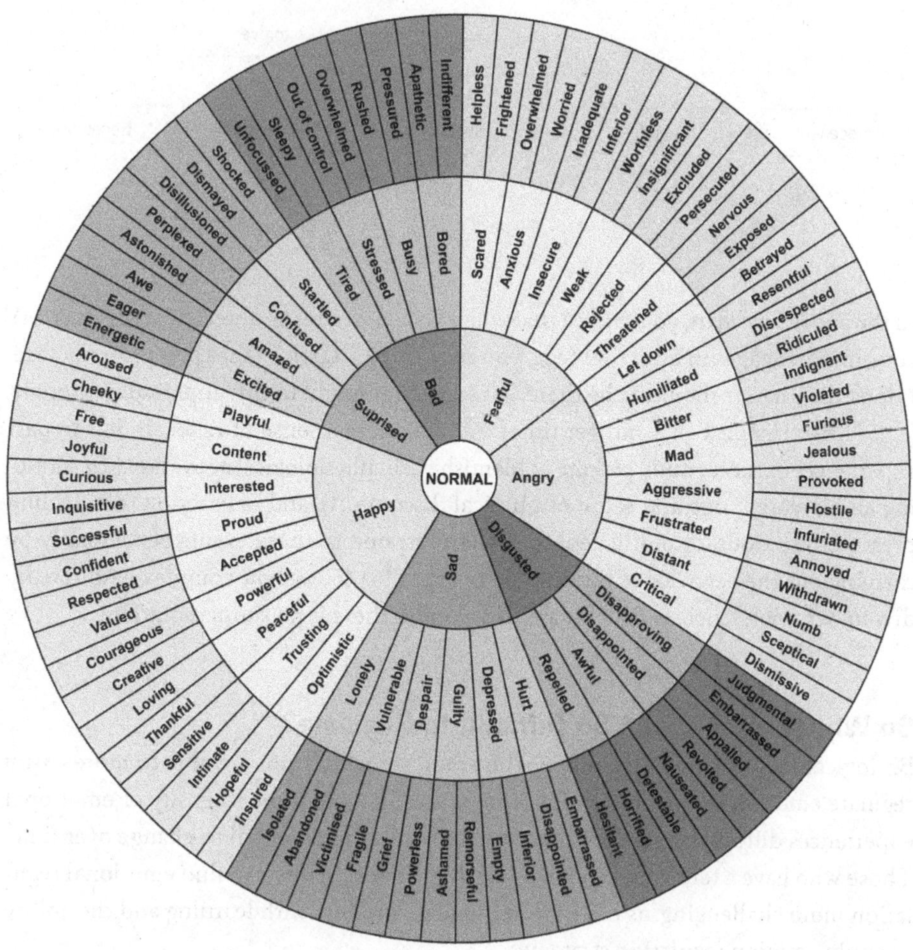

Emotional Regulation Skills

Emotion regulation is the ability to understand how you may influence which emotions you experience, how you experience them, and how you express them behaviorally. Emotion regulation skills are strategies that you can learn to more effectively manage emotions that do not help you achieve your goals or live the life you want. When emotions feel overwhelming or feel "out of control," this is called dysregulation. In order to be able to use emotion regulation skills more adeptly, it is important to first understand your own emotions and their functioning.

Emotions are sometimes referred to as "full system responses" because of the ways in which our minds and bodies are connected (Linehan 1993).

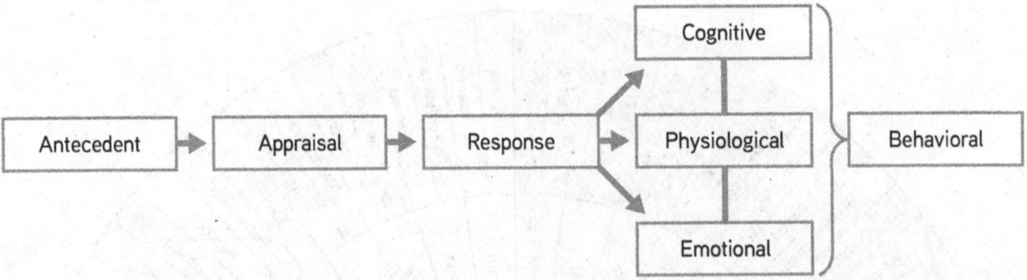

In the above flowchart, you can see that when you encounter an antecedent (e.g., mirror), your mind engages in appraisal (e.g., you may think, "Look at that bump on my face. I don't like that. It shouldn't be there."). You then respond to this appraisal in thought (e.g., "I need to pick this and get rid of it," imagining a sense of relief similar to past experiences of successfully picking at blemishes), in physiological activation (e.g., noticing an increased urge and sense of physical discomfort), and in emotion (e.g., feeling pressured, anxious, or motivated). You then respond to these events behaviorally by carrying out the behavior of picking the bump. This shows how complex emotionally driven behaviors, such as BFRBs, are. No wonder there is no simple solution!

So Why Are Emotions So Difficult to Regulate?

Biological factors can play a role in the extent to which you are able to more easily regulate emotional experiences. Emotional sensitivity and the intensity of emotional experiences differ from person to person and have the potential to change over time. Those who have a tendency to experience high emotionality can find emotional regulation more challenging, as the experience may interfere with learning and the ability to apply emotion regulation strategies.

Emotional regulation skills deficits may exist and working on building such skills may be warranted. Some people learn these skills more easily than others or may have had more opportunities to learn these skills in a wider variety of contexts in their life. Life experiences may have sent unhelpful messages about emotions, such as the invalidating belief that you can control the way you think, feel, or behave if you simply have enough willpower. And, thus, you've not had the opportunity to address emotion regulation in a meaningful way.

Mood state, energy levels, and one's capacity for willingness to learn and apply new emotion regulation skills may be relevant factors in developing satisfactory emotion regulation skills. Regulating emotions takes quite a bit of work. It is possible that the demands of your life have left you feeling that you do not have the motivation or energy to change your experience. For example, maybe you've really wanted to address your BFRB, but you've found yourself unable to attend therapy on a consistent basis or carve out time to work on skills development.

Emotional overload can pose an obstacle to effectively managing emotions. You may find yourself experiencing such intense emotions that you are unable to utilize other skill sets, such as problem-solving or reasoning skills. Instead, you may become frozen or stuck in that negative emotion, unable to move past it. It can also become a self-perpetuating cycle. If every time you feel sad and shameful about your BFRB, you feel so overwhelmed that you isolate yourself and avoid others, you do get to avoid scrutiny by others in doing so. Or, every time you get distressed and pick, that provides an immediate sense of satisfaction as well as distraction, and therefore you're more likely to respond in this way when you are distressed, reinforcing both the overwhelming emotions and the ineffective management of them. In other words, we have a tendency to do what we've always done.

PRACTICE

TOOLS FOR THE TERRAIN

- Identify and Respond to Emotions
- The Role of Emotions
- Increase Positive Emotions
- Decrease Vulnerability to Negative Emotions
- States of Mind
- Opposite Action
- Problem Solving

Identify and Respond to Emotions

Let's practice noticing the emotions that you experience and the ways in which you respond to those emotions.

Select an emotion that you experienced today or sometime recently that was an antecedent to your BFRB.

....

....

What other words might be used to describe that emotion?

....

....

What were the prompting events for your feeling?

....

....

What were your beliefs about that event that prompted your feeling?

....

....

How did you experience that emotion? Describe how your body felt, physically. What were your thoughts about that emotion?

....

....

How did you express your emotion? Internally and/or externally?

....

....

What were the short-term and long-term after-effects/consequences of your emotion?

....

....

Did the emotion and its intensity fit the situation?

....

....

Did the emotion influence your behavior? If so, how?

....

....

Was this response in line with your values and who you want to be?

....

....

As you can see, emotions are complex. They involve a felt sense as well as thoughts, other emotions, and physical sensations. We give them meaning and that meaning influences the ways in which we act. Let's take a look at the complexity of emotions. In the following chart, describe your emotional experiences and their relationship to your thoughts and actions.

★ The Complexity of Emotions

Emotion	Physiological Response This includes physical sensation, facial expressions, and body language	Thoughts This includes thoughts, images, and memories	Urges What do you *feel like you want to do* when you have this emotion?	Behaviors What do you *actually do* when you have this emotion?	Consequences What are the short- and long-term effects of your behavior?
Sadness	*Heavy feeling in chest, tearful, body pulled inward*	*People think I am a weirdo; I see how they look at me* *Everyone thinks I am on drugs*	*I want to just avoid the world and pick at my skin and nails*	*I lie down on my sofa, turn on the TV and look at my skin for bumps to pick* *I avoid contact with anyone, even my friends.*	*Short term—I feel good because I am at home and I get satisfaction from picking* *Long term—I feel worse because my skin and nails have additional damage and I miss people*

The Role of Emotions

Emotions serve many functions and fundamentally influence how you experience your world. They can provide you with motivation to move toward something desirable or away from something that is unpleasant. They alert you to possible physical or emotional danger and can be felt deeply and instinctively (fear, disgust). Emotions aid in communication with others and can elicit powerful social reactions that ensure reproduction and survival (attraction). They can optimize your functioning toward a sense of fulfillment and well-being (happiness). Emotions can alert you to something that is unfair (anger) or contrary to your values (guilt), or to a behavior that does not fit into cultural norms (shame). They facilitate social connections by helping you to understand others' emotional expressions so that you may meet their needs (empathy). The ways in which we physically demonstrate emotions, such as facial expressions, are powerful, universal communication tools.

Think of an emotion you experienced today or recently experienced. Why did this emotion arise? What intended function might it have been serving?

....

....

By being able to study and examine your emotions in this way, you will gain a little more space to resist reflex reactions and, instead, respond to them in more adaptive ways. Emotion regulation skills training is a core component of DBT, which was created by Marsha Linehan in the late 1970s (Linehan 2014). Along with their companion skill sets, mindfulness, distress tolerance, and interpersonal effectiveness, DBT skills can be useful in helping individuals to develop a range of strategies to more effectively manage their difficult emotions.

Increase Positive Emotions

Efforts to increase positive emotions can be a useful way to help improve emotional states and build a life worth living. While we are typically aware of some of the means by which to engage in pleasurable activities, it is easy to get caught up in the day-to-day routine or find ourselves spending most of our time and energy just managing stressors and struggles. That is not much fun.

Even with your daily struggles, it is important for you to recognize that there are many ways to increase positive emotions. That's right: both can be there at the same time, even though you may find you have a tendency to hold on to negative emotions. We do not have to wait to feel good in order to engage in enjoyable activities. Allow yourself to increase positive emotions through increasing your pleasurable activities.

Pleasurable Activities

Below is a list to get you started as you begin to brainstorm all of the ways to live a life that allows you to experience some fun and joy. Circle the items that you enjoy, find interesting, or may be curious to try.

- Go to the park.
- Walk around the mall.
- Go to a movie.
- Redecorate a room.
- Play with a pet.
- Listen to music.
- Play an instrument.
- Sing.
- Go for a drive.
- Read a book, poem, or magazine.
- Create art.
- Knit or crochet.
- Go to a museum.
- Play video games.
- Practice gratitude.
- Spend time with enjoyable people.
- Get outside in nature.
- Snuggle with someone.
- Create an adventure.
- Take or look at photos.
- Play a board game.
- Work on a puzzle.
- Take a bath.
- Dance.
- Color.
- Listen to comedy.
- Watch children or animals play.
- Go to a spa or sauna.
- Watch or play sports.
- Play a card game.
- Recall funny or loving memories.
- Buy yourself flowers.
- Give someone a gift.
- Volunteer.
- Bake or cook something you enjoy.
- Look at the stars.

- Go fishing.
- Pray.
- Meditate.
- Journal.
- Attend a concert or play.
- Birdwatch.
- Engage in a hobby (painting model cars, Lego).
- Look for seashells.
- Sit in the sun.
- Rollerblade or roller skate.
- Enjoy a cup of coffee or tea.
- Practice learning a language or accent.
- Go for a swim.
- Ride a bike.
- Smell your favorite perfume, essential oil, or flower.
- Build a bonfire.
- Plant flowers or garden.
- Color a mandala.
- Collect stones or fossils.
- Build or walk a labyrinth.
- Do tai chi or qigong.
- Practice martial arts.
- Teach someone a skill.

Are there any activities that you would add to this list?

....

....

Let's explore activities that you've enjoyed in the past, things you currently do, and possible new activities that you may find pleasurable:

What is one of your favorite memories that makes you laugh or brings you joy?

....

....

How do your mind and body feel when you recall that experience?

....

....

What made that experience pleasurable? What were the people, places, and spaces in that memory?

....

....

What are some of your current activities that feel pleasurable or restorative?

....

....

What new activities can you explore to create more joy in your day-to-day life?

....

....

Is there anything that excites you that is coming up in the near future?

....

....

Decrease Vulnerability to Negative Emotions

As we have discussed, it is important to take care of your body and mind so that you can optimally manage stress and emotions. There are factors that influence how reactive and vulnerable you are to your emotional experiences. If you experience intense emotions, and/or see them as one of the key factors in your BFRB cycle, it is worth reviewing the vulnerabilities you identified in Chapter 6 and looking a little deeper into how they impact your emotional experience. Here are the key areas of vulnerability to review if you notice your emotions tend to influence you in undesirable ways:

- sleep
- nutrition
- exercise
- substances and addictions
- psychological factors and co-occurring mental health conditions
- acute and chronic stressors and medical conditions.

States of Mind

Another way to practice emotional regulation is to identify your states of mind. By exploring your mind without judgment, you are able to assess yourself more accurately and determine where your mind is leading you and if that matches your desired goals. There is no good or bad state of mind; each has its pros and cons.

EMOTIONAL REGULATION CODE AND STATES OF MIND

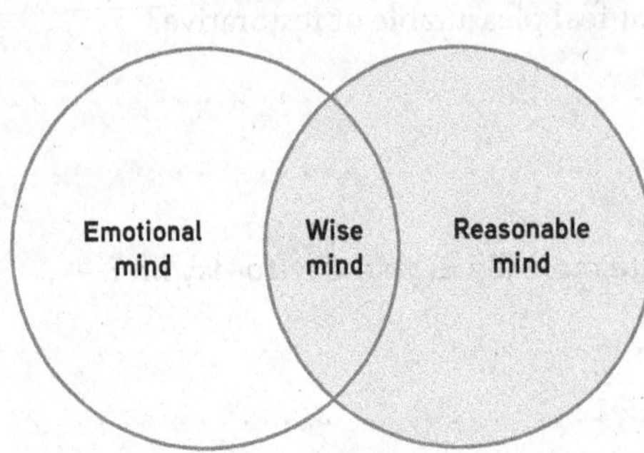

Emotional mind:

- What you *feel* to be true
- Facts are distorted by feeling
- Does the emotion help you be effective in the short term vs. long term?

Reasonable mind:

- What you think or believe to be fact
- Intellectual, logical, rational, problem solving
- Easier when we feel good

Wise mind:

- What you *know* to be true
- Intuitive knowing, integration of logic and emotion
- More effective outcomes

Linehan (2014)

Wise mind occurs when you are able to balance your states of mind in order to make effective decisions. In order to recognize and get into this state of being, you must first recognize your emotional and reasonable states of mind.

Emotional mind occurs when your emotions are controlling your urges, thoughts, and behaviors. Being more emotionally and physically vulnerable will increase the likelihood that you will respond with this state of mind. We have many examples of this in our own lives and in observing others (e.g., feeling angry and lashing out at someone, or feeling intense love and showing devotion toward others). While there are many advantages to this state, problems arise when there is a short-term gain but long-term negative outcome or when the emotion is just too painful for you to effectively respond to the situation. You may notice that being in this state creates a sense of urgency, difficulties focusing on other things, or strong sensations in your body.

Can you think of a recent time in which you experienced emotional mind?

....

....

Do you notice a relationship between this mind state and your BFRB?

....

....

Reasonable mind occurs when logic and reason control your urges, thoughts, and behaviors. This aspect of your mind is easier to access when you are less vulnerable and are feeling good. This part of your mind allows you to solve logical problems and follow instructions (e.g., follow a recipe, complete a puzzle). While this may sound good, the lack of emotion will limit how you experience and respond to the world around you. You may be in this state of mind if you are pushing away your own feelings or sensations, have difficulty empathizing with others, or feel emotionally flat.

Can you think of a recent time in which you experienced reasonable mind?

....

....

Do you notice a relationship between this mind state and your BFRB?

....

....

Wise mind is a balanced state of mind that integrates both logic and emotion. You are able to see the value of both states and draw upon many different ways in which you experience the world. This gives you a deep sense of knowing, openness, and clarity. You may notice a sense of intuition, and while it cannot be experienced at all times, you do possess the ability to access wise mind and it can be enhanced through skillful practice and mindfulness. This involves settling into the middle path through breathing, naming your emotions, and approaching a situation with willingness and confidence. This may occur at times when you recognize you are stressed at work and take a break to care for yourself, or walk away from a fight with a friend.

Can you think of a recent time in which you experienced wise mind?

....

....

How do you think wise mind can guide you in your BFRB journey?

....

....

Opposite Action

Using opposite action is another great way to regulate emotions by acting overtly in a way that is inconsistent with the distressing or unhelpful emotion. It is important to understand that you are not attempting to block or suppress the uncomfortable emotion, but you are simply expressing another emotional and behavioral response. When you feel bad, you may notice yourself acting in ways that intensify that bad feeling (e.g., feeling sad and staying in bed all day). This promotes that stuck feeling and an unhelpful cycle of behavior. By using opposite action, you change the way that you act, which will change the way you feel. This can be used to slow down your emotional mind, modulate emotions, and break unhelpful cycles that limit you or cause you harm.

Emotion	Action Urge	Opposite Action
Anxiety/fear	Avoid, leave the situation	Approach, remain in the situation
Sadness	Withdraw and isolate	Seek socialization and support, get active
Disgust	Criticize or reject self or others	Increase exposure, welcome discomfort
Envy	Act defensively, minimize others	Practice gratitude, express happiness for others
Anger/frustration	Lash out or attack	Be polite, show kindness, be gentle, show empathy
Shame	Avoid situations and hide from others	Reach out to others, share your experience with others who will understand

Linehan (2014)

Opposite action is an effective skill that needs to be practiced over and over again in order to change the reaction pattern and intensity of your initial emotion and action urge. Use this skill when the emotion and urge are not justified by the facts of the situation or are unhelpful. This is the treatment strategy often used in treating phobias, OCD, depression, and other conditions that cause strong emotional reactions and patterns of behavior that maintain the problem (i.e., exposure therapy, behavioral activation). There are steps you can take when you find yourself feeling overwhelmed by these unhelpful emotions and action urges. Here's an example:

1. **Identify the situation.**
   I had an argument with a friend.
2. **Identify my emotion(s) and action urge(s).**
   I notice sadness and anger. I feel as though I want to pull my hair to distract and soothe myself. I notice that I want to be alone for the rest of the day.
3. **Identify my states of mind.**
   The action urges are coming from my emotional mind and would not be effective in helping me to feel better. They would not be consistent with my value of friendship or with my goal of reducing hair pulling.

4. **Identify opposite action(s).**
   I can choose to call my friend and calmly talk about what happened, how I felt, and what I would like to have happen. I can make plans for the day to ensure I have social support and choose a few BFRB tools to use while I work through this emotion.

Let's put opposite action into practice for you!

Recall a time when you found yourself feeling overwhelmed by a situation:

....

....

What was the emotion that you experienced in that situation (sadness, anger, shame, anxiety)?

....

....

How would you describe your experience of that emotion (tightness in chest, crying, racing thoughts)?

....

....

What action urges did you notice? What did you feel like doing (avoid, yell, BFRB)?

....

....

What state of mind were you experiencing? Would acting on your emotional urges have been useful and effective in this situation? Would it have taken you toward your values or goals?

....

....

Can you identify an opposite action to your action urges? If so, what might you have done?

....

....

When using opposite action, it's most effective to go "all in" and "do it all the way." How might you have carried out this opposite action in a complete and convincing way through your thoughts, body posture, behavior, etc. (e.g., if socially anxious, go to a party, make eye contact, have the thought, "I've got this!", interact with others, smile)?

....

....

In what situations can you continue to use opposite action? How can you ensure you practice this new way of responding?

....

....

The idea behind acting in the opposite direction of your emotional urge is to engage in this alternative behavior until your emotion eventually changes its quality or is diminished. This is often referred to as "habituation." This may not sound like the most natural thing to do; remember that the only reason we feel like hiding ourselves when we are ashamed or avoiding the situation when we are anxious is because it *feels* right. But that is not a good enough reason to simply go with the behavior—in fact, the way in which our feelings prompt us to act is not always helpful. Remember, our emotions are not always our best guides. See what happens when you respond in an opposite way. Experiment.

Problem Solving

Problem solving is a skill that is used to determine the best course of action in a difficult situation when your emotion is justified or when you have not had much success in changing your thoughts, feelings, or behaviors in a problematic situation. This requires a focused effort and flexibility of thought, without judgment, in order to consider your best course of action in changing a situation or dealing with people differently. There is a method to problem solving.

Step 1: Observe, describe, and define the problem.

What is the problem or situation that you wish to change?

....

....

In order to most effectively solve a problem, you need to first explore what exactly you are dealing with in this situation. We can use the ABCs (antecedent, behavior, consequence) of behavioral analysis to better understand your problem.

What happened right before you found yourself in this situation?

....

....

What are your thoughts about the situation?

....

....

What are your emotions, primary and secondary, related to this problem?

....

....

What did you do or not do in response?

....

....

What were the consequences in both the short term and long term?

....

....

Step 2: Identify what is problematic about this situation. What makes this problem or situation unpleasant for you?

....

....

Step 3: What were your obstacles to solving the problem? What has kept you from meeting your goal?

....

....

Step 4: Identify your goals in problem solving. What are some simple, realistic goals that you can achieve in the short term?

....

....

Step 5: Brainstorm many possible solutions. Come up with any possible solutions, even include unrealistic or silly options, that could help you achieve your goal. Have fun with this and do not judge your ideas.

....

....

Step 6: Evaluate your options. Now read through your list and select the best possible solutions. You may consult with the wise mind, conduct a cost vs. benefit analysis, do a Choice Point, or rank-order them to reflect which options are most likely to work.

....

....

Step 7: Choose a solution to put into action. Which solution did you choose?

....

....

What is your initial step and what other small, manageable steps can you take as you move toward your goal in using this solution?

....

....

What strategies can you use if and when barriers arise in this action plan?

....

....

What are your backup options?

....

....

Step 8: Evaluate the results.

If your action plan worked, that is great! What helped you to be successful in solving this problem?

....

....

If the action plan did not work, go back to your brainstorming list and repeat the process. What is the next possible solution you can try?

....

....

Remember that problem solving is not always a linear process. That is okay. There are many things that we learn along the way that may increase our chances of success through using a strategic approach. You can use this worksheet to help you in this process:

Problem Solving

✶ What is the problem?	
What is the behavior analysis? (antecedents, behaviors, consequences)	
What is problematic about this situation?	
Are there any obstacles to solving this problem?	
What do you hope to achieve?	
Brainstorm possible solutions	
Evaluate your options and rate their potential for success	
Choose a solution to implement and determine steps to carry out the plan	
Evaluate the results	

When facing problematic situations in life, it is important to remember that you have choices. You can choose to solve the problem if you can change the situation, accept the problem if it is something you cannot change, modify the way you think or feel about the problem, remain stuck in your cycle of unhelpful thoughts, feelings, and behaviors, or make choices that make things worse for yourself. If you are like most people, you can probably come up with examples of times in which you selected each one of those options. We encourage you to use the skills in this workbook to guide you in a direction that decreases your suffering and the negative impact of your BFRB.

Emotion Strategies Observations

★

Antecedent Emotions ➔	➔ Emotions Strategies
Anxiety	*Opposite action*
Envy	*Problem solving*

ACTION PLAN

Regulating Intense Emotions

What key points in this chapter really spoke to you? What are the highlights *you* most want to keep in mind that are important for you and your BFRB?

. . . .

. . . .

What did you learn about yourself as you **explored**?

. . . .

. . . .

What **practices** will you commit to working on this week to move you toward your destination?

. . . .

. . . .

What is your **action plan**? What steps will you take to put these practices in place?

. . . .

. . . .

When and how often will you engage in these practices?

. . . .

. . . .

As you experiment with regulating emotions, monitor your observations in the Strategies and Skills Observation Log.

Strategies and Skills: Emotions Observation Log

Date and Time	Antecedent Emotions	Strategy	Observations

CHAPTER 14

Developing and Maintaining Satisfying Relationships

EXPLORE

Interpersonal effectiveness involves the ability to improve or maintain relationships while, at the same time, working toward achieving a desired outcome. In our work with people with BFRBs, we have had many clients share the impact their BFRB has had on their relationships and also how their relationships impact their BFRBs. Our relationships play a central role in our values, happiness, and sense of living a full life. When our relationships are healthy, we feel supported and more resilient to stress and life struggles. When relationships are distant, unhealthy, or non-existent, it can be a major source of suffering. If we do not have a strong social support system, it is important to work toward developing one.

In order to improve your interpersonal effectiveness, it is good to first understand what building healthy relationships looks like. Here is a list of skillful behaviors that may improve your feeling of self-respect and the quality of connections you make with others.

Being skillful in achieving objectives with others includes:

- asking others to do things
- saying no to unwanted requests effectively
- being heard and taken seriously
- building relationships
- strengthening current relationships
- ending destructive relationships
- not letting pain and problems build up
- resolving conflicts before they become overwhelming
- walking the middle path
- creating and maintaining balance in relationships
- balancing acceptance and change in relationships.

Although these relationship goals are ideal, there are obstacles that can arise that interfere with interpersonal effectiveness. These interferences may include:

- lack of clear communication skills
- indecision about your own needs
- interference from emotions and reactivity
- prioritizing short-term goals over long-term goals
- low distress tolerance
- failure to consider consequences
- other people in your environment who enable or disrupt
- your thoughts and beliefs about how your request will be met
- not feeling deserving of getting what you want or need.

Let's take a look at the quality of your relationships and the extent to which they are meeting your needs.

What do you think you do well in your relationships with others?

....

....

In what areas do you struggle in your relationships?

....

....

Do you notice an association between your BFRB and your relationships?

....

....

If you notice thoughts, feelings, and behaviors that negatively impact your ability to develop and strengthen relationships, or you have toxic relationships that require more distance, there are skills you can use to improve your interpersonal effectiveness. Like all skills, interpersonal skills also require practice. There will be times where using these skills will quickly improve social situations, but also know that there will be some relationships that will take time to adjust to new communication styles.

PRACTICE

TOOLS FOR THE TERRAIN

- Relationship Effectiveness: GIVE Skills
- Assertiveness Training
- Objective Effectiveness: DEAR MAN Skills
- Self-Respect Effectiveness: FAST Skills
- Distancing Yourself from Toxic People
- Social Support

Relationship Effectiveness: GIVE Skills

GIVE skills, from DBT, help you to maintain or improve healthy relationships. This includes boundary setting and being able to respectfully say no to another person's request or being able to ask something of someone. GIVE skills include:

- **G**entle
- **I**nterest
- **V**alidate
- **E**asy manner.

Be **G**entle: Be gentle by objectively and calmly stating what you want. Choose your words wisely; be mindful that what you say and how you say it is non-threatening. This includes resisting physical or verbal attacks, name-calling, eye-rolling, judging, or using guilt. Showing respect toward others will increase the likelihood of them complying with your request. If they do not agree to your request, use your skills to exit the situation gracefully and respectfully.

Show **I**nterest: Show interest in what the other person is sharing with you. Listen to what they are saying and monitor verbal and nonverbal cues. Use conversation facilitators, such as maintaining eye contact, leaning in, smiling, nodding, and verbally acknowledging what someone has said to show the other person that you are engaged in active listening. Resist multitasking, looking at your mobile phone, or becoming distracted by other tasks. Hold on to your own emotional reactions while they are speaking if they are getting in the way of active listening or achieving a long-term goal in a relationship.

Validate: Validate by trying to understand their point of view and convey this verbally. This does not necessarily mean that you agree or accept what they are saying (the "what") but that you are treating them as an equal and understand their reasoning (the "why"). Practice turn taking in the conversation and use reflective listening to repeat back what they are saying or assess for the main point they are trying to convey. And remember to validate not only with words but also with action when warranted. For example, when someone lets you know that they are feeling overwhelmed with household chores, you may empathize with this experience but also offer to help them with tasks or encourage them to take a break.

Use an **E**asy manner: Use an easy manner, which shows friendliness and assertiveness. Show willingness and acceptance to have a respectful conversation. Be gentle with yourself and others, smile, and know that you can end even a difficult conversation in a loving way. For example, at the end of a difficult conversation in which there is a disagreement, you may thank them for their willingness to talk about this uncomfortable topic and let them know that you continue to value them and their friendship.

Can you think of a situation in which you could use GIVE skills?

....

....

How do you think the other person would respond to you? How would you feel about your own behavior?

....

....

GIVE Skills: Plan Ahead

Consider upcoming situations in which you would like to plan to be interpersonally effective in your communications with others. Use the following chart to plan for the use of GIVE skills.

★

Situation	How Might You Be Gentle?	How Might You Show Interest?	How Might You Validate?	How Might You Use an Easy Manner?

Assertiveness Training

Assertiveness is an important life skill that involves the ability to communicate in a manner that is direct, honest, and respectful while maintaining the ability to manage one's own emotional reactions and one's boundaries. The ability to be assertive does not often come naturally to individuals, but it is a skill that can be developed with practice. Numerous research studies have demonstrated that improving assertiveness skills can decrease anxiety in social contexts, increase feelings of self-worth, decrease stress, improve physical health, and help one to engage in more values-based activities (Alberti and Emmons 2017).

In order to build assertiveness, it is important to understand the different styles of communication.

Styles of Communication

Communication Style	Thoughts	Feelings	Behaviors	Goals
Passive	The desires and opinions of others are more important; lack of trust in your own decision-making and judgment	Fears of conflict or of being rejected by others; low self-esteem; angry, powerless, helpless; resentful from feeling used in relationships	Apologize, self-deprecate or deny that you disagree; do not express what you want or need; avoid eye contact, speak softly, make yourself small	Avoid rejection or conflict; other people have control and responsibility
Passive aggressive	Belief that one is entitled and not responsible for one's actions	Resentful of others; fear of being rejected or having conflict if one was to be more direct	Not accepting responsibility through denying, defensiveness, distraction, or forgetting; may mimic passive style with nonverbal behaviors	Get what one feels is deserved without having to take responsibility
Aggressive	One's own needs are more important or correct; beliefs that desires of others are silly, stupid, or wrong	Anger, rage, frustration toward others; striving toward the victory of being correct; may later feel justified or remorseful	Attacking, dismissing, insulting, disrespecting behavior toward the needs of others; loud voice, penetrating eye contact; intimidating body language that may be seen as threatening	Have others agree; take control over others and "win" at any expense to others

Assertive	Willingness to take personal responsibility; equal rights for people to express their wants, needs, and desires	Improved self-esteem, integrity, respectful feeling toward self and others; willingness and openness	Honestly expressing wants, needs, and beliefs; having self-control and not needing others to agree	Maintain respect for self and others by directly expressing beliefs, needs, and wants without needing others to see the situation the same way

Which one of these styles do you often find yourself using in your communication patterns with others? What are the thoughts, feelings, behaviors, and goals that you hold? Do you think this is an effective way to interact with the people in your life? Does it fit with your values?

....

....

What is the relationship between your style(s) of communication and your BFRB?

....

....

In what ways might you benefit from exploring a different communication style and practicing assertiveness skills?

....

....

Objective Effectiveness: DEAR MAN Skills

This interpersonal skills set used in DBT helps to outline the ways in which you can use direct and assertive communication to ask someone for something that you want or say no to a request that they are making of you. This requires practice, and you are encouraged to write out your response or rehearse these statements in your mind, practice them in a mirror, or rehearse with someone else. DEAR MAN skills include:

- **D**escribe the situation
- **E**xpress clearly
- **A**ssert wishes
- **R**einforce
- **M**indfulness
- **A**ppear confident
- **N**egotiate.

Describe the situation: Briefly and objectively describe the situation by only including the facts and providing enough context to help the individual understand your perspective and the reason for your statement or request. Directly share what the problem is and what your hope for resolution may be without blaming or using accusatory statements. Keep it short and to the point to avoid confusion or defensiveness.

Express clearly: Express your thoughts and feelings using "I statements." An "I statement" is a statement that expresses your personal reactions to a given situation and conveys what it is that you want from the interaction. Share your emotional reaction and why you are making a request or saying no.

Assert wishes: Ask for what you want or say no, clearly. Don't make assumptions, use passive-aggressive language, or assume others can read your mind and know your wishes. Use clear, concise language in the form of a question rather than stating a demand or using sarcasm.

Reinforce: Reward the person in advance by explaining the potential positive outcomes of agreeing to your request or accepting your refusal. Communicate that there are benefits to complying with your request or respecting your decision to say no.

Mindful: Stay focused on what you want to accomplish with this conversation. Calmly repeat your request or say no as many times as necessary. There is strength in repeating and maintaining your position. Ignore distractions, diversions, defensiveness, or attempts to change the topic. Maintain calm focus on your objective.

Appear confident: Respectfully maintain eye contact and use a confident vocal tone when making your request. Hold your body in an assertive, upright, and open stance. It is okay if you feel anxious or uncomfortable; the skill is to appear confident and deserving of respect, even if you do not 100 percent feel that way inside.

Negotiate: When such discussions are not progressing, be willing to offer or invite the other person to offer another solution to consider that may solve the problem in a different manner. You may also break your request down into smaller steps or asks in order to move in the direction of getting what you want. You might also offer something in return for the person agreeing to your request.

Can you think of a situation in which you could use DEAR MAN skills?

....

....

How do you think the other person would respond to you? How would you feel about your own behavior?

....

....

Let's look at how you might utilize DEAR MAN skills. Choose a situation in which you will make a request of someone or decline a request. Consider how you may do so with interpersonal effectiveness. As these skills can be challenging, we've included an example.

DEAR MAN Skills: Plan Ahead

Describe the Situation	*Whenever I touch my head, my spouse tells me to stop and tells me I used to have such a beautiful head of hair.*
Express Yourself Clearly	*I have a condition that causes hair pulling and hair loss. It's not helpful to be told to just stop or to be reminded of what my hair used to look like.*
Assert Your Wishes	*Please refrain from telling me to stop or telling me I used to look beautiful. Will you do this for me?*
Reinforce	*I would appreciate you considering this request. It would make me a lot happier and improve my ability to effectively manage my hair pulling.*
Maintain Mindfulness	*If they disagree or become defensive, I can remind them of my request or ignore any diversions from the request.*
Appear Confident	*I will look my partner in the eyes, sit up straight, refrain from apologizing, and use clear language as I assert this request.*
Negotiate, if Necessary	*If my partner has a difficult time agreeing to this request, I can ask if, instead of telling me to stop, they could say, "Is there something I can do for you?" or offer me an item from my BFRB toolbox.*

Self-Respect Effectiveness: FAST Skills

Self-respect effectiveness involves communicating with others in a manner that results in the ability to maintain or increase your self-respect after the interaction has passed. FAST skills help remind you to act in ways that allow you to keep your self-respect in interpersonal relationships when asking for something that you want or when saying no. FAST skills include:

- (be) **F**air
- (no) **A**pologies
- **S**tick to values
- (be) **T**ruthful

(Be) **F**air to yourself and to the other person in the attempts to have difficult discussions or to problem solve. Respect and validate the thoughts and feelings of yourself and others at all times. Sacrificing your own self-respect by taking advantage of others or not asserting yourself will decrease your effectiveness and contribute to a negative self-concept.

(No) Apologies: Don't over apologize for making a request, saying no, or being you. Apologizing may be appropriately and effectively used to take responsibility for having done something wrong. In other circumstances, such as apologizing before making a request or setting a limit, apologizing may serve to minimize the power of your statement and your perceived value, and diminish your self-respect over time.

Stick to values: Hold on to your own values and opinions. Do not step outside of your values or beliefs in order to get someone to like you or agree. Maintain your self-respect by identifying and sharing where you stand in a situation and allow others to hold their own values.

(Be) Truthful: Sometimes, people are dishonest to protect themselves or others from negative feelings. Don't lie, act helpless, make up excuses, or exaggerate when trying to get someone to comply with a request or deny another person's request. Communicating in dishonest ways over time will diminish your self-respect and quality of relationships. If you struggle with truthfulness, be mindful of this quality and limit how often you are dishonest. Take responsibility for yourself and own up to your thoughts, feelings, and behaviors.

Can you think of a situation in which you could use FAST skills?

....

....

How do you think the other person would respond to you? How would you feel about your own behavior?

....

....

FAST Skills: Plan Ahead

Consider upcoming situations in which you would like to plan to be interpersonally effective in your communications with others while maintaining your self-respect. Use the following chart to plan for the use of FAST skills.

★

Situation	How Might You Be Fair?	How Might You Express (No) Apologies?	How Might You Stick to Values?	How Might You Be Truthful?

Distancing Yourself from Toxic People

Everyone deserves healthy relationships. While having healthy relationships is a cornerstone for happiness, having toxic, abusive relationships is sure to bring misery into your life. Setting limits and boundaries with others, including ending relationships, is an appropriate means of maintaining healthy relationships. If you find yourself in an abusive relationship or a relationship that is characterized by interpersonal violence or intimidation and are in need of support and guidance to safely end the relationship, contact the National Domestic Violence Hotline at 1-800-799-7233 (SAFE).

Do you have a toxic or abusive relationship from which you need to exit or create distance?

....

....

What steps can you take, either on your own or with the assistance of others, to effectively address this unhealthy situation?

....

....

Social Support

Social support is essential to living well with a BFRB. Many individuals live with the secret of having a BFRB, as they fear rejection by others should their "secret" be discovered. As a result, living with a BFRB can lead to feelings of loneliness and isolation. But it doesn't have to be this way.

Sharing the vulnerability of your BFRB with a trusted friend or family member can provide much-needed comfort and compassion. Many people also find that gaining connection to others who have the shared experience of living with a BFRB is vital to their "recovery." It can be a powerful addition to the healing process beyond self-help efforts or engaging in individual psychotherapy. There are many resources for social support available both online and in communities across the world.

Is there a friend or family member currently in your life who you think may serve this supportive role?

....

....

What steps can you take to find a support network, either online or in your community?

....

....

Interpersonal Effectiveness Strategies

★

Antecedent TIMES (Interpersonal Situation) ➔	**➔ Interpersonal Effectiveness Strategies**
A well-intentioned family member keeps grabbing my hand each time they see me bite my nails	*Use DEARMAN to request that they refrain from grabbing my hand* *Assert myself by saying that this is not actually helpful and there are other ways they can better support me*

ACTION PLAN

Developing and Maintaining Satisfying Relationships

What key points in this chapter really spoke to you? What are the highlights *you* most want to keep in mind that are important for you and your BFRB?

....

....

What did you learn about yourself as you **explored**?

....

....

What **practices** will you commit to working on this week to move you toward your destination?

....

....

What is your **action plan**? What steps will you take to put these practices in place?

....

....

When and how often will you engage in these practices?

....

....

As you experiment with interpersonal effectiveness skills, monitor your observations in the Strategies and Skills Observation Log.

★ Strategies and Skills: Interpersonal Observation Log

Date and Time	Antecedent Interpersonal Situation	Strategy/Skill	Observations

CHAPTER 15

Accepting and Effectively Managing Distress

EXPLORE

While our levels of stress wax and wane over time, there may be times in which you feel as though your levels of distress seem intolerable, leaving you feeling overwhelmed and unable to act effectively. This may be when you are most vulnerable to your BFRB and to coping in ways that are not aligned with your values and goals—those DOTS (e.g., avoiding, isolating, unhelpful negative thinking, and engaging in your BFRB).

Identifying Your Distress

Think about the stressors in your life. How do you know when you are experiencing high levels of distress? What is that like for you? When your stress levels peak, what thoughts, images, memories, emotions, sensations, and urges show up?

....

....

What situations typically trigger this level of distress for you? Consider all the different areas of your life—relationships, work/education/finances, leisure activities, physical health, emotional health, or other areas of your life.

....

....

When levels of distress peak, what do you do?

....

....

Are there times when you unintentionally worsen a distressing situation? For example, you may unintentionally increase your distress by internally engaging in self-criticism, comparing yourself to others, thinking about the past or future in a catastrophic or negative manner, focusing on unpleasant bodily sensations and urges, or thinking of your experience as being hopeless or unbearable? Or you may do something externally to worsen your situation, such as acting out, yelling at someone, avoiding, using drugs or alcohol, overeating, spending money you didn't budget for, or some other action that does not resolve the problem but, rather, prolongs dealing with it.

....

....

In these moments of high distress, you may consider using grounding skills and practice strategies to increase willingness, acceptance, or emotion regulation. However, there may be times when your emotions are so intense that you feel unable to practice these strategies. There may be moments when you feel as though you are in an emotional crisis. You may be in such a state if:

- you notice your emotions are very intense
- you notice physical pain, discomfort, racing heartbeat, tightness in your chest
- you notice racing thoughts, confusion, or think you "don't know what to do"
- you notice a sense of urgency and thoughts like, "I can't stand this. This has to stop now!"
- you believe you are unable to resolve a problem or improve your present moment.

In moments like these, it can be difficult to effectively use strategies and continue to move toward what's important to you. These moments may be best served by using distress tolerance skills.

PRACTICE

TOOLS FOR THE TERRAIN

- TIPP Skills
- Self-Soothing Skills
- Distraction Skills—ACCEPTS
- Improving-This-Moment Skills—IMPROVE

Distress Tolerance Skills

Originating from DBT, distress tolerance skills may help you to navigate highly distressing situations or painful moments so that you may more easily ride out the moment without unintentionally increasing your anxiety or worsening the situation by getting stuck in a BFRB episode. These skills *are not* intended to serve as a means to solve a stressful problem or help you move toward what you want, but they can be helpful in the short term to manage your intense TIMES when you are feeling extremely upset or overwhelmed and unable to use other skills.

TIPP Skills

TIPP skills are intended to be practiced during times of very intense distress—in those times of emotional crisis when it may feel as though you are unable to even think about other skills or strategies that may be useful in the moment. The goal of TIPP skills is to quickly shift your physiological response to reduce the intensity of your emotional experience. TIPP skills include:

- **T**ip the temperature
- **I**ntense exercise
- **P**aced breathing
- **P**rogressive muscle relaxation.

Tip the temperature is a practice in which you utilize cold water or ice to trick your body into quickly activating your parasympathetic nervous system and the "relaxation response." You may do this by holding your breath and leaning down into a cold bowl or sink filled with ice water for at least 30 seconds. Or alternatively, you may fill a large freezer bag with ice and place it on the surface of a table and lower your face onto the bag, ensuring that your forehead, eyes, and cheeks are making contact with the ice for at least 30 seconds. If neither of these strategies are feasible, you may try to splash cold water on your face to promote this response.

In this practice, very cold water initiates rapid physiological changes by mimicking the sensation of being immersed in cold water and triggering a human (and other mammalian) survival response. Thus, tipping the temperature is a quick way to decrease your body temperature, heart rate, and blood pressure when highly activated. Note that when considering the use of this skill, use caution and consult with your physician first if you have a medical condition that would render this contraindicated. How might you most easily practice tipping the temperature?

....

....

Intense exercise, either aerobic or strength training, for a brief period of 10–15 minutes or longer can help to expend the body's energy when keyed up and calm both the body and mind. Consider taking a brisk walk, doing jumping jacks or sit-ups, dancing, or playing a pick-up game of basketball to change your body's level of activation. What might you do to engage in intense exercise?

....

....

Paced breathing is another skill to decrease your nervous system activation. Practicing slow, diaphragmatic breathing can activate the relaxation response. To practice paced breathing, inhale slowly and deeply, first into your belly and then into your chest. Pause. And exhale slowly, aiming for a longer exhalation. You may consider counting your breath—inhaling to a count of four, pausing, and exhaling to a count a six to elongate the breath rate.

....

....

Progressive muscle relaxation (PMR) is a skill that teaches the differentiation between the feeling of muscle tension and the feeling of muscle relaxation. It is an exercise in which you encourage the relaxation response by slowly moving through each muscle group of your body, tensing and relaxing each area for a brief period of time. Below, you will find a PMR script to record and follow along with while listening or to practice with a friend. There are also many PMR exercises that can be found on the internet in both video and audio format.

Progressive Muscle Relaxation

Take a moment to settle into your seat. Close your eyes if that's comfortable for you or cast your gaze downward. Notice how your body feels in this moment, noting any points of tension or pain. Now, take a deep breath into your belly, filling your lungs, and exhaling as you release your breath. Take several more breaths like this, inhaling through your nose and exhaling through your mouth. Allow your breath to be slow, rhythmic, and natural.

Let's begin by bringing your attention to your hands and arms. Create two fists and bend your elbows up toward your shoulders, clenching the muscles of the hands, lower arms, and biceps. Hold them tightly. Notice the tension in your fingers, around the palms, and knuckles. Notice the tension in your forearms and upper arms. Hold this tension for several moments. Tighten. And now release. Let your arms rest at your sides. Wiggle your fingers and relax the muscles of your hands, letting go of that tension more and more. Notice the sensation of loosening. Sit with this feeling, letting go further and further. Observe the difference between tension and relaxation.

When you're ready, bring your attention to your shoulders. Lift your shoulders up toward your ears. Notice the sensation of tightness or discomfort. Hold on to that sensation, lifting your shoulders as high as you can. Hold this tension for several moments. Tighten. And now release. Roll your shoulders back. Notice them fall. And loosen the muscles, allowing the shoulders and arms to rest comfortably. Sit with this feeling, letting go further and further. Observe the difference between tension and relaxation.

Now let's turn your attention to your neck. Slowly bring your head back to a point of tension, bringing your gaze upward to the ceiling or sky. Hold that state of tension for several seconds. When you're ready, slowly bring your head forward into a neutral position. Tip your neck to the left, drawing your ear toward your left shoulder. Feel the gentle stretch and tension. Hold this for several seconds and slowly bring your head back to a neutral position. Bring your chin toward your chest, feeling the stretch in your neck and upper back. Hold that for several seconds and slowly bring your head back to a neutral position. Now tip your head, moving your right ear toward your right shoulder. Feel the stretch on this side. Notice the sensation for several seconds and slowly bring your head back to neutral.

Now turn your attention to the muscles of your face. First, let's notice the muscles around your forehead, raising your eyebrows up toward the top of your head. Notice the tension across your forehead. Hold this tension. And allow your eyebrows to fall, loosening the tension across the upper parts of your eyes and head. Notice the difference between tension and relaxation. Clench your eyes tightly, holding them closed with tension across your face for several moments. Notice the discomfort. And release the tension, relaxing the muscles around your eyes. Next, open your mouth as widely as you can, noticing the tension created in your jaw. Feel the pull across the lower portions of your head for several moments. And relax, loosening the tension across your mouth and jaw. Notice the difference between tension in the muscles around your head and face and the sensation of relaxation.

Now turn your attention to your chest and upper back. Bend your arms, push your elbows behind you, and arch your back. Notice the tension across your chest and back as you squeeze your elbows toward each other, tightening the muscles of your upper back. Hold that tension for several moments. Notice the discomfort. And release the tension, loosening the muscles further and further. Observe the difference between tension and relaxation.

Next, focus on the muscles of the stomach. Tighten the muscles of your stomach, by pulling your stomach muscles in, noticing the tension across your stomach and around your sides. Hold on to that tension for several moments. And now release the tension, relaxing the stomach and noticing your ability to breathe freely and easily. Observe the difference between tension and relaxation.

Turn your attention to your buttocks. Tighten the muscles around your hips and your seat, noticing the tension around your body. Squeeze the muscles for several moments. And now relax the muscles, releasing any tension. And observe the difference between tension and relaxation.

Now turn your attention to your legs. Lift your legs up, straightening your knees, feeling the tension across your legs, from your thighs down to your ankles. Hold the tension across your legs for several moments. And now relax your legs and allow them to rest. Loosen any tension and allow yourself to notice the difference between tension and relaxation.

Lastly, curl your toes under, tightening all the muscles of your feet and ankles. Squeeze the muscles, noticing the discomfort. Hold this tension for several moments. And release. Allow your feet to relax and rest comfortably. Notice the difference between tension and relaxation.

Let's return to your breath as you sit comfortably in your seat. Breathe in and out as you imagine a wave of relaxation washing over you from head to toe, sweeping away any remaining tension or discomfort. Breathing in and out. Bring your attention back into the moment, feeling a little more relaxed and renewed. And, when you're ready, open your eyes and return your attention to the room.

Self-Soothing Skills

Self-soothing skills are intended to provide sensory comfort. Just like the sensory strategies you've already explored, these strategies provide sensory input that may override your present emotional experience. Consider expanding your sensory options by exploring your five senses:

- Vision: Examine paintings, photographs, or interesting visual patterns, or bird watch.
- Hearing: Listen to music, play an instrument, or attend to the sound of silence.
- Smell: Use your favorite lotion, light a fragrant candle, brew coffee, or smell flowers.
- Taste: Mindfully eat your favorite food, chew flavorful gum, or suck on a hard candy.
- Touch: Pet an animal, get a hug, or put on your softest clothing.

Use the following chart to explore other self-soothing skills:

Self-Soothing Strategy	Skills
Vision	
Hearing	
Smell	
Taste	
Touch	

Distraction Skills—ACCEPTS

Although distraction is not a solution to any problem, it can provide you with a brief period of time to press pause and reset—to take a break by shifting your attention away from something very upsetting and prevent you from getting stuck in your BFRB cycle. Distraction skills are not intended to be practiced for an extended period of time, as overindulging in distraction has the potential to be counterproductive and serve as avoidance or away moves, pushing away your discomfort and keeping you from moving toward your values. Think of distraction skills as a quick reset so that you may realign yourself and your emotions with your own interests. Distraction skills are easily recalled by using the acronym ACCEPTS, which stands for:

- Activities
- Contributions
- Comparisons
- Encourage different emotions
- Push away
- Think different thoughts
- Sense other sensations.

Activities that distract are those actions that move you toward something else that is important to you. They may be something you enjoy that you do even in the midst of suffering. Consider those committed-action activities. What do you do that is meaningful to you? Consider those pleasurable activities. What actions bring you enjoyment? These activities may be involved or they may be simple. Examples of activities that distract may include reading, watching TV, listening to music, going for a walk, talking to a friend, or attending a sporting event or concert. What may serve as distraction activities for you?

....

....

Contributions are those behaviors that pivot your attention away from your own distress and toward someone or something else external to you which you can contribute to, improve, or otherwise enhance. They allow you to make room for your discomfort and move toward something else so that you do not hyper-focus on your internal distress. In what ways might you contribute to a collective effort or cause that is meaningful to you? How might you help or support other people in your family, community, or world? Examples of distracting with contributions may include calling a loved one and expressing gratitude to them for their friendship, writing a thank you note to a colleague for their appreciated teamwork, bringing flowers to a local eldercare facility, making a donation to a nonprofit organization that does charitable work you admire, or volunteering your time to assist a local community organization. What may serve as contributions for you?

....

....

Comparisons are cognitive strategies that enable you to practice perspective taking; this may be particularly useful when you are feeling overwhelmed, as you may find that you have a tendency to become inflexible and unable to see your situation from other vantage points when feeling this way. Distraction with comparisons may involve thinking about how the ways in which you are presently managing your distress compare with times in the past when you've coped less effectively or when you've had fewer strategies and resources to use. How might you use this information to provide yourself with support for the present? Consider how you may feel after a long period of time. In other words, how might you feel long after this difficult moment has passed? Or think about that which you have in your life for which you are grateful. How does that compare with other times in your life or with that which others have? How might you utilize comparisons?

....

....

Encouraging different emotions is a distraction skill that may help you to unhook from the immediate distress of your current situation. Rather than focusing on your distress, consider activities that may help you to experience a preferred emotion. Rather than listening to the sad lyrics of your favorite ballad, play upbeat music that you think of as happy or relaxing if you are feeling keyed up or on edge. Ask yourself, "What am I feeling right now?" And, "What can I do that would usually feel good or help me to feel a pleasant emotion?" Other examples may include watching stand-up comedy if you're feeling sad, playing with your pet if you're feeling lonely, or taking a warm bubble bath if you're feeling cold and irritable. What might you do to encourage different emotions?

....

....

Push away is the practice of temporarily taking a break from something overwhelming for a brief period of time in the event that working on it in the present moment is not serving you well. Have you ever found yourself struggling to focus on something while your attention is preoccupied by something else? Setting limits by allowing yourself to put a matter aside for a discrete period of time can promote effectiveness and self-regulation. Consider writing a "to-do" list and note which items are immediately actionable, which can be addressed at another time, and whether it is a good time to work on each item. If you notice thoughts racing through your mind before bed, consider writing these thoughts down and putting them away to think about in the morning. The purpose of the push-away skill is to develop the ability to set appropriate limits and boundaries for yourself in order to optimize your functioning and promote healthy problem solving. What might you do to push away and set healthy limits for yourself?

....

....

Think different thoughts is the action of shifting your attention to another mental activity. For example, if you find yourself distressed by anger and frustration, and noticing loud critical thoughts about your appearance, engage in a mental task that requires your full attention such as playing a word game, working on a puzzle, or solving riddles or word problems. The goal of thinking different thoughts is to busy your mind with another mental activity that is incompatible with your upsetting thoughts—that which cannot be focused on simultaneously. In what ways might you think different thoughts?

....

....

Sense other sensations is the final distraction skill. The goal of sense other sensations is to provide yourself with another intense sensation that may take your mind off your distress. In moments of emotional crisis, you may choose to take a hot or cold bath/shower, get a massage, hold an ice cube in your hand, eat something spicy or sour, engage in vigorous exercise, or stand outside in the wind. In what ways might you sense other sensations?

....

....

Use the chart below as a quick reference to your ACCEPTS skills:

Distraction Strategy	Skills
Activities	
Contributions	
Comparisons	
Encourage different emotions	
Push away	
Think different thoughts	
Sense different sensations	

Improving-This-Moment Skills—IMPROVE

IMPROVE skills are intended to orient you toward taking a step in the direction of improving your present-moment experience. These skills include efforts to improve the moment with:

- Imagery
- Meaning
- Prayer
- Relaxation
- One thing in the moment
- Vacation
- Encouragement.

When feeling distressed, it can feel empowering to do something to improve your immediate moment by making a small move toward a more pleasant internal experience.

Improving the situation with **I**magery in your **i**magination can provide such a movement. Consider engaging in a guided-imagery exercise, imagine being in your favorite place or with people you care about, visualize a relaxing scene, envision coping effectively, or imagine your worries floating up into the clouds. Using your imagination can help you to disengage from your situation and encourage flexibility. How might you improve with imagination?

....

....

....

Improve the situation by making **M**eaning of it, even though the experience may be difficult. Even in the darkest of moments, there may be something to be gained from having been through it. In these moments, consider if there is a "silver lining" or something that may be learned. Find that meaning. An example of this may be that a difficult experience brings to light those in your life who are there for you to support you and help you to feel understood. How might you improve your situation by searching for meaning?

....

....

Improving the situation with **P**rayer refers to the act of connecting with one's own spirituality. Whether that be through connection to a religion or higher power, to a deep sense of self and inner wisdom, to nature, or to our common humanity, getting in touch with a sense of spirituality can help to facilitate a sense of shared experience, reducing feelings of loneliness and isolation. How might you improve your situation with prayer?

....

....

Improve the situation with **R**elaxation: Relaxation practices are an excellent way to change your inner experience quickly and provide relief to emotional as well as physical pain. These include a wide range of activities that are intended to provide you with a break from stressful situations and engage you in an activity you typically find calming or relaxing. Practicing paced breathing, PMR, mindfulness, or engaging in a quiet activity that brings enjoyment such as having a warm cup of cocoa or tea while reading a good book are examples of relaxation practices. What are ways in which you may improve situations with relaxation?

....

....

One thing in the moment is a skill used to focus on the moment. Sometimes, when individuals experience a high degree of distress, their minds drift to both the past and the future, piling on thoughts and worries that can worsen their sense of the current crisis. Thus, focusing one's full attention on the present-moment experience, mindfully, including the five-senses experience of what you are doing and letting any thoughts of your past or future come and go, can be a useful strategy to effectively manage the moment. How might you practice improving situations with one thing at a time?

....

....

Improve your situation by taking a brief **V**acation. This doesn't need to be a trip to an exotic island. By vacation, we mean taking a break from your situation and from all of the competing demands of your life. Step away from the office for a brief period of time. Turn off your phone. Stay in bed for an extra half hour. Order takeout, play some soft music, and dim the lights. Do something that allows you to feel a little distance from the pressure of your day to allow your mind and body to reset and recharge. What might you do to improve a situation with vacation?

....

....

Improve your moment by providing yourself with **E**ncouragement. In moments of distress, we can sometimes be hard on ourselves. Instead, be that voice of encouragement, prop yourself up by expressing confidence in yourself, tell yourself you can get through this even though it's difficult, provide yourself with self-compassion, and don't forget to say it like you mean it. Everyone needs encouragement. You are your closest, most important source of that support. How might you improve your circumstances with encouragement?

....

....

Use the chart below as a quick reference to your IMPROVE skills:

Improve Strategy	Skills
Imagery	
Meaning	
Prayer	
Relaxation	
One thing in the moment	
Vacation	
Encouragement	

Unfortunately, pain and distress are parts of life that everyone experiences. Sometimes our greatest efforts to escape pain paradoxically prolong it and create misery. Learning to accept pain and discomfort and riding out the experience does not mean that you want it or approve of it. Distress tolerance skills may enable you to more effectively sit with pain, hold it gently, and enable it to pass. When empowered in this way, you don't have to feel stuck in a state of suffering.

Distress Tolerance Strategies

Antecedent Emotion →	→ Distress Tolerance Strategies
Feeling overwhelmed during a BFRB episode, thinking that I may as well give up and keep picking	*Use tip the temperature and engage in improving-this-moment skills*

ACTION PLAN

Accepting and Effectively Managing Distress

What key points in this chapter really spoke to you? What are the highlights *you* most want to keep in mind that are important for you and your BFRB?

What did you learn about yourself as you **explored**?

What **practices** will you commit to working on this week to move you toward your destination?

What is your **action plan**? What steps will you take to put these practices in place?

When and how often will you engage in these practices?

....

....

As you experiment with distress tolerance skills, monitor your observations in the Strategies and Skills Observation Log.

Strategies and Skills: Emotions Observation Log

★

Date and Time	Antecedent Intense Emotions	Strategy/Skill	Observations

STEP IV

LIVE YOUR BEST LIFE

CHAPTER 16

Building Confidence and Overcoming Difficult Situations

EXPLORE

Self-Efficacy

Everyone wants to feel effective, like they are successful in their endeavors. This serves to help us maintain our motivation. Working on something particularly challenging—like changing the relationship you have with your BFRB—is no different than other challenges in life that you set out to address. You likely began to work on this goal feeling motivated and thinking positively about your ability to do this and about the potential for success. However, as time passes, skepticism and doubt may creep in as you experience the "ups and downs" of day-to-day efforts. This is "normal." Most people experience this as they begin to work on behavior change, such as efforts to change lifestyle behaviors like diet, exercise, or sleep routines. You may begin to lose your "umph," that positive outlook and energy you initially put into your efforts. You may even begin to question whether you can be successful in making this change. That, too, is "normal." It's natural to want to avoid struggling because the TIMES show up and can overwhelm. Thoughts of doubt, feelings of frustration, or memories of setbacks may come to mind, and you might consider pushing away this distress by giving yourself permission to engage in your BFRB (which may provide you with some short-term relief).

> **TOP TIP**
>
> To win the "long game," keep your "eye on the ball," regardless of the distractions going on around you that could throw you off course. Consistency is key and working on yourself is a process.

Remind yourself that to be successful in the long term is to learn to allow yourself to experience these moments and everything they entail, even the frustrations, and respond by supporting yourself and keeping your efforts sustained so that you learn to manage these internal experiences differently as they rise and fall.

Building a sense of self-efficacy, the belief that you have the capacity to do that which is needed to meet your goals, is essential to maintaining motivation and overcoming challenges. When struggles arise, you may find yourself questioning your self-efficacy, but you can strengthen this belief and your resilience in the face of adversity by engaging in activities that build mastery—that sense of "I CAN do this!"

PRACTICE

TOOLS FOR THE TERRAIN

- Supportive Statements
- Building Mastery
- Coping Ahead of Time
- Learning from Experience: Chain Analysis
- Breaking the Chain
- Repairing and Healing the Consequences
- Missing-Link Analysis

Supportive Statements

High-quality supportive statements include: acknowledgement, acceptance, and confidence in your ability to manage the TIMES. An example of a self-supportive statement is, "Having a BFRB setback can be difficult for me, but I know that I can manage the difficult thoughts and feelings of this experience and move forward effectively." Practice supporting yourself in this way. Think of it as a personal mantra.

What supportive statement can you develop and practice for yourself?

....

....

Building Mastery

The skill of building mastery is important in developing self-confidence, competency, and a sense of personal control. Over time, this skill increases emotional resilience and improves your sense of happiness. You develop mastery through the successful completion of somewhat challenging tasks. As you experience mastery, you are willing to give effort to new tasks because of the confidence and positive emotions built from previous successes. Do not fall into the perfectionism trap when building mastery. Choose an activity you can do every day and something you believe you can be successful in accomplishing. You are encouraged to break down large tasks into smaller chunks and give yourself permission to feel good about all of the steps you are taking each day. Remember to set yourself up for success and know that you can increase difficulty gradually as you take on challenges.

This "look what I can do" feeling of accomplishment may come from learning something new or further developing an existing skill. Building this sense of confidence and competency will help improve your resilience to challenging TIMES. You can choose crafts, music, yoga, gardening, cooking, athletics, household tasks, or any other tasks that can build your feelings of being capable, confident, and in control.

What are some things in your life that bring you a sense of accomplishment? These may be activities related to work, home, leisure, anything that makes you feel productive, satisfied, and/or gives you a sense of achievement—such as solving a problem, constructing a puzzle, or learning to play a tune on an instrument.

....

....

Are there any activities that you've wanted to do—things that are just for you—such as learning a foreign language, playing the piano, writing poetry, or improving your physical strength or flexibility?

....

....

What emotions do you associate with mastery?

....

....

What thoughts can you carry with you from these accomplishments as you try to take on new experiences?

....

....

Set an intention to make time for yourself each day, even if for only ten minutes, to build this sense of self-efficacy and self-satisfaction. Plan to do at least one thing per day that will give you this sense of accomplishment. Here are some tips to guide your plan:

- Choose something challenging but possible.
- Set reasonable goals for this practice and plan for success rather than failure.
- Foster your own growth and learning experiences by gradually increasing the challenge over time.
- If you begin to find the challenge too difficult, consider what you might do differently to enable you to continue to progress. Perhaps approach the activity from another perspective or choose something a bit easier to accomplish so that you may move more easily toward that next step.

What mastery-building activities might you incorporate into your daily practice? Use this chart to track your progress:

....

....

★

Mastery Activity	Monday	Tuesday	Wednesday	Thursday	Friday	Saturday	Sunday
Practice guitar	✓	✓	✓	✓	✓	✓	✓

Coping Ahead of Time

TOP TIP

You cannot always control what *will* happen, but you can learn to flexibly and effectively respond to what *does* happen.

Sometimes we find ourselves anxiously anticipating a specific stressful situation. Maybe you find yourself nervous about an upcoming social event or a performance review at work. In such circumstances, you find that your mind, being the busy, protective part of you that it is, tries to prepare you for the "worst." In other words, the "what ifs" show up and you worry about what could happen—not necessarily what is likely to happen. And this anticipation causes you to feel more anxious, more uncertain, and less in control. While there will be some degree of uncertainty and a range of possible ways in which these actual events may play out, you can prepare yourself by planning ahead for difficult situations so that your BFRB does not become the way in which your stress is manifested.

Note that there is a difference between worrying ahead of time and coping ahead of time. Worrying thoughts may lead you to questions that are unresolvable in advance of the situation (e.g., What if I fail? What if someone notices my bald spot? What if my makeup runs down from my eyebrows? What if someone notices my scars or my chewed-up cuticles?). Your aim here is not to endlessly consider the possibilities but rather to identify the ways in which you will respond to (cope with) any unwanted TIMES that could arise related to the context of the situation (before, during, or after the situation has occurred). After all, you cannot control what *will* happen, but you can learn to flexibly and effectively respond to what *does* happen.

Describe a situation you believe may be problematic and may lead to your BFRB. When will this situation occur?

....

....

What do you know about the situation (what are the observable facts)?

....

....

What are the uncertainties about the situation (what does your mind worry could happen)?

....

....

What are your fears about what could happen related directly to the situation and in regard to your BFRB? (Think about the "what ifs" and "thens" as well as the "worst-case scenarios.")

....

....

Are these feared outcomes possible or probable?

....

....

Describe the TIMES that may show up in the situation which may interfere with practicing your BFRB strategies or otherwise carrying out effective behavior.

....

....

Develop a Coping-Ahead Plan

Imagine in your mind that you are in the difficult situation you had anxiously anticipated. Picture this as clearly as you can, using all of your mind's eye's senses. Picture what is around you. What do you see? Hear? Taste? Touch? Smell? Imagine this as clearly as you can. Rather than engaging in worry about what could possibly "go wrong," practice coping effectively in your mind. Imagine what you will do to respond to the situation and with the discomforts that arise. What might you do?

....

....

Practice what you will think, say, feel, and do. You can practice this as often as you'd like in advance of the situation. Next, practice with other problems that may arise as well. And, if you are feeling keyed up or on edge following these imaginal exercises, practice grounding, relaxation, meditation, or mindfulness to center yourself back into your present moment.

Learning from Experience: Chain Analysis

When life throws you a curveball and events don't go as expected, you may not always respond as effectively as you could. You may notice that in such circumstances, you are left with feelings of sadness, shame, anger, or regret. You may make promises that you will never allow this to happen again, yet you may subsequently find yourself in a similar situation. Does this sound familiar to you?

Chain analysis is a powerful tool used to closely examine these events. Through this process, you will be able to identify the moments in which you may have practiced a strategy or skill rather than resorting to your BFRB. And, when there are consequences that need attention, you will learn ways to repair and heal them.

Like so many other skills, this begins with self-awareness. By reflecting on what has occurred when undesirable situations arise, you can identify factors that have contributed to them, which will enable you to respond differently in the future and potentially prevent yourself from repeating these patterns. You will begin to notice what is in your control, and what isn't, so you can stop yourself going down the same old path.

Chain Analysis

Let's examine, retrospectively, a situation that did not go as intended—perhaps one that led to your BFRB. In this example, we'll call your BFRB the "target behavior." Target behaviors are behaviors that you'd like to explore—the "why did this happen" behavior. Target behaviors can span a range of situations, such as picking/pulling/biting, isolating oneself, yelling at a loved one, drinking to excess, or any other behavior that you would have liked to have been different.

Describe, in detail, the target behavior.

Describe the prompting event (**Antecedent—External Factors**). What happened immediately before the behavior began that prompted it? What were you doing? What was going on around you?

Describe your TIMES MAP (**Antecedent—Internal and External/Contextual Factors**). What were your thoughts, images, memories, emotions, sensations, movement and automaticity, awareness of vulnerabilities, and people, places, and spaces just *prior* to your target behavior?

Describe the chain of events in detail, beginning at the prompting event and ending with the target behavior.

An example of a chain may look like this:

> I was feeling tired from not sleeping well the previous night. 🔗 I was in the powder room washing my hands, when I looked up into the mirror and noticed what appeared to be a patch of thinned hair. 🔗 I had the thought, "This is ugly." 🔗 I noticed feelings of embarrassment, guilt, and feeling unattractive. 🔗 I began to examine the thin spot more closely in the mirror. 🔗 I noticed what appeared to be a thick, wiry hair. 🔗 I noticed the thought, "This hair doesn't look right and is sticking out from the rest." 🔗 I ran my fingers through my hair to try to get the hair to lie flat with the rest of my hair, but it continued to stick out. 🔗 I noticed the thought, "This hair has to go." 🔗 I pulled the hair and dropped it to the floor. 🔗 I noticed feeling satisfied. 🔗 I noticed the thought that other hairs around it did not look right. 🔗 I noticed I was feeling frustrated. 🔗 I pulled several more hairs.

Now, it's your turn:

What were your TIMES MAP (**Consequences—Internal and External/Contextual Factors**) immediately following the behavior and after a period of time? Describe your thoughts, images, memories, emotions, sensations, movement and automaticity, awareness of vulnerabilities, and people, places, and spaces *after* your target behavior?

How did you respond to the target behavior occurring, both immediately and after a period of time? What did you do? (**Consequences—Behavioral Response**)

What impact, if any, did the behavior have on your environment (**Consequences—External Factors**)? Did this impact anything that is important to you, such as your relationships, your work, your home, your belongings, or the belongings of others?

Describe the consequences of the target behavior.

An example of consequences may look like this:

Immediately after pulling, I noticed the thought, "I made it worse! I can't control this." 🔗 I noticed feeling frustrated and sad. 🔗 After a period of time, I decided to decline the offer to go out to dinner with friends and I stayed home alone and watched TV. 🔗 I noticed I continued to feel sad and alone. 🔗 I noticed feeling hopeless. 🔗 I noticed permission-giving thoughts and I told myself that I didn't care if I pulled. 🔗 I pulled more hair as I watched TV that evening. 🔗 I noticed the thought that I missed out on an evening with my friends, who said they missed seeing me.

Chain Analysis

★ Identify the links in the chain of events that led to your target behavior.

Target behavior:

Antecedent—Internal Factors:	Antecedent—External and Contextual Factors:

Chain of Events:

Consequences—Internal Factors:	Consequences—Behavioral Response:	Consequences—External and Contextual Factors:

Breaking the Chain

Review your behavior chain. Each link in the chain holds an opportunity—an opportunity for you to press pause, make a change, and break the chain in similar future situations. Let's explore:

Identify an antecedent link in the chain. Is there a practice strategy or skillful behavior you may have used to break the chain and prevent the problem behavior?

At each link, what might you have done differently to address your TIMES MAP in a way that would have been more aligned with what is important to you? What practice strategy or skillful behavior might you have used?

....

....

Breaking the Chain

★ Identify each chain link and consider practice strategies and skills that may break the behavioral sequence.

Chain Link	Practice Strategy or Skillful Behavior
I was feeling tired from not having slept well the previous night	*Prioritize going to bed before midnight to get sufficient sleep*
I noticed the thought, "I made it worse! I can't control this"	*Cognitive restructuring, grounding and acceptance of difficult thoughts, or leaves on a stream mindfulness practice*
I noticed the thought, "This hair has to go"	*Practice urge surfing, HRT, opposite action, or perspective taking*

Practice, Practice, Practice: Consider creating coping cards with a chain link on one side and practice strategies/skillful behaviors on the other side. You may consult the cards in the future when you notice these antecedent links arise.

Repairing and Healing the Consequences

The goal of this practice is to identify what you might do to repair any important negative consequences of the behavior. Look at both internal (yourself) and external (others) consequences and consider what you might do to improve the situation. Let's explore the event:

What was the impact of this experience? What were the consequences to yourself or others?

....

....

Is there anything you can do to remedy the problem or the harm caused to yourself or others?

....

....

Repairing and Healing the Consequences

★ Identify each consequence and consider repair strategies or healing behaviors to repair the personal, interpersonal, and other contextual consequences.

Consequence	Repair Strategy or Healing Behavior
I felt bad about myself and missed out on an evening with my friends, who said they missed seeing me.	*I can practice loving kindness meditation. I can also call my friends and ask if they'd like to go to a movie tomorrow. I can tell them that they are important to me.*

Missing-Link Analysis

In some circumstances, you may notice the thought that you know what you "could have" or "should have" done but you did not do those things. In order to prevent this pattern from recurring, let's explore why that might be.

How do you think the outcome might have been different if you had broken the chain earlier through the use of skillful means to care for yourself differently or distance yourself from a toxic situation?

....

....

Did you notice the chain was occurring?

....

....

If so, did you then consider ways in which you could respond adaptively to the antecedent TIMES MAP?

....

....

If not, consider behavioral cues. What might you do to alert yourself to this in the future? For example, might you use a stimulus control strategy, such as placing a Post-it note reminder on your mirror?

....

....

Were you able to think of ways to break the behavior chain as the sequence was occurring? In other words, ask yourself, "Did I know what to do?"

....

....

If so, what got in the way of taking adaptive action? Did you notice any TIMES that prevented you from carrying out those strategies in order to break the chain? Were there other factors that posed a barrier?

....

....

If not, consider ways in which you can increase your ability to recall how to respond differently. For example, create coping cards to which you can refer with a list of common antecedents and "go-to" practice strategies or skillful behaviors.

....

....

Were you willing to experience your uncomfortable TIMES and direct your behavior toward strategies and skills?

....

....

If not, what might you do to increase your willingness and your ability to sit with your TIMES? For example, you might consider practicing mindfulness, willing hands, or a half-smile.

....

....

ACTION PLAN

Building Confidence and Overcoming Difficult Situations

What key points in this chapter really spoke to you? What are the highlights *you* most want to keep in mind that are important for you and your BFRB?

....

....

What did you learn about yourself as you **explored**?

....

....

What **practices** will you commit to working on this week to move you toward your destination?

....

....

What is your **action plan**? What steps will you take to put these practices in place?

....

....

When and how often will you engage in these practices?

....

....

As you experiment with these strategies, monitor your observations in the Strategies and Skills Observation Log.

Strategies and Skills: Observation Log

Date and Time	Antecedents	Strategy	Observations

CHAPTER 17

Mastering Your BFRB Skills

EXPLORE

To master your BFRB skills, you'll need to gain confidence in your ability to use them when you most need them—when the going gets a little tough. Now that you've had the chance to examine your BFRB patterns, choose individualized practice strategies, prepare yourself for challenging events, and troubleshoot difficult situations, it's time to invite your TIMES in—yes, on purpose—so that you can practice these skills with willingness and intention. You can challenge yourself to master your BFRB skills by using them in response to intentional exposure to BFRB antecedent cues (in a thoughtful, methodical way).

PRACTICE

TOOLS FOR THE TERRAIN

- Urge Surfing—Revisited
- Exposure and Response Prevention
- Perceptual Retraining
- Maintenance and Setback Guide

Urge Surfing—Revisited

We'll begin by revisiting urge surfing but supercharging this practice by changing your attentional focus. To prepare for this practice, we'd like you to imagine your antecedents.

What is the typical situation that currently most often sets the stage for your BFRB? Where are you? What are you doing?

....

....

Who and what is around you? What do you see? Hear? Touch? Smell? Taste? Describe where you are when the urge arises, in detail.

....

....

What TIMES do you notice?

....

....

Now that you are becoming experienced with strategies that may be used to increase your distress tolerance and your ability to surf your BFRB urge, it's time to challenge yourself to master this skill. We'll do this by revisiting the urge-surfing exercise—but, this time, instead of observing an itch sensation as it changes over time, we will provoke your BFRB urge and observe it, mindfully, without responding to it. Remember, the purpose of any mindfulness exercise is to be fully present in our bodies, in the moment, and able to be an observer of our experience, without judgment or response. You can do this—you've been training for this. Ready? Here we go!

Begin by bringing your attention to your breath. You may close your eyes or just sit comfortably with your eyes downcast and fixed on an object below. Notice your breath as you breathe in and breathe out. In and out. Let's focus on the moment. What are you hearing right now? How does your body feel? Can you notice the temperature in the room? What are you thinking? Let's examine your experience, mindfully, with curiosity, just noticing it, without responding to it. Watch it ebb and flow.

Now bring your BFRB urge to mind. Picture a challenging situation in which you have the urge to act on impulse and engage in your BFRB. Where are you? What are you doing? Who and what is around you?

Notice any thoughts you are having about pulling, picking, or biting, and about your history with this struggle. Notice the emotions you are experiencing. What are they? Where in your body do you notice that they manifest most—as though they have a location? Notice any other physical sensations. Do you notice tension? Do you notice an urge?

Try to bring that urge to mind and focus on that urge as though you are holding a magnifying glass to it. Notice the intensity of that urge. Notice where you feel it. What does it feel like? Just observe it. Notice how the urges are like waves: they rise, they crest, and they fall. Stay with that experience and observe the waves coming and going. They rise and fall, even though you are not responding to them in the moment—the urges rise and they fall, they subside. They may rise again, but they will subside again, coming and going. You are a surfer, noticing, riding the waves. Try to enjoy the freedom of observing and accepting these experiences—the urges, and all of the thoughts, feelings, and sensations, that also rise and fall—with no need to react or respond to them.

As you experience and observe your urges, you may notice that sometimes they are more intense than other times. Some may feel like a ripple in the water, while others may feel like a tidal wave.

But, you, you remain the same, just observing and noticing that you can be mindful of the moment without responding. You are merely a container for all of your experiences as they come and go. You are the unchanging constant.

Notice that you can be fully present with all of your experiences, even the difficult thoughts, feelings, sensations, and urges, without reacting.

Now, let go of the experience you've created in your mind's eye and return your attention to your breathing. Take a few breaths, in and out. Notice your body's movement as you breathe. And, now, you can open your eyes and bring your attention back into the room.

Consider what that experience was like for you. Moment to moment, you always have the power to choose how you respond to both your inner and outer worlds.

Practice this exercise. Pay attention to the TIMES, acknowledge them, make space for them, and learn to ride the rise and fall of BFRB-associated internal experiences without responding to them. The more you practice, the more you learn that you have the ability to experience your BFRB cues. Over time, they will become less distressing and easier to ride out because "You've got this!"

Exposure and Response Prevention

Exposure and response prevention (ERP) is the process of systematically confronting your triggers and refraining from responding by engaging in your BFRB. The E (exposure) is the practice of exposing yourself to your discomforts, your TIMES. The RP (response prevention) is the act of refraining from the behaviors that have previously brought you relief in response to these discomforts (pulling, picking, other BFRBs, or avoidance). The goals of ERP are to decrease your avoidance behaviors (so that you can begin to live life more fully again), learn to get more comfortable with your triggers (because they will naturally occur in your day-to-day life), and decrease your tendency to over-respond (because being stuck in your BFRB is no fun at all). To review those triggers, or antecedents, as we've come to know them, refer to your TIMES MAP (thoughts, images, memories, emotions, sensations, movement and automaticity, awareness of vulnerabilities, and people, places, and spaces).

Here's where you put on that superhero suit. This is where you'll be brave and creative, ushering in your discomforts so that you can use your powers to respond differently. Consider ways in which you can cue your BFRB (yes, you're going to poke the beast)—to intentionally provoke the TIMES in order to practice responding differently, more adaptively, more in line with what's important to you. You'll want to start with some exposures that are only mildly evocative and work your way up to those that are more challenging. But you can do it. We know you can.

Exposures may include: direct contact with your BFRB cues; or engaging in activities that you've avoided because of your BFRB. It can be a little challenging to create a list of exposure ideas at first—to help you get started, consider where your discomfort lives. For example, exposure to cues may include examining the rough spots on your arm (direct contact with a BFRB cue). Or, if you are afraid of being seen without makeup for fear that someone may notice your scabs and scars, think negatively of you, or say something critical, that's also a discomfort to address with exposure. An exposure task might then be going to the convenience store to buy milk without wearing makeup or anything else to camouflage your face (exposure to an avoided experience).

Let's brainstorm. Here are some examples of what exposure exercises might look like for someone who pulls their eyelashes:

Level of Exposure	Exposure Activity
Low challenge	*Drawing a picture of an eye with slightly uneven eyelashes*
	Looking at a photo of uneven eyelashes
Medium challenge	*Look at eyelashes in the mirror from an 18-inch distance*
	Examining eyelashes in a mirror at a very close distance
	Going to the grocery store without eye makeup
High challenge	*Touching eyelashes with the back of the hand*
	Going to visit a friend without makeup

Now, it's your turn. Create a list of exposures—ways of eliciting the TIMES that typically lead to your BFRB. Rate the level of challenge for each item as **low**, **medium**, or **high**, as well as your willingness to confront this trigger in the service of living the life you want, unfettered by your BFRB, on a scale from **0 (not at all willing)** to **10 (very much willing)**.

Exposure Practice

Exposure Activity	Level of Challenge (Low, Medium, High)	Willingness (0–10)

cont.

Exposure Activity	Level of Challenge (Low, Medium, High)	Willingness (0–10)

Now that you've developed an exposure plan, which activity would you be willing to confront first? Ideally, begin with an item that is rated high on willingness and relatively low on distress, and work your way up to more challenging activities.

As you engage in each item of ERP practice, notice how your distress levels and willingness levels change over time and track that. You should see that with repeated exposures your distress tends to decrease and your willingness tends to increase. Success! You're strengthening your resistance muscles and living the life you want, unhindered by your BFRB!

As you allow your TIMES to ebb and flow with practice, ERP may seem easier and your discomfort more manageable with repetition. You may also learn that you are willing and better able to manage any TIMES that arise. You may increase and diversify the challenge—for example, increase the time in public, go to various public places, engage in a variety of BFRB-cuing exposures. As you build your ability to ride out the TIMES, you may find that you no longer need to disengage or push away your discomforts or utilize your well-practiced skills and strategies. Instead, you've learned to bring whatever discomforts arise with you as you live life more freely.

Use the following chart to track your ERP practice:

Exposure and Response Prevention

★

Exposure Practice	Pre- and Post-Exposure Challenge Level (Low, Medium, High)	Pre- and Post-Exposure Willingness (0–10)

Perceptual Retraining

Like ERP, perceptual retraining involves confronting BFRB cues. Specifically, perceptual retraining is a practice in which you will change your relationship with the visual cues to your BFRB.

Like other BFRB practice strategies and skills, perceptual retraining is not necessarily relevant for everyone. However, if you find yourself over-attentive to specific target areas of the body and find that reflective surfaces are the bane of your existence, this may be a useful exercise for you. For example, you pick skin on your face and become hyper-focused on your appearance each time you catch a glimpse of yourself in a mirror, and you judge this area of your body harshly, oftentimes in an unrealistic manner. You may focus on one particular target area, almost to the exclusion of seeing other areas of your body. You may use items like magnifying mirrors or other reflective surfaces that offer you a distorted view of yourself (no one looks good in a magnifying mirror). You may check your appearance excessively, avoid your reflection altogether, or struggle with both.

While engaged in this inspection of your appearance, you may become absorbed in your BFRB in an attempt to fix imperfections but paradoxically cause more damage to your body, all the while criticizing yourself, your appearance, and your actions. In an attempt to feel better, you unintentionally make yourself feel worse. You may lose valuable time, missing out on school, work, or quality time with others because of the time spent with mirrors and engaged in your BFRB. You may become stuck in feeling like this is all others see and that they share these negative judgments of you. But you are so much more than a head of hair or a less-than-perfect complexion.

Practice: Perceptual Retraining

The goal of perceptual retraining is to practice confronting those visual cues and widening your lens—to see a more holistic view, practicing mindful attention and non-judgment of the experience, of really seeing yourself and to refrain from maladaptive responses to this reflection, such as engaging in your BFRB, checking, camouflaging, and other avoidance behaviors. You are going to be looking at your entire body objectively, without judgment and without getting stuck focusing on those target areas that you tend to scrutinize. As with ERP, this exercise may bring up your BFRB urges or TIMES for you to ride out, without responding to them by engaging in the behavior.

Place yourself at a comfortable, moderate distance (approximately 12–18 inches) from a typical mirror (one that does not magnify or otherwise distort the image), so that you can see a holistic perspective. Ensure that you are visible and unobscured by clothing, makeup, or other coverings that may camouflage or help you avoid viewing your reflection. Check in with your level of anxiety or apprehension (low, medium, high) and your level of willingness (on a scale of 0–10) to fully experience your observations at the outset of the exercise, during the exercise, and following the exercise.

Take five to ten minutes for this activity. Describe yourself, starting at the top of your head and proceeding downward to your feet, including each area of your body, in objective, non-judgmental language. For example:

> My head is round. I have medium-length, brown hair that flanks my face and rests on my shoulders. I have two arched, dark-brown eyebrows that sit above two light-brown eyes. I have a set of eyelashes that curl upward, extending from my eyelids. I have a round nose that extends downward and ends between two pinkish cheeks. My skin is beige. I have a pink blemish on my left cheek that is round and about three centimeters in diameter. My mouth sits below my nose and philtrum. My lips are pinkish red. My chin...

PERCEPTUAL RETRAINING TIPS

- Be on the lookout for judgmental language. If you do notice words that carry a negative emotional valence, return to that description and restate it in an objective way.
- If you get stuck on a specific spot, use a one-sentence description and move on to the next area.
- Do not avoid, push away, or try to diminish triggers or discomfort. Acknowledge it and move forward.
- Allow your TIMES to come and go, maybe even embrace them as part of your human experience.
- Practice new ways to relate to the experience, to sit with it, to ride it out, to see it in a non-threatening way, so that it no longer has control over you.
- This is where you will find freedom from the negative impact of your BFRB.

Maintenance and Setback Guide

The term "relapse prevention" is used in the field of cognitive-behavioral psychology to describe the process of reducing the likelihood of experiencing a full recurrence of symptoms, but this term is a misnomer. If you engage in your BFRB after a period of abstinence, all is not lost; you are not back to being completely entrenched in your BFRB without the knowledge of what you can do to address it. You experienced a setback. Setbacks are not failures and can be expected (and accepted) as part of progress toward "recovery." Setbacks can provide information that can be used to explore, evaluate, and motivate you toward action planning. Take care not to get caught up in your judgmental mind, criticizing yourself for what has happened. When a setback occurs, you actually already *know* what to do. You have that knowledge.

Let's review:

Thoughts—Thoughts that show up in your mind Images—Images that come to mind in your mind's eye Memories—Narratives from past experiences Emotions—Emotions that you notice yourself experiencing Sensations and Urges—Bodily sensations or urges	Internal Experiences
Movement and Automaticity—Movements, body postures, and activities Awareness of Vulnerabilities—Biological influences such as genetics, co-occurring medical conditions, sleep, nutrition, exercise People, Places, and Spaces—Where you are, who and what is around you	External/Contextual Experiences

External/contextual experiences (the MAP) provide a path to uncomfortable internal experiences. Internal experiences that are uncomfortable are responded to by performing the BFRB in an effort to gain comfort/relief from discomfort.

Setback Guide Action Plan

1. Revisit the My Matrix exercise in Chapter 2 to anchor yourself toward your values.
2. Review motivation planning and current stage of change.
3. Log your BFRB for one week with a BFRB Information-Gathering Log.
4. Revisit your current BFRB cycle.

Antecedents may include:
Thoughts
Images
Memories
Emotions
Sensations and Urges

1. Antecedents
Antecedents serve as cues or triggers for the behavior.

Vulnerabilities may include:
Movement and Automaticity
Awareness of Vulnerabilities
People, Places, and Spaces

3. Consequences
Both positive and negative consequences occur, which serve to reinforce the stimulus-response pattern.

2. Behavior
The behavior is carried out in a specific sequence of events in an attempt to avoid the experience of discomfort and to self-regulate.

5. What are your current MAP factors?

 ....

 ....

6. What are your current antecedent TIMES?

 ....

 ....

7. What are the reinforcing consequences (both short term and long term)?

 ....

 ....

8. What practice strategies and/or skillful behaviors might you use that align with the identified antecedents TIMES MAP?

 ....

 ....

9. What has been useful in the past? If some skills or strategies are no longer helpful, why might that be and what can you do to modify them?

....

....

ACTION PLAN

Mastering Your BFRB Skills

What key points in this chapter really spoke to you? What are the highlights *you* most want to keep in mind that are important for you and your BFRB?

....

....

What did you learn about yourself as you **explored**?

....

....

What **practices** will you commit to working on this week to move you toward your destination?

....

....

What is your **action plan**? What steps will you take to put these practices in place?

....

....

When and how often will you engage in these practices?

....

....

CHAPTER 18

Living the Life You Want

As you continue your life's journey with or without a BFRB, keep in mind that you are a work in progress—we are all a work in progress—continually moving toward the best you that you want to be. Your best self is ever-evolving, changing over time, and shaped by each experience, each person who touches your life, and each and every moment of joy as well as pain. Even in the event that your BFRB has greatly improved or has diminished from your daily experience altogether, you, like all people, are complex. You are an ever-changing wonder whose future is somewhat uncertain and therefore able to be cultivated through your moment-to-moment opportunities to move toward what matters to you.

Your 100th Birthday Party

Imagine it is your 100th birthday party (happy birthday!) and you are surrounded by family and friends who have come to celebrate you and your life. One by one, your loved ones each rise to share a few words with everyone in attendance. As they each speak, they share their experiences with you and anecdotes about your life, what matters most to you, what they most admire about you, and what you mean to them. They share what you're all about. Imagine them saying what you most want to hear about who you are, what you stand for, and what is most important to you. What do they say?

....

....

Now, go back to what you've written and read what they've said. Really imagine the celebration of your life and the impact you've had on others. Consider what your friends and loved ones have shared about you.

Did any of these people mention that you struggled with a BFRB? Did any of them mention the hair loss, skin damage, or other physical manifestation of the consequences of the behavior? Did any of them mention any of the criticisms of you or your BFRB that you sometimes hold for yourself in the privacy of your mind?

We're going to go out on a limb and guess that the answer is "no." But, why? Your

BFRB has been such a big part of your life—so much so that you've dedicated your time and effort to this book (and made it to our final chapter!). Why didn't they all talk about it?

There's so much more to you than your hair, your skin, or your nails. Your BFRB, whether it is active or not, does not define who you are, what you stand for, or what you hold most dear in life. It does not change your ethics, your integrity, your charitable nature, or any other values you hold as those to live by every day. Chances are these imagined speeches, which are carefully delivered, share your love and kindness toward others, your sense of humor, your unwavering support, dedication, and all of those characteristics that are important to you in your daily life. That is what matters.

In your life, you will experience pain and discomfort, some of which may be related to your BFRB. Pain reminds us that we are alive and able to experience the breadth of living. But it's the other stuff that counts. So make some room for your difficult moments; they will come and go. And go live the life you want.

Bibliography

Alberti, R. E., & Emmons, M. L. (2017). *Your Perfect Right: Assertiveness and Equality in Your Life and Relationships* (10th ed.). Oakland, CA: New Harbinger Publications, Inc.

American Psychiatric Association. (1987). *Diagnostic and Statistical Manual of Mental Disorders* (3rd ed., revised).

American Psychiatric Association. (2013). *Diagnostic and Statistical Manual of Mental Disorders* (5th ed.).

Anālayo, B. (2020). Buddhist antecedents to the body scan meditation. *Mindfulness, 11*, 194–202.

Arabatzoudis, T., Rehm, I. C., & Nedeljkovic, M. (2021). A needs analysis for the development of an internet-delivered cognitive-behavioural treatment (iCBT) program for trichotillomania. *Journal of Obsessive-Compulsive and Related Disorders, 31*, 100689.

Aristotle, Ross, W. D., & Brown, L. (2009). *The Nicomachean Ethics*. Oxford, New York: Oxford University Press.

Asplund, M., Rück, C., Lenhard, F., Gunnarsson, T., Bellander, M., Delby, H., & Ivanov, V. Z. (2021). ACT-enhanced group behavior therapy for trichotillomania and skin-picking disorder: A feasibility study. *Journal of Clinical Psychology, 77*(7), 1537–1555.

Aydin, E. P., Demirci, H., Begenen, A. G., Kenar, J. G., *et al.* (2022). Facial emotion recognition difficulties may be specific to skin picking disorder, but could also be related to the presence of alexithymia in trichotillomania. *The European Journal of Psychiatry, 36*(2), 130–136.

Azrin, N. H., Nunn, R. G., & Frantz, S. E. (1980a). Treatment of hairpulling (Trichotillomania): A comparative study of habit reversal and negative practice training. *Journal of Behavior Therapy and Experimental Psychiatry, 11*(1), 13–20.

Azrin, N. H., Nunn, R. G., & Frantz, S. E. (1980b). Habit reversal vs. negative practice treatment of nailbiting. *Behaviour Research and Therapy, 18*(4), 281–285.

Bezerra, A. P., Machado, M. O., Maes, M., Marazziti, D., *et al.* (2021). Trichotillomania-psychopathological correlates and associations with health-related quality of life in a large sample. *CNS Spectrums, 26*(3), 282–289.

Bloch, M. H., Panza, K. E., Grant, J. E., Pittenger, C., & Leckman, J. F. (2013). N-Acetylcysteine in the treatment of pediatric trichotillomania: A randomized, double-blind, placebo-controlled add-on trial. *Journal of the American Academy of Child and Adolescent Psychiatry, 52*(3), 231–240.

Bottesi, G., Cerea, S., Ouimet, A. J., Sica, C., & Ghisi, M. (2016). Affective correlates of trichotillomania across the pulling cycle: Findings from an Italian sample of self-identified hair pullers. *Psychiatry Research, 246*, 606–611.

Budde, H., & Wegner, M. (2018). *The Exercise Effect on Mental Health: Neurobiological Mechanisms* (1st ed.). New York, Abingdon: Routledge.

Carlson, E. J., Malloy, E. J., Brauer, L., Golomb, R. G., *et al.* (2021). Comprehensive Behavioral (ComB) treatment of trichotillomania: A randomized clinical trial. *Behavior Therapy, 52*(6), 1543–1557.

Cavic, E., Valle, S., Chamberlain, S. R., & Grant, J. E. (2021). Sleep quality and its clinical associations in trichotillomania and skin picking disorder. *Comprehensive Psychiatry, 105*, 152221.

Chesivoir, E. K., Valle, S., & Grant, J. E. (2022). Comorbid trichotillomania and attention-deficit hyperactivity disorder in adults. *Comprehensive Psychiatry, 116*, 152317.

Christenson, G. A., & Mackenzie, T. B. (1994). Trichotillomania. In M. Hersen, & R. T. Ammerman (eds.) *Handbook of Prescriptive Treatment for Adults* (pp.217–235). New York, NY: Plenum Press.

Christenson, G. A., MacKenzie, T. B., & Mitchell, J. E. (1994). Adult men and women with trichotillomania: A comparison of male and female characteristics. *Psychosomatics, 35*(2), 142–149.

Crosby, J. M., Dehlin, J. P., Mitchell, P. R., & Twohig, M. P. (2012). Acceptance and Commitment Therapy and Habit Reversal Training for the treatment of trichotillomania. *Cognitive and Behavioral Practice, 19*(4), 595–605.

Delong, L. & Bukhart N. (2013) *Tongue Chewing: Causes, Treatments, and Information for Patients.* Modified from Delong L. & Burkhart N. (2013). *General and Oral Pathology for the Dental Hygienist* (2nd ed.). Baltimore, MD: Lippincott, Williams and Wilkins.

Erdogan, H. K., Arslantas, D., Atay, E., Eyuboglu, D., *et al.* (2021). Prevalence of onychophagia and its relation to stress and quality of life. *Acta Dermatovenerologica Alpina, Pannonica, et Adriatica, 30*(1), 15–19.

Falkenstein, M. J., Conelea, C. A., Garner, L. E., & Haaga, D. A. F. (2018). Sensory over-responsivity in trichotillomania (hair-pulling disorder). *Psychiatry Research, 260*, 207–218.

Falkenstein, M. J., Mouton-Odum, S., Mansueto, C. S., Golomb, R. G., & Haaga, D. A. (2016). Comprehensive behavioral treatment of trichotillomania: A treatment development study. *Behavior Modification, 40*(3), 414–438.

Farhat, L. C., Olfson, E., Nasir, M., Levine, J. L. S., *et al.* (2020). Pharmacological and behavioral treatment for trichotillomania: An updated systematic review with meta-analysis. *Depression and Anxiety, 37*(8), 715–727.

Flessner, C. A., Lochner, C., Stein, D. J., Woods, D. W., Franklin, M. E., & Keuthen, N. J. (2010). Age of onset of trichotillomania symptoms: Investigating clinical correlates. *The Journal of Nervous and Mental Disease, 198*(12), 896–900.

Flessner, C. A., Woods, D. W., Franklin, M. E., Cashin, S. E., & Keuthen, N. J. (2008). The Milwaukee Inventory for Subtypes of Trichotillomania-Adult Version (MIST-A): Development of an instrument for the assessment of "focused" and "automatic" hair pulling. *Journal of Psychopathology and Behavioral Assessment, 30*(1), 20–30.

Franca, K., Chacon, A., Ledon, J., Savas, J., & Nouri, K. (2013). Psychodermatology: A trip through history. *Anais Brasileiros de Dermatologia, 88*, 842–843.

Frey, A. S., McKee, M., King, R. A., & Martin, A. (2005). Hair apparent: Rapunzel syndrome. *The American Journal of Psychiatry, 162*(2), 242–248.

Ghanizadeh, A. (2008). Association of nail biting and psychiatric disorders in children and their parents in a psychiatrically referred sample of children. *Child and Adolescent Psychiatry and Mental Health, 2*(1), 13.

Grandner. M. (2019). *Sleep and Health.* New York, NY: Elsevier Science & Technology.

Grant, J. E., & Chamberlain, S. R. (2020). Prevalence of skin picking (excoriation) disorder. *Journal of Psychiatric Research, 130*, 57–60.

Grant, J. E., Chamberlain, S. R., Redden, S. A., Leppink, E. W., Odlaug, B. L., & Kim, S. W. (2016). N-Acetylcysteine in the treatment of excoriation disorder: A randomized clinical trial. *JAMA Psychiatry, 73*(5), 490–496.

Grant, J. E., Dougherty, D. D., & Chamberlain, S. R. (2020). Prevalence, gender correlates, and co-morbidity of trichotillomania. *Psychiatry Research, 288*, 112948.

Grant, J. E., Odlaug, B. L., & Kim, S. W. (2009). N-acetylcysteine, a glutamate modulator, in the treatment of trichotillomania: A double-blind, placebo-controlled study. *Archives of General Psychiatry, 66*(7), 756–763.

Grant, J. E., Peris, T. S., Ricketts, E. J., Lochner, C., *et al.* (2021b). Identifying subtypes of trichotillomania (hair pulling disorder) and excoriation (skin picking) disorder using mixture modeling in a multicenter sample. *Journal of Psychiatric Research, 137*, 603–612.

Grant, J. E., Valle, S., Aslan, I. H., & Chamberlain, S. R. (2021a). Clinical presentation of body-focused repetitive behaviors in minority ethnic groups. *Comprehensive Psychiatry, 111*, 152272.

Grant, J. E., Valle, S., & Chamberlain, S. R. (2021). Nutrition in skin picking disorder and trichotillomania. *Frontiers in Psychiatry, 12*, 761321.

Grant, J. E., Valle, S., Chesivoir, E., & Ehsan, D. (2022). Tetrahydrocannabinol fails to reduce hair pulling or skin picking: Results of a double-blind, placebo-controlled study of dronabinol. *International Clinical Psychopharmacology, 37*(1), 14–20.

Gupta, M. A., & Gupta, A. K. (2019). Self-induced dermatoses: A great imitator. *Clinics In dermatology, 37*(3), 268–277.

Haaland, A. T., Eskeland, S. O., Moen, E. M., Vogel, P. A., *et al.* (2017). ACT-enhanced behavior therapy in group format for trichotillomania: An effectiveness study. *Journal of Obsessive-Compulsive and Related Disorders, 12*, 109–116.

Hallopeau, H. (1889). Alopecia by scratching (trichomanie ou trichotillomania). *Ann Dermatol Syphililgr, 10*, 440–441.

Halteh, P., Scher, R. K., & Lipner, S. R. (2017). Onychophagia: A nail-biting conundrum for physicians. *The Journal of Dermatological Treatment, 28*(2), 166–172.

Harris, R. (2008). *The Happiness Trap*. London: Robinson Publishing.

Harris, R. (2009). *ACT Made Simple: An Easy-To-Read Primer on Acceptance and Commitment Therapy*. Oakland, CA: New Harbinger.

Harris, R. (2017). *The Choice Point 2.0: A Brief Overview*. ACTMindfully. Accessed on 20/2/2023 at www.actmindfully.com.au/free-stuff/worksheets-handouts-book-chapters.

Harris, R., & Hayes, S. C. (2019). *ACT Made Simple: An Easy-To-Read Primer on Acceptance and Commitment Therapy* (2nd ed.). Oakland, CA: New Harbinger Publications.

Hayes, S. C., & Smith, S. (2005). *Get Out of Your Mind and into Your Life: The New Acceptance and Commitment Therapy*. Oakland, CA: New Harbinger Publications.

Hayes, S. C., Strosahl, K. D., & Wilson, K. G. (1999). *Acceptance and Commitment Therapy*. New York: Guilford Press.

Heard, H. L., & Linehan, M. M. (2019). Dialectical Behavior Therapy for Borderline Personality Disorder. In J. C. Norcross & M. R. Goldfried (eds.) *Handbook of Psychotherapy Integration* (pp.257–283). Oxford, New York: Oxford University Press.

Hegde, A. M., & Xavier, A. M. (2009). Childhood habits: Ignorance is not bliss—A prevalence study. *International Journal of Clinical Pediatric Dentistry, 2*(1), 26–29.

Hoffman, J., Williams, T., Rothbart, R., Ipser, J. C., *et al.* (2021). Pharmacotherapy for trichotillomania. *Cochrane Database of Systematic Reviews, 2021*(9), CD007662.

Houghton, D. C., Alexander, J. R., Bauer, C. C., & Woods, D. W. (2018). Body-focused repetitive behaviors: More prevalent than once thought? *Psychiatry Research, 270*, 389–393.

Houghton, D. C., Mathew, A. S., Twohig, M. P., Saunders, S. M., *et al.* (2016). Trauma and trichotillomania: A tenuous relationship. *Journal of Obsessive-Compulsive and Related Disorders, 11*, 91–95.

Johnson, J., & El-Alfy, A. T. (2016). Review of available studies of the neurobiology and pharmacotherapeutic management of trichotillomania. *Journal of Advanced Research, 7*(2), 169–184.

Jones, W. H. S. (ed.) (1868). *Hippocrates Collected Works I.* Cambridge: Harvard University Press.

Kabat-Zinn, J. (2005). *Wherever You Go There You Are* (10th ed.). New York: Hyperion.

Keuthen, N. J., O'Sullivan, R. L., Ricciardi, J. N., Shera, D., *et al.* (1995). The Massachusetts General Hospital (MGH) Hairpulling Scale: 1. Development and factor analyses. *Psychotherapy and Psychosomatics, 64*(3–4), 141–145.

Keuthen, N. J., Rothbaum, B. O., Falkenstein, M. J., Meunier, S., *et al.* (2011). DBT-enhanced habit reversal treatment for trichotillomania: 3- and 6-month follow-up results. *Depression and Anxiety, 28*(4), 310–313.

Keuthen, N. J., Rothbaum, B. O., Fama, J., Altenburger, E., *et al.* (2012). DBT-enhanced cognitive-behavioral treatment for trichotillomania: A randomized controlled trial. *Journal of Behavioral Addictions, 1*(3), 106–114.

Keuthen, N. J., Rothbaum, B. O., Welch, S. S., Taylor, C., *et al.* (2010). Pilot trial of dialectical behavior therapy-enhanced habit reversal for trichotillomania. *Depression and Anxiety, 27*(10), 953–959.

Keuthen, N. J., Tung, E. S., Tung, M. G., Curley, E. E., & Flessner, C. A. (2016). NEO-FFI personality clusters in trichotillomania. *Psychiatry Research, 239*, 196–203.

Koob, G. F., Sanna, P. P., & Bloom, F. E. (1998). Neuroscience of addiction. *Neuron, 21*, 467–476.

Kwon, C., Sutaria, N., Khanna, R., Almazan, E., *et al.* (2020). Epidemiology and comorbidities of excoriation disorder: A retrospective case-control study. *Journal of Clinical Medicine, 9*(9), 2703.

Lee, D. K., & Lipner, S. R. (2022). Update on diagnosis and management of onychophagia and onychotillomania. *International Journal of Environmental Research and Public Health, 19*(6), 3392.

Lee, E. B., Homan, K. J., Morrison, K. L., Ong, C. W., Levin, M. E., & Twohig, M. P. (2018). Acceptance and Commitment Therapy for trichotillomania: A randomized controlled trial of adults and adolescents. *Behavior Modification, 44*(1), 70–91.

Lee, M. T., Mpavaenda, D. N., & Fineberg, N. A. (2019). Habit reversal therapy in obsessive compulsive related disorders: A systematic review of the evidence and CONSORT evaluation of randomized controlled trials. *Frontiers in Behavioral Neuroscience, 13*, 79.

Leibovici, V., Murad, S., Cooper-Kazaz, R., Tetro, T., *et al.* (2014). Excoriation (skin picking) disorder in Israeli University students: Prevalence and associated mental health correlates. *General Hospital Psychiatry, 36*(6), 686–689.

Lerner, J., Franklin, M. E., Meadows, E. A., Hembree, E., & Foa, E. B. (1998). Effectiveness of a cognitive behavioral treatment program for trichotillomania: An uncontrolled evaluation. *Behavior Therapy, 29*(1), 157–171.

Linehan, M. (1993). *Skills Training Manual for Treating Borderline Personality Disorder.* New York: Guilford Press.

Linehan, M. (2014). *DBT Skills Training Manual* (2nd ed). New York: Guilford Press.

McGuire, J. F., Ung, D., Selles, R. R., Rahman, O., *et al.* (2014). Treating trichotillomania: A meta-analysis of treatment effects and moderators for behavior therapy and serotonin reuptake inhibitors. *Journal of Psychiatric Research, 58*, 76–83.

Neal-Barnett, A., Flessner, C., Franklin, M. E., Woods, D. W., Keuthen, N. J., & Stein, D. J. (2010). Ethnic differences in trichotillomania: Phenomenology, interference, impairment, and treatment efficacy. *Journal of Anxiety Disorders, 24*(6), 553–558.

Neff, K., & Germer, C. (2022). The role of self-compassion in psychotherapy. *World Psychiatry: Official Journal of the World Psychiatric Association (WPA)*, *21*(1), 58–59.

Ngoc, V. T. N., Hang, L. M., Bach, H. V., & Chu, D. T. (2019). On-site treatment of oral ulcers caused by cheek biting: A minimally invasive treatment approach in a pediatric patient. *Clinical Case Reports*, 7(3), 426–430.

Ostafin, B. D., & Marlatt, G. A. (2008). Surfing the urge: Experiential acceptance moderates the relation between automatic alcohol motivation and hazardous drinking. *Journal of Social and Clinical Psychology*, 27(4), 404–418.

Oxford University Press. (n.d.). *Oxford Advanced Learner's Dictionary*. Accessed on 20/2/2023 at www.oxfordlearnersdictionaries.com.

Pacan, P., Grzesiak, M., Reich, A., Kantorska-Janiec, M., & Szepietowski, J. C. (2014). Onychophagia and onychotillomania: Prevalence, clinical picture and comorbidities. *Acta Dermato-Venereologica*, *94*(1), 67–71.

Pacan, P., Grzesiak, M., Reich, A., & Szepietowski, J. C. (2009). Onychophagia as a spectrum of obsessive-compulsive disorder. *Acta Dermato-Venereologica*, *89*(3), 278–280.

Petersen, J. M., Barney, J. L., Fruge, J., Lee, E. B., Levin, M. E., & Twohig, M. P. (2022). Longitudinal outcomes from a pilot randomized controlled trial of telehealth acceptance-enhanced behavior therapy for adolescents with trichotillomania. *Journal of Obsessive-Compulsive and Related Disorders*, *33*, 100725.

Polk, K. L., & Schoendorff, B. (eds). (2014). *The ACT Matrix: A New Approach to Building Psychological Flexibility Across Settings and Populations*. Oakland, CA: New Harbinger Publications.

Pozza, A., Giaquinta, N., & Dèttore, D. (2016). Borderline, avoidant, sadistic personality traits and emotion dysregulation predict different pathological skin picking subtypes in a community sample. *Neuropsychiatric Disease and Treatment*, *12*, 1861–1867.

Prochaska, J. O., & DiClemente, C. C. (2005). The Transtheoretical Approach. In J. C. Norcross & M. R. Goldfried (eds.). *Handbook of Psychotherapy Integration. Oxford Series in Clinical Psychology* (2nd ed.) (pp.147–171). Oxford, New York: Oxford University Press.

Rahman, O., McGuire, J., Storch, E. A., & Lewin, A. B. (2017). Preliminary randomized controlled trial of habit reversal training for treatment of hair pulling in youth. *Journal of Child and Adolescent Psychopharmacology*, 27(2), 132–139.

Ricketts, E. J., Snorrason, Í., Mathew, A.S., Sigurvinsdottir, E., *et al.* (2021). Heightened sense of incompleteness in excoriation (skin-picking) disorder. *Cognitive Therapy and Research*, *45*, 759–766.

Rucklidge, J. J., & Kaplan, B. J. (2016). Nutrition and mental health. *Clinical Psychological Science*, 4(6), 1082–1084.

Shulman, J. D., Beach, M. M., & Rivera-Hidalgo, F. (2004). The prevalence of oral mucosal lesions in U.S. adults: Data from the Third National Health and Nutrition Examination Survey, 1988–1994. *Journal of the American Dental Association (1939)*, *135*(9), 1279–1286.

Sleep Foundation. (2022). Using Cannabis as a Sleep Aid. Accessed on 20/2/2023 at www.sleepfoundation.org/sleep-aids/cannabis-and-sleep.

Snorrason, Í., Ólafsson, R. P., Flessner, C. A., Keuthen, N. J., Franklin, M. E., & Woods, D. W. (2012). The Skin Picking Scale-Revised: Factor structure and psychometric properties. *Journal of Obsessive-Compulsive and Related Disorders*, *1*(2), 133–137.

Snorrason, Í., Smári, J., & Ólafsson, R. P. (2010). Emotion regulation in pathological skin picking: Findings from a non-treatment seeking sample. *Journal of Behavior Therapy and Experimental Psychiatry*, *41*(3), 238–245.

Snorrason, Í., Smári, J., & Ólafsson, R. P. (2011). Motor inhibition, reflection impulsivity, and trait impulsivity in pathological skin picking. *Behavior Therapy, 42*(3), 521–532.

Solley, K., & Turner, C. (2018). Prevalence and correlates of clinically significant body-focused repetitive behaviors in a non-clinical sample. *Comprehensive Psychiatry, 86*, 9–18.

Stemberger, R. M., Thomas, A. M., Mansueto, C. S., & Carter, J. G. (2000). Personal toll of trichotillomania: Behavioral and interpersonal sequelae. *Journal of Anxiety Disorders, 14*(1), 97–104.

Stiede, J. T., Woods, D. W., Idnani, A. K., Pritchard, J., Klobe, K., & Kumar, S. (2022). Pilot trial of a technology assisted treatment for trichotillomania. *Journal of Obsessive-Compulsive and Related Disorders, 33*, 100726.

Swedo, S. E., Leonard, H. L., Rapoport, J. L., Lenane, M. C., Goldberger, E. L., & Cheslow, D. L. (1989). A double-blind comparison of clomipramine and desipramine in the treatment of trichotillomania (hair pulling). *The New England Journal of Medicine, 321*(8), 497–501.

Teng, E. J., Woods, D. W., & Twohig, M. P. (2006). Habit reversal as a treatment for chronic skin picking: A pilot investigation. *Behavior Modification, 30*(4), 411–422.

Teng, E. J., Woods, D. W., Twohig, M. P., & Marcks, B. A. (2002). Body-focused repetitive behavior problems. Prevalence in a non-referred population and differences in perceived somatic activity. *Behavior Modification, 26*(3), 340–360.

The WHOQOL Group. (1998). Development of the World Health Organization WHOQOL-BREF quality of life assessment. *Psychological Medicine, 28*(3), 551–558.

Thomson, H. A., Farhat, L. C., Olfson, E., Levine, J. L. S., & Bloch, M. H. (2022). Prevalence and gender distribution of trichotillomania: A systematic review and meta-analysis. *Journal of Psychiatric Research, 153*, 73–81.

Twohig, M., Petersen, J. M., Fruge, J., Ong, C. W., *et al.* (2021). A pilot randomized controlled trial of online-delivered ACT-enhanced behavior therapy for trichotillomania in adolescents. *Cognitive and Behavioral Practice, 28*(4), 653–668.

Twohig, M., Woods, D., Marcks, B., & Teng E. (2003). Evaluating the efficacy of habit reversal: Comparison with a placebo control. *The Journal of Clinical Psychiatry, 64*(1), 40–48.

Van Ameringen, M., Mancini, C., Patterson, B., Bennett, M., & Oakman, J. (2010). A randomized, double-blind, placebo-controlled trial of olanzapine in the treatment of trichotillomania. *The Journal of Clinical Psychiatry, 71*(10), 1336–1343.

Van der Pols, J. C. (2018). Nutrition and mental health: Bidirectional associations and multidimensional measures. *Public Health Nutrition, 21*(5), 829–830.

Wilson, E. (1875). *Lectures on Dermatology: Delivered in the Royal College of Surgeons of England in 1874–1875*. London: J. & A. Churchill.

Woods, D. W., Ely, L. J., Bauer, C. C., Twohig, M. P., *et al.* (2022). Acceptance-enhanced behavior therapy for trichotillomania in adults: A randomized clinical trial. *Behaviour Research and Therapy, 158*, 104187.

Woods, D. W., Flessner, C. A., Franklin, M. E., Keuthen, N. J., *et al.* (2006). The Trichotillomania Impact Project (TIP): Exploring phenomenology, functional impairment, and treatment utilization. *The Journal of Clinical Psychiatry, 67*(12), 1877–1888.

Woods, D. W., Wetterneck, C., & Flessner, C. (2006). A controlled evaluation of Acceptance and Commitment Therapy plus habit reversal for trichotillomania. *Behaviour Research and Therapy, 44*(5), 639–656.

Zielinski, M. R., McKenna, J. T., & McCarley, R. W. (2016). Functions and mechanisms of sleep. *AIMS Neuroscience, 3*(1), 67–104.

Subject Index

thoughts, images, memories
strategies 149, 151, 166–7

Author Index